THE
WORLD'S
BIGGEST
CASH
MACHINE

ALSO BY CHRIS BLACKHURST

Too Big to Jail

CHRIS BLACKHURST

THE WORLD'S BIGGEST CASH MACHINE

MANCHESTER UNITED, THE GLAZERS, AND THE STRUGGLE FOR FOOTBALL'S SOUL

MACMILLAN

First published 2023 by Macmillan
an imprint of Pan Macmillan
The Smithson, 6 Briset Street, London EC1M 5NR
EU representative: Macmillan Publishers Ireland Ltd, 1st Floor,
The Liffey Trust Centre, 117–126 Sheriff Street Upper,
Dublin 1, D01 YC43
Associated companies throughout the world
www.panmacmillan.com

ISBN 978-1-0350-1117-9 HB
ISBN 978-1-0350-1118-6 TPB

1 3 5 7 9 8 6 4 2

A CIP catalogue record for this book is available from the British Library.

Typeset in Minion Pro by Jouve (UK), Milton Keynes
Printed and bound by CPI Group (UK) Ltd, Croydon, CR0 4YY

Visit **www.panmacmillan.com** to read more about all our books
and to buy them. You will also find features, author interviews and
news of any author events, and you can sign up for e-newsletters
so that you're always first to hear about our new releases.

To Annabelle

Contents

viii | Contents

'The world's biggest cash machine' is adapted from a quote from the ex-Manchester United and England player Paul Parker: 'All United are, really, is the highest-profile ATM machine in world football. Not bad, is it? Come in, tap a few numbers and take out millions in dividends.'

Introduction

I've always been gripped by spectacular business deals and the super-wealthy. I'm not sure why. I guess it stems from having state schoolteachers as parents and growing up in a family that was removed from the commercial world. My mother was one of three sisters – two teachers and a nurse. My father was an only child and became a geography teacher. Making money wasn't in my DNA.

As a child, I would watch episodes of *Whicker's World* open-mouthed, as Alan Whicker, the smooth, debonair presenter, revealed a world seemingly populated only by the super-rich. These were people who were extremely rich or – as they're now known – hyper-rich. They didn't just have yachts, they had super-yachts; their houses weren't houses but palaces; their cars had wheels and were made of metal, but they did not look like any car I'd ever seen – not in Barrow-in-Furness in Cumbria.

Years later, when I first started work at a City law firm, I was exposed to some of them. One client was Tiny Rowland, a fearsome, freewheeling global tycoon. Rowland was a domineering figure who cared little for those who got in his way – shareholders and non-executive directors included. Not for nothing was his company once described by a former prime minister as the 'unacceptable face of capitalism'.

While my solicitor employer was extremely successful and its partners were wealthy, they were small fry compared to Rowland. Their job was to serve him, to do his bidding. He and his company had interests right across the planet.

The role of his lawyers was to pave the way, to make things happen for him and to clear up the mess if things went wrong. Lawyers, accountants, insurers, bankers, stockbrokers, public relations people, all of them have their own stars who claim hefty salaries and bonuses and equity payouts but, when all is said and done, they're servants, always at their clients' beck and call.

When I became a journalist I met characters like Sir Richard Branson, Bill Gates, Rupert Murdoch, Mohamed Al-Fayed, the media tycoon (and – as it transpired – fraudster) Robert Maxwell, industrialist Lord Hanson and financier Lord Rothschild, among many others. Some, I got to know well. Frequently, they would talk about where opportunities might lie, where they thought the world was heading, where their next bag of treasure might be unearthed.

It was riveting and unnerving. They seemed to operate on a higher plane than anyone else; anyone, that is, except their fellow buccaneers. I got to know the hedge-fund and commodity kings as well. They, too, would speak about landing massive profits, of making huge killings, in having called the market right and destroying the opposition. They were fascinating because they operated in an alternative universe.

I was not one of them. It's always amazed me, the lack of fear, the brass neck, the big *cojones* of these people. I didn't possess such qualities, not like that; not where taking risks and making money were concerned.

Occasionally, there comes along a business coup that is so audacious as to take the breath away. When you hear about it, you want to learn more, you want to know how. It's the knockout, the one that makes even the Titans sit up. Invariably, it is counted in billions not millions. It's a piece of commercial chutzpah, sheer bravado and cunning, marking the grabbing of a chance, an opening, that no one else saw or had.

It's the mega-hedge-fund play: taking a massive 'short' position and delighting as the stock falls; a piece of super-prescient trading in shares and financial futures. It's a legendary market hit, a spot of deal-making brilliance that's legal but – in terms of sheer audacity – akin to the cleverest heist.

On 20 September 2004, I was a guest in the Directors' Box as Manchester United played Liverpool under floodlights at Old Trafford.

It was a wonderful, raw, full-throttled occasion, befitting one of the fiercest rivalries in world sport. The two mightiest North-West of England teams, two giants of English football, separated only by a short motorway, with long, glorious, trophy-winning histories behind them, comprised of superstars, with fans following them in every part of the world, battling head-to-head.

The air was crackling with anticipation. Rio Ferdinand was returning to the United line-up after an eight-month ban. The prodigiously talented Cristiano Ronaldo was playing. The Welsh wizard, Ryan Giggs, was making his 600th appearance for the club. Only the formidable Wayne Rooney was missing, injured. On the Liverpool side, Steven Gerrard, their talisman, was leading the line, Jerzy Dudek was keeping goal for the 100th time, and they were fielding their major summer signing, Djibril Cissé, the French league's top goal-scorer the previous season.

Sitting in the Directors' Lounge beforehand, enjoying fine wine and food amid tables occupied by Manchester and Merseyside TV celebrities, and well-known business and political figures, it felt like being a member of royalty. Not the Buckingham Palace sort, but a more tangible, down-to-earth, northern variety. We were with the gods, privileged and elite. It was giddying and special. There was no denying the sense of power, the sheer thrill, the buzz, in walking out into the Directors' Box in front of a huge, roaring crowd of 67,000.

The massive structure of Old Trafford, or as Manchester United's slick marketing folk like to promote it, the 'Theatre of Dreams', was packed, and the noise was constant and deafening – even more so when United won 2–1, thanks to two Mikaël Silvestre-headed goals versus an own goal from John O'Shea. Afterwards, the world-famous players came in to mingle and to chat, showered, sleek and impossibly athletic – and my sense of being Very Important was compounded.

I was there because Finsbury, United's London corporate public relations firm, had invited me. United was almost certainly facing the prospect of a full-blown takeover bid from the United States, and they wanted me, as City editor of the *London Evening Standard*, together with a journalist from the *Financial Times*, to meet the 'home' management team.

United had been 'in play', as they say in the City, for a while. Rupert Murdoch was interested but was stymied by the regulator. Two mighty Irish business personalities, both multibillionaires, J. P. McManus and John Magnier, owned a sizeable stake. They had enjoyed a close friendship with the United manager Sir Alex Ferguson, but then that had turned nasty.

Meanwhile, the little-known Florida businessman Malcolm Glazer had started acquiring United's shares. Glazer was relatively anonymous, even in his native US. He owned the NFL's Tampa Bay Buccaneers but remained firmly in the background. He appeared to have no natural affinity with soccer. In the media, he was portrayed as a hard-headed, calculating, publicity-shy money man.

What had begun on May 2003 as a small, seemingly benign investment was turning hostile – since then Malcolm and his sons had been steadily building a substantial position. It was becoming apparent that the obscure Glazers were no pushovers, and that they might even be intent on trying to acquire United, the biggest football club, the biggest sports club brand, in the world.

The United establishment did not like what was happening – the Glazers stayed determinedly in the shadows, rarely speaking to the media, never courting publicity, strictly religious, not the sorts, it was widely assumed, to be associated with owning glamorous, high-profile Manchester United. In the Old Trafford stands, in the United pubs, the devoutly Jewish, resolutely low-key Glazers were already being derided as 'weirdos'.

It was clear, talking to them that evening, that the United directors did not have a clue as to what the Glazers' plans were, what type of proprietors the Americans might be. I was nervously quizzed as to what I knew about them, which was nothing at all. In the lounge, alongside the lights sparkling on the large luxury watches and gold rings, the clinking of leaded glasses, the smell of aftershave, the warm handshakes and hugs and chatter, there was tension in the air, an edginess that had nothing to do with what was taking place on the pitch.

It would be a further nine months before the Glazers secured their prize. They achieved it by moving softly, by stealth at first, then by striking an audacious deal. The business community was shocked, while 'daylight robbery' was one of the more polite terms used by United's supporters and within football. The Americans, emerging from nowhere, had seen off well-known contenders and constructed an astonishing play, one that meant they could snaffle the great Manchester United by using hardly any of their own money. Smarter still was the likelihood that they'd done it by borrowing heavily to put up their share; that the Glazers weren't even that rich.

For all its popularity, football as a financial proposition is not for the faint-hearted. History is littered with examples of supposedly brilliant commercial minds who piled into the game, believing it afforded easy pickings, only to be cleaned out. There have been winners, but not many. The joke is that if you want to become a millionaire, start with a billion and buy a football club.

Unlike in the major league sports in the US, English football clubs can go down as well as up. Indeed, United themselves have been relegated five times (once under their original Newton Heath Lancashire and Yorkshire Railway FC moniker), and most recently in 1974. The 'Theatre of Dreams' has also known desolation and emptiness.

Football isn't as easily adaptable to the analytical *Moneyball* approach as, say, baseball or American football. It can't be so readily broken down and dissected. Matches are free-flowing and fast, often decided by moments of instinct, endeavour and pure skill, but also by human error and the vagaries of the referee and linesmen, and these days by those assisting them via video.

Like many major professional sports, football as a business is populated at the top by sharks. It's the habitat of agents and salesmen, deal-makers, brash persuaders and manipulators, men in sharp suits who pride themselves on their ruthlessness and their nose for a profit. The clubs are often bossed by these swaggering characters writ large – men, always men, who are used to getting their own way and brushing aside anything and anyone in their path.

Traditionally, the owners liked to lay claim to an affinity for their club, its place at the heart of *their* 'community', its connection to *their* people. Often, owners purchased teams from where they grew up, the team being the one that they had followed as a child, and their parents and grandparents before them. Nobody could come in and tell them how to run their club, and certainly it wouldn't be expected that someone from far away, who knew next to nothing about football, who had no link with the area, the club, or its heritage and devoted fan base, would sweep in and oust them.

The real stars of a club are, of course, the players. Now aided and abetted by their agents, they usually display little loyalty to a club or area, trying to earn as much as they can before they grow too old or are injured. They enjoy vast pay packets but they're young, and often single men. They like to splash their cash – on clothes, watches, cars, mansions – and they like to party. Invariably, from time to time, their scandalous behaviour can cause a headache for the club and for the owner.

Managers, too, are big characters, who are paid well and require careful handling. The successful ones need to be retained, and that means doing whatever it takes to secure their services and fend off the competition. They must be happy, to be allowed to have their way – buying and selling the players they want. Not easy, if it's your money the manager is spending, possibly squandering. The temptation to try and wrest back control is strong.

Owners, too, must placate the agents, ensuring they get the first call about a player's availability, and then ensuring they are not working against the club, encouraging an in-demand star to seek a transfer, sign for another club. All this and more, much more, comes to the proprietor's door. This, and the fact that they've also made themselves public property by purchasing a club followed by thousands – if not millions – of fans.

Football remains the people's game. The typical British matchday ritual of going to the pub and downing pints of beer, walking to the ground, eating a cardboard pie or soggy burger, stopping by the pub again on the journey home, is hardly glamorous; it's certainly not of interest to those intent on making fortunes. They can build their smart executive boxes and lay on a different type of experience, but, for now, the heart of the sport, in Britain at least, lies with those ordinary fans in the stands, who follow their team day in, day out, rain and shine.

All clubs, too, no matter how grand, are at the mercy of the crowd, their supporters, who can set the narrative, and who are perfectly capable of driving out players, managers and yes, owners too. In fact, the fans believe they are the rightful owners, it's *their* club – the fat cats in the Directors' Box are merely guarding it for future generations.

A friend of mine, Paul Casson, enjoyed a successful business career in the US, doing very well in the mobile phone industry. In a moment of madness, as he puts it, he bought lowly Barrow, our hometown club. He saved it from bankruptcy. Not that his benevolence cut much ice with the fans. From the very outset they wanted to know which star players he was going to acquire and if not, why not? As far as the fans were concerned, he was rich and he could pay – no matter that he had a budget, a limit on what he would spend.

That attitude extended even to the local council. The ground needed totally rebuilding. Paul made an offer to the Labour-run local authority. He would pay half, if they paid half, and on non-matchdays the new stadium could be used by the community. No, said the council: you're rich, you pay for it.

The local media were his friend one minute, his sternest critic the next. So it was with the supporters. If Barrow were winning, all was well. Lose and keep on losing, and they would be after his blood. It was his responsibility to hire the manager. He would pick a candidate, only for problems to arise. Eventually, Paul quit, heavily out of pocket. He still maintains he enjoyed the ride, though – well, some of it.

Into such a maelstrom entered the unheralded, downbeat, uncon-nected, totally alien Glazers. I've always wondered how exactly they managed it. How and why they bought Manchester United, and how and why they stayed the course in the face of unprecedented abuse and hostility.

I'm not a United supporter (Barrow, always, then later, Fulham), but I do remember being allowed to stay up late to witness, on a grainy black-and-white TV, United win the European Cup, forerun-ner of the Champions League, in 1968 at Wembley Stadium against Portugal's Benfica, the first English club to do so.

I grew up watching and marvelling at United's George Best, Bobby Charlton, Denis Law, Nobby Stiles, Pat Crerand, Alex Stepney and the stewardship of their manager, Matt Busby. I knew about the Munich air crash, and how members of the team and club staff had perished, including the great Duncan Edwards, a boy wonder, widely regarded as the best player in England. And how, afterwards, Busby had picked himself up, and the club too, and had rebuilt and taken Manchester United to the very top of the game.

No other club had that back story or could engender the same emotion. No other team possessed that cachet and romance. Then, latterly, came the class of '92, the wunderkinds of David Beckham, Ryan Giggs, Nicky Butt, Paul Scholes and the Neville brothers, Gary and Phil, and the haughty panache of the French master Eric Can-tona, the speed of thought of Wayne Rooney, the physicality of Roy Keane and the audacity of Ronaldo, all marshalled by the redoubtable Alex Ferguson.

The United fans did not take to their strange new owners. Some chose to don the former Newton Heath colours of green and gold, angrily demonstrating and protesting. Some went further and formed their own club, FC United of Manchester. Star players were sold to pay off the debts, or not bought to keep costs down; the fans constantly complained that the rarely seen, distant Glazers were tight with money; that they lacked vision, that they didn't care, that they were too profits-driven, more interested in paying themselves fees and dividends. After Ferguson left in 2013, managers came and went; and, for all its grand size, the Old Trafford stadium wasn't updated. In terms of comfort and facilities, it began to lag behind those of United's Premier League and European peers.

In 2021, the Glazers alienated United fans still further, and football followers everywhere, with a plan, hatched with other bosses, to form a 'European Super League' (ESL) of some of Europe's biggest clubs. It wasn't the first time that owners had broached the subject of creating a breakaway competition, but this was more serious and carefully planned. For its founders, there would be no relegation from the ESL. United and the other clubs involved, and more particularly their American owners, were guaranteed an initial twenty-three-year bonanza, playing an elite competition among themselves and sharing enormous payouts for TV rights.

Opposition was furious and from all quarters – fans, media, pundits, ex-players, managers (who had been kept in the dark about the scheme) and politicians, including the UK prime minister and government. Football was being hijacked by a bunch of people intent only on enriching themselves; they had no love for the spirit of the game, founded on the disappointment of defeat and the thrill of winning. The opprobrium directed at the Glazers, who were among the ringleaders, was especially vitriolic and personal, leading to fans breaking into Old Trafford and seeking their removal, and the rescheduling of the season's prestige match against Liverpool. Within days, the scheme collapsed, although there is still suggestion of it being redesigned and resurrected.

The ESL episode served to harden the fans' enmity. They hated the Glazers, always had, always would. Now, it got worse.

Despite the riots and ferocity, the enduring appeal of United always shone through, unabated. Everywhere you go in Britain, apart from Liverpool, men and boys, women and girls wear United's red shirts (sponsored for seven years by Chevrolet – for a record $559 million, or £64 million a year). Everywhere across the world, too. I was on holiday in Turkey and stopped for a coffee in the middle of nowhere. The roadside snack bar had a rack of football shirts. There were strips from all the Turkish clubs, but only one foreign one: Manchester United. Here, in the far-flung recesses of Turkey, not a Manc to be seen anywhere. During the Libyan revolution of 2011, many of the rebels were wearing replica Manchester United tops.

All over the world there are United fan clubs. The United players are global household names, pin-ups for the beautiful game. United songs are sung in bars in every city on every continent. Old Trafford is the largest league ground in Britain, a giant temple to the Red Devils. They don't have a crummy shop outside; they have the Megastore, and it is always busy. It is their matches the TV companies want first; and for their loyal followers, United have their own subscription TV channel. More airtime and column inches are dedicated to the ups and downs of United than to any other club. When Liverpool beat United recently, I counted on the *Daily Mail* Sports stream eleven items focusing on United and what went wrong, as against three on Liverpool and how well they played.

In November 2022, the Glazers said they were undertaking a 'strategic review' and invited offers for the club. *Forbes* suggested United would fetch as much as £5 billion. Around £6 billion was said to be what the Glazers were seeking. Some suggested that with advances in technology and how the sport is watched, United could be worth a lot more.

At the very least, that's several billions of pounds from not putting in much at all, and after extracting many millions in cash for you and your family down the years. Brilliant.

This is the story of how the Glazers pulled it off, how they purchased, and then made billions from, Manchester United. How they have a racehorse and an almighty personal falling out to thank for their amazing good fortune.

But it's also about the exploitation of 'the people's game'; how they have treated a sport and the greatest club in the world as one giant family ATM. How they tore the soul out of football.

ONE

Red Devils

In the North-West of England, there's no escaping Manchester. It's the magnet, the draw, 'Britain's Second City' as it likes to think, even though it's not. There's no avoiding its people either. They're cocky, infectious, funny, direct, unafraid.

Mancunians, or Mancs, are no respecters of status. If they believe you're too big for your boots they will let you know, often in quite pointed terms.

The night we went to watch United play Liverpool, the smooth, urbane Finsbury PR boss, Roland Rudd, and Peter Thal Larsen from the *Financial Times* and I were met at Manchester Airport. It was early evening, there was a major game on, it was raining, the city traffic was terrible. Roland grew exasperated and, in his finest, plummy southern tone, he suggested to the driver he knew a quicker way to the Lowry Hotel, where we were checking in and dropping our bags. The driver turned and said, 'Listen mate, I don't know what you do, I don't know who you are, but I don't care. This is what I do,

I drive this car. I will get you there, so please shut up and leave it to me.'

Try as it might, Manchester will never do proper posh. There will always be a rough edge, the people of Manchester will always let you know what they really think. There are pockets that are smart, and as luxurious and design conscious as anywhere in the world. No matter. They have a saying in case someone gets above themselves: 'All fur coat and no knickers'.

Manchester: musically the home of the Smiths, the Stone Roses, Joy Division, Oasis, as well as the Hacienda, Madchester, Factory Records and Anthony J. Wilson (RIP). It was historically the world's first industrial city; architecturally it is where high-end fashion boutiques stand within walking distance of Strangeways high-security prison; culturally it is the site of TV's *Coronation Street*, and now the Salford Quays and MediaCity development, home to large parts of the BBC, which includes the Lowry Arts Centre and Imperial War Museum North. Manchester, the once grimy, stinky mill town, home to a prestigious university that has produced twenty-five Nobel laureates. Scuzzy, glorious Manchester.

Brash and in your face, working-class Manchester fears no one. Which is why Manchester's story is marked by political protest and struggle and mass gatherings.

In 1819, more than 60,000 pro-democracy and anti-poverty campaigners assembled in St Peter's Fields in the city to hear speeches by the likes of Henry 'Orator' Hunt, the parliamentary reformer. The local infantry and yeomanry had other ideas; they attacked the crowd on horseback, armed with clubs and sabres. Many hundreds of people were injured in the ferocious attack, and up to twenty men and women died.

The 'Peterloo Massacre', as it was termed, became embedded in national folklore, a rallying point for the left, for the Chartist, trade union, women's suffrage, anti-Corn Law, Communist and Cooperative movements, all of them straight out of Manchester. It led to the establishment of the *Manchester Guardian* – later *The Guardian* – newspaper.

It's where Friedrich Engels and Karl Marx studied together in the Reading Room at Chetham's in 1845. The same Marx who wrote what could be the anti-Glazer, Manchester United supporter credo: 'Everyone will own productive property in common, and everyone will work that property. No one will be able to exploit the labour of others to accumulate private wealth. No one will be alienated because everyone has a claim of ownership in everything that is produced.'

It was in Manchester where, in opposition to slavery, the local mill workers, at great personal financial cost, refused to touch raw cotton picked by American slaves. Where the cotton-mill owners bankrolled the world's biggest art exhibition, attended by 1.3 million people. Where 10,000 unemployed men and women marched against the introduction of 'means testing' – an event immortalized in the great, furious, polemical scream of a novel, *Love on the Dole*.

It was in Manchester where Pope John Paul II, on the first papal visit to the UK, in May 1982, held a mass for 250,000, among them a young Liam Gallagher. When Gallagher later played with Oasis on the very same spot to another huge audience he said, 'Last time I was here I came to see the Pope. He was all right but he didn't have many tunes.' Typical Liam, typical Manc.

It was also where, on North Road in 1878, the Lancashire and Yorkshire Railway Company's Newton Heath works set up a football and cricket club. The idea was that the workers could better themselves, staying off the drink, at least while the matches were being played. They wore the company colours of green and gold. The first team grew in stature, largely through the device of the L&YR offering jobs in their factory to those from further afield who could play football. As a result, Newton Heath or 'Heathens' contained non-local talent, from Wales, Scotland and elsewhere.

Soon, a row developed over ownership of the club: Newton Heath officials were ambitious and built two stands for spectators; the railway company was disapproving and unwilling to back their construction. 'Heathens' and L&YR parted, and from that point on, anyone could play for the club, not just employees of L&YR.

Today, some United fans cloak themselves in nostalgia for the old Newton Heath, wearing green and gold, to profess allegiance to a club that was more 'of the people'. That it might have been, but it was also hopelessly run. The club survived, just, but only thanks to the generosity of its fans. Newton Heath found salvation eventually in the shape of John Davies, owner of a brewery and married to a Tate & Lyle sugar heir. He took charge, paid off the club's debts, and changed the strip to red and white. He proposed altering the name, and at a special meeting of fans and directors, Manchester United was born.

Under Davies's sound financial stewardship, United prospered. Once he'd installed Ernest Mangnall as manager, the club's fortunes on the pitch improved as well.

Mangnall was a person of contrasts. He was stylish, liking a cigar and wearing a straw boater. But he was also a fitness fanatic and autocratic. He was, in approach, not unlike Alex Ferguson.

In May 1908, United secured their first league title. They followed that with the FA Cup in 1909, beating Bristol City at Crystal Palace. In *Manchester United: The Biography*, the writer and devoted United fan Jim White records the reaction of *The Times* to the invasion of thousands of Mancunians in support of their team: 'There are no people in the world like the northerners. They spend their money; they have their quaint ways. They bring stone jars of strong ale and sandwiches an inch thick packed in the wicker baskets which can be used for conveying carrier pigeons.'

Whatever the state of the United fans, the players were different. When presenting the cup, Lord Charles Beresford, commander-in-chief of the Channel Fleet, declared: 'I do not think I have seen finer specimens of British humanity than those who played in this game.'

On their return to Manchester, more than 300,000 people turned out to see the victory parade, with the cup being held aloft by players, management and directors on a carriage pulled by six grey mares.

Euphoria was short-lived, as the team, led by the Welsh winger Billy Meredith, demanded an end to the salary cap imposed by the club owners. They formed the Professional Footballers' Association (PFA) and sought affiliation with the General Federation of Trade Unions (GFTU). Out of Manchester: trade unionism. Out of United: the football players' union, the PFA.

The owners, in the form of the Football Association, hit back, banning the new organization and telling club chairmen to fire any players who had joined. In Manchester, the United players were locked out of their ground in Bank Street, close to the city centre. Their response was to break in and seize property in lieu of payment, including the FA Cup.

It was typical hot-headed, hotbed Manchester. Protest and the sacking of offices, especially those of the boss class, were regarded as legitimate acts, as 'fair game'. The revolt ended in defeat for the players, and victory for the FA. In 1909, the United owner, Davies, emboldened by the mass celebrations for the FA Cup triumph, commissioned a new stadium, over the city border in neighbouring Salford. Thanks to his astute financial management, Davies was able to pay for it from cash, without borrowing.

Built on land bought from the Earl of Trafford, the ground, designed to house 100,000 spectators, was described by the *Sporting Chronicle* as 'the most handsomest, the most spacious and the most remarkable arena I have ever seen. As a football ground it is unrivalled anywhere in the world.'

Thus, it became engrained in United folklore that the Reds play, and deserve to play, in the finest stadium anywhere; and, what is more, they do so for a club that is debt-free.

Many years later, and such was the level of success under Sir Alex Ferguson and, before him, Sir Matt Busby, that the modern image of Manchester United had become one associated with unalloyed triumph.

It hadn't always been the case. Indeed, United's supporters developed a taste for uprising against owners they deemed to be responsible for failure as far back as the 1930s. Those same supporters who vent their fury that the Ferguson era was not sustained would do well to study what occurred to their favourite club after the Mangnall reign and the ending of the First World War, when United entered a prolonged slump.

In 1922, United were relegated. They were not even the top local team in the Second Division – Stockport County could claim that position. Old Trafford, built for 100,000 spectators, was regularly hosting just 11,000. In the febrile Mancunian atmosphere, inflated expectation and the desire to place blame saw rumours abound that the pitch was cursed; there were calls for it to be dug up.

Meanwhile, Manchester City were riding high. The Blues had secured the services of Meredith, Mangnall and other former United stalwarts; they had moved across the city and were winning on and off the park, drawing large crowds. Again, the red mist provoked by the dominance of blue is a phenomenon that has deep roots.

In 1924, too, supporters and minority shareholders combined to seek representation on the United board. They received short shrift.

On it went. So-so displays in matches were accompanied by growing dissatisfaction on the terraces. United were back in the First Division but going nowhere – and not winning with anything like the panache their supporters demanded.

The fun in following United or, as one fan put it in a complaint to the club's Annual General Meeting, the 'sentiment', was fast disappearing. Matters came to a head in 1931. United performed dismally, conceding twenty-five goals in their first five games and losing twelve matches in a row.

The joint Manchester United Supporters Club and Shareholders Association had had enough. It demanded the board quit and that the FA scrutinize the financial dealings of the club. Led by George Greenhough, a taxi firm owner, they published a five-point plan: new manager, better player recruitment system, sign quality players, election of a new board and a rights issue to fund recovery.

True to the city's radical heritage, a call was made for a mass boycott of the home fixture against Arsenal, then the country's top team. Supporters were split as to whether a boycott was the right and proper thing to do. Notices and calls to action were circulated among the fans. The feeling was universal: though there was discontentment at the performance of the club, the beef was not with the players but with the directors. After that, though, there was a split, between the most extreme factions and the bulk of the ordinary fans.

At a public meeting to discuss the planned action, Greenhough claimed there were 3,000 at Hulme Town Hall, while the *Manchester Evening News* settled on 1,200. The resolution was carried, to boycott the plum Manchester United v. Arsenal fixture.

Strangely, as with most of the modern-day protests, it had more bark than bite. There were additional police on duty, and they were positioned on the turnstiles to spot troublemakers, but that was the extent of it. The players were cheered when they appeared, while the directors were treated with disdain. The crowd was down on the normal number for the glamour tie, but it was still United's biggest gate of the season; for the great body of supporters, the match came first. They wanted their entertainment, their weekly release, and they were not prepared to lose it. In the *Manchester Evening News*, Greenhough's movement was derided as 'a total failure'. *Athletic News* noted that 'the much-discussed boycott was on, but nobody noticed it.'

Despite their scepticism, Greenhough had put down a marker. His revolution petered out, but he showed that United fans were no respecters of hierarchy; they were unafraid to voice their anger and, even though the numbers involved were relatively small, he had effectively corralled enough people to provoke debate and spark headlines.

As it turned out, United the team went from bad to worse, losing consistently and getting relegated. The crowd, in a venue built for 100,000, now reached a low point of 3,900. Inevitably the club was running up debts; in 1931, it owed £30,000 for the building of the new North Stand at Old Trafford. Stories abounded of the depths to which it had sunk; that there was no cash for the players and staff Christmas lunch; supporters were washing the team kit to save on the laundry costs; the players were not getting paid; the gas supply to Old Trafford was disconnected because the bills were unpaid. Consistent failings on the pitch coupled with the global slump, the worst in history, which led to business closures nationwide and sky-high unemployment. The club was on its knees, seemingly destined for bankruptcy.

Salvation came in the guise of James Gibson, co-owner of a Manchester clothing firm called Briggs, Jones and Gibson. He invested a total of £30,000 to help save the club, but it had strings attached.

Gibson was not especially interested in the game of football, neither was he a particular follower of United. What concerned him was the city of Manchester and the fortunes of its inhabitants. He was persuaded that having a flourishing United was good for civic pride; even better if the team was comprised of young, local lads, reflecting the values and concerns of the people who would support the club. Gibson was signalling what was to follow, laying the foundations for the romance and legend of the later great teams. Again, something of Gibson seeped into the United DNA.

A wealthy man, he could have stopped there. But the community spirit in him pushed Gibson further. He was happy to put cash in, provided others followed his lead, and if the fans approved. For the first time the supporters were getting a proper say in the running of the club.

Four others came forward and put in £2,000 – a considerable sum in those days. United was now a club owned by rich people, but one that seemed to be determinedly for the people. For their part, the supporters responded in kind, flocking back to Old Trafford, rekindling the love for their team. The attendance for the first game with Gibson in situ on Christmas Day 1931 was almost ten times that terrible low of 3,900, up to 33,123 for a League Division Two match against Wolves which United won 3–2.

United was making a fresh start, re-establishing pride in the 'Manchester United' name. But however appealing the philosophy, it did not guarantee results. On the pitch, United was still enduring a torrid time, going right to the wire, to the very last game of the 1933–4 season, and only just managing to avoid yet another defeat and relegation to the Third Division.

It was a turning point of sorts. The club clawed its way back, and in doing so it drew on local youth players, further fuelling the legend. Gibson and the club secretary, Walter Crickmer, set up the Manchester United Junior Athletic Club in 1937, to nurture local talent. A predecessor of the Youth Academy, it produced a steady stream of players, among them Charlie Mitten, Johnny Aston and Stan Pearson.

In its first season in a local amateur league, the youth team scored an incredible 223 goals.

At the senior level, progress was mixed, with the club winning promotion as champions at the end of the 1935–6 season, only to be relegated again the following year. However, by the end of the 1937–8 season, United finished second in the league and were promoted once more to the First Division, where they would stay for the following thirty-six years. The outbreak of war in September 1939 meant that only three games were played in the 1939–40 season; for those who did not go to join the fighting, a special non-competitive War League was organized, which would dominate fixture lists until the end of the 1945–6 season.

Old Trafford had been requisitioned as a military depot, but football was still played there. A German bombing raid in December 1940 caused some damage, but a further raid in March 1941 wrecked much of the stadium, including the main stand, and after that Manchester United had to play its games at Maine Road, home to Manchester City. It was not until 1949 that the stadium had been repaired sufficiently for the players to return, though it still had no roof.

In broad terms, the team had had a good war, in the sense that none of its players had been killed or seriously injured, and it emerged with a fine squad and a new manager.

Once of Manchester City and Liverpool, Matt Busby had been managing the Army side when he had been contacted by United in December 1944. Words like 'thinker' and 'calm' are used to describe Busby, and that's how I remember him from TV interviews. He would always be wearing his trademark tracksuit or looking dapper in a woollen overcoat, jacket and trilby hat. His answers were measured and careful; he was not given to histrionics.

He'd been a successful player, and now he was turning to management. Busby displayed clarity of mind and determination, setting out his own terms for the job. He wanted to be left alone, to choose the team, to sort out transfers. He desired a free hand – something that would prove anathema to those later owners of the club, the Glazers, who liked to be consulted and involved in the buying and selling of players. He also made it clear that he was not to be judged immediately; that success would not come overnight but would take five years minimum.

Busby officially became the United manager on 1 October 1945, after he was demobbed. He was hands-on, his own man. Attempts by directors to get involved with team selection or tactics were dealt with politely but firmly. Always he was able to count on Gibson for backing.

The Busby era was encapsulated by his favourite phrase: 'Just go out and play.' Romantic as it is to regard his simple instruction as almost boyish and joyous, it masked an underlying steel. Busby was just as details driven as the modern manager, taking the players through breakdowns of the opposition, analysing their strengths and weaknesses.

His mantra took the credit, though, when United beat Blackpool 4–2 in 1948, in one of the greatest FA Cup finals, when they came up against the England duo of Stanley Matthews and Stan Mortensen. It was a terrific contest, with United living up to their image as a buccaneering, stylish, all-out attacking side. At half-time Blackpool led 2–1, only for United, after being told to 'just go out and play', to dominate the second half and win.

Another victory parade through the centre of Manchester ensued. This was one with a difference, when the team diverted to Gibson's house – he was at home, ill, having missed the final. It was an important, symbolic moment. Seven of this team were local Mancs. There was a togetherness – of a club, its owners, players, manager, supporters, and the city itself.

Busby was an impatient character, not given to resting on his laurels. No sooner had United triumphed than he began to dismantle the team, believing it to be too old, to focus on building a new, younger edition.

Bobby Charlton, Duncan Edwards, David Pegg, Billy Whelan, Eddie Coleman . . . Busby created a team of local youths. No matter that several of them were not from Manchester at all. They were all treated as locals; ordinary lads who lived in digs and would ride bikes to and from the United training ground, The Cliff in Salford, and hang out in the local dance halls and cinemas afterwards.

Busby made sure they behaved as normal kids, and that success did not go to their heads. And Manchester embraced them for it. They were seen as the city's own, to be loved, nurtured and protected. It added to the sense of United being the people's club. That spirit was fostered as well by how United played – with élan and verve. Their modus operandi was all-out attack. In 1955–6, they lost just one game between Christmas and the end of the season, winning the league by a huge eleven points.

Two nicknames were coined for them: Busby Babes and Red Devils. Busby himself preferred the latter, seeing it as conveying style and mischief.

In 1956, the club was invited by UEFA to play in Europe, for the second season of the newly formed European Cup. The English football establishment, notably the football league, was not best pleased, but was powerless to resist.

Here was United blazing a trail, setting forth to compete on a bigger stage, one that would in time come to dwarf the domestic competitions in terms of prestige and financial worth. The first match was against Anderlecht, the top Belgian side, in Belgium. United won 2–0. In the return leg, played at City's ground in Maine Road because Old Trafford did not have floodlights, United were imperious, unstoppable, winning 10–0, and watched by 43,365 spectators. Clearly Manchester was captivated by the glamour of European nights, and enamoured with the bewitching football that its young team was producing. Again, it was not only United that was setting a different standard, playing in a different league; the city and its people were sharing the journey. The nation, too.

In the quarter-final, United overcame Athletic Bilbao in a two-leg thriller in early 1957, prompting this, from Henry Rose, the *Daily Express* football correspondent: 'My hands are still trembling as I write. My heart still pounds. And a few hours have passed since, with 65,000 other lucky people, I saw the greatest soccer victory in history, ninety minutes of tremendous thrill and excitement that will live for ever in the memory. Salute the eleven red-shirted heroes of Manchester United. The whole country is proud of you.'

United had won the English Football League First Division, they were in the final of the FA Cup, and now the semi-final of the European Cup. For a while, it appeared as though this swashbuckling team would win the lot. In the end it was not to be, and they were well beaten by Real Madrid, which prompted a bout of soul-searching in Busby. What had impressed him was not only Real Madrid's better football, but also how thoroughly the club was immersed in the community. All levels of Madrid society appeared to have a say in the running of the club, which was owned by the supporters.

It appeared to Busby that even Manchester City had closer ties with Mancunians; United was becoming synonymous with money, even back then. Busby resolved to do more to improve local relations and return the club to its roots, to the people who lived around it. Tragically, happenstance was to do that in a way that no one would have wanted or foreseen. If the plane carrying the players, management and press on the way back from playing Red Star Belgrade had not skidded off the runway at Munich after a refuelling stop, what then? It is impossible to speculate.

Twenty-three people perished as a result of the Munich air disaster of 6 February 1958, among them eight players, including Duncan Edwards, then considered England's coming superstar. As a song composed in their memory put it, 'the flowers of English football, the flowers of Manchester' were lost.

Arguably, these terrible events cemented the United legend. The accident and the club's recovery afterwards came to define the badge on the shirt, what it stood for, what it meant.

Tragedies have befallen other clubs – in England alone, the Hillsborough catastrophe and the Bradford City stadium fire, both of which involved far greater loss of life. Perhaps the difference is that, at Munich, players were among the dead, star players, magic boys, heroes in death as in life. The club's supporters, Manchester and beyond – all regarded the players as somehow theirs. As Bobby Charlton put it: 'Before Munich, United were seen as Manchester's club. Afterwards, everyone felt as if they owned a little bit of it.'

Rio Ferdinand remarked that Munich was 'the starting point, really, for the tradition, the start of setting down the standard for Manchester United Football Club.'

In the aftermath of the disaster, Manchester United could have collapsed or faded into quiet obscurity, but – perhaps distilling that wartime sense of 'carrying on' – they not only survived the tragedy but prospered.

The task of rebuilding the club fell initially to Jimmy Murphy, Busby's ebullient, popular assistant who had not been on the Belgrade trip. Busby had been critically injured in the crash but, even as he lay stricken on a Munich hospital bed, he urged: 'Keep the flag flying, Jim, till I get back.'

Thus was the romance, the spirit of renewal, born. The first match, a fortnight after the aircraft burst into flames, was at home against Sheffield Wednesday. Murphy picked seven youth-team players, two recent signings and two Munich survivors. Somehow, at a packed Old Trafford, the cobbled-together outfit won. In the stands, in the terraced streets of Manchester, across the country and the world, even amid traditional foes, there was joy.

Shortly afterwards came the awful blow that Duncan Edwards, who had been critically injured and clung on for fifteen days, would not be coming back.

From then on, United would try and play a certain, courageous way – 'attack, attack, attack' was the Old Trafford call – in tribute to those who died. That's how Bobby Charlton saw it, saying he always gave everything he had 'for Manchester United and the lads who didn't make it.' When, today, the players' form dips or they become too defensive, it is not long before some reference is made to the 'United way' or the 'Busby way', code for the spirit of 1958.

United refused to be cowed. The survivors were not going to allow what had happened to destroy the club or the legacy of the players who had perished. Within weeks of the crash, they'd fought their way to the FA Cup final in May 1958. That day they wore specially emblazoned club badges on their shirts, showing a phoenix. Their storybook defiance earned them supporters from all over. No matter they lost, in the end, 2–0 to Bolton Wanderers.

Within football there was enormous and heartfelt sympathy for United, but in some quarters it was also accompanied by animosity, born out of a kind of twisted jealousy, that United now had a popular kudos and stature that other clubs could never match. Some opposition fans mimicked the sounds and movement of an airplane crashing; others mocked 'the Munichs' on commemorative T-shirts.

For the club itself, after the initial support and sympathy, the first few years after the disaster were grim. United was still in shock, and the training ground and Old Trafford were unhappy places. The play-ers did not sparkle on the pitch and attendances, which had risen immediately after the accident as people wanted to rally round, dropped. Gradually, though, the mood, and with it the results, lifted.

Matt Busby, finally having left hospital after nine weeks' recupera-tion, had resumed a full managerial role in the 1958–9 season. His chest had been crushed, a lung had collapsed and he'd been on life support. Twice, he'd had the last rites read to him. When he started to recover, he was guilt-stricken at what had been lost, by his decision to play in Europe. He struggled with the thought that he had lived and so many others had not. He turned his back on the game, but gradually, he came round – his wife, Jean, told Busby how much his family needed him and by walking away from football, from United, he was letting down those who had perished. He owed it to them to return.

He began to rebuild the team, buying a young, brilliant goal-scorer, Denis Law, from Torino in 1962, and from Celtic the midfielder Paddy Crerand in February 1963, to feed Law long balls from the back. Alongside Law stood David Herd (forward), Bobby Charlton (attacking midfielder), Bill Foulkes (centre half), Nobby Stiles (defen-sive midfielder), Tony Dunne (left back), and goalkeeper Harry Gregg. It was the makings of a strong side. What tipped it over into greatness was the arrival of George Best.

The wonderfully talented, mercurial 'kid', the blue-eyed boy genius from Belfast, was the first true 'celebrity' footballer, with his pop-star hairstyle, dashing good looks and attendant wild lifestyle. He belonged to United. George was United.

On his own, Best was special, but put him alongside the disci-plined, unyielding oak of Charlton and the snapping terrier of Law, and you had a corporate marketeer's dream. The Englishman, the Irishman and the Scotsman, as Law liked to joke. Then set this 'holy trinity' against the quiet stoicism of Busby and resurrection that followed the horror of Munich, and you had the trappings of an epic tale. Manchester, the world, were enthralled.

There was another more prosaic first. Old Trafford became the first football ground in the country, in 1965, to acquire corporate hospitality boxes. United was catering for ambition. Redbrick, smokestack Manchester was being elevated. Together, club and city were on a shared odyssey.

Liverpool might have The Beatles, but United had their own non-singing version in Best, and a feverish atmosphere around the club and its matches to rival a Beatles concert. For anyone not wedded to a particular team, they could – and did – choose to follow the most glamorous of all.

The foundation for everything that followed was laid on 29 May 1968 at Wembley. The old stadium was packed with over 92,000 people, mostly United supporters, who had somehow got tickets for the European Cup final. They were pitched against Portugal's Benfica, which was making its fifth appearance in a European Cup final; for United it was a first.

It was fitting the match was at the scene of England's World Cup victory two years earlier. That was the national team, this was the nation's team. In Bideford Gardens, in Barrow-in-Furness, I was allowed to stay up and watch. I was not alone – United had most of the country and an international audience rapt.

It was more than a mere ninety minutes of twenty-two men chasing a leather football round a rectangle of grass. It was a decade after disaster; a celebration for a manager who almost lost his life and saw his boys lose theirs, a glorious showcase for a team of extraordinary talent. Words like 'faith', 'spirit' and 'destiny' were bandied about.

United had to win, of course they did. For ninety minutes it was close, 1–1. But in extra time, George Best, Brian 'Kiddo' Kidd and

Bobby Charlton all scored to make it 4–1, unleashing a communal outpouring of emotion of the kind that perhaps only sport can deliver. As the beers and tears flowed, it was clear that Manchester United was special, that among football clubs it was unique, a club with a history, blighted by terrible tragedy, yet possessed of remarkable, almost mythical powers of recovery that resonated down the ages. In that moment of triumph, United's hegemony was sealed. There were football clubs – and there was Manchester United.

TWO

Anyone but Maxwell

The triumph at Wembley in May 1968 was short-lived. What might have been a springboard to repeated glory became instead a descent into unimagined humiliation.

Several of those players on that never-to-be-forgotten night were already nearing the end of their careers. Meanwhile, George Best was battling his demons: alcohol, gambling, and the kind of unrelenting attention that would be hard for the most stable character to endure. The upshot was, he had become ever more unreliable. Although Busby tried to introduce younger legs, elevating members of the club's youth system into the first team, it proved impossible to match the once-in-a-generation team that had lifted the European Cup, full of stars who were among the best in Europe, if not the world.

Now aged sixty, Busby stepped back from managing the team, instead installing himself as the club's general manager. This made for an unsatisfactory situation, for whoever came along next would be managing the team under the gimlet eye of Busby. He still had the power; whatever he said, went. Busby opted for an unknown as his successor: Wilf McGuinness, the youth team coach, who was on something of a hiding to nothing. He wanted to introduce new coaching ideas; they were dismissed. He tried to assert his authority by making Charlton do press-ups in front of the others; Charlton was not pleased. He snubbed Jimmy Murphy – not a way to treat a hero from Munich. He fell out with Best; the superstar absented himself.

Eventually, after a period of mayhem, Busby rode back in, taking charge full time and consigning the hapless McGuinness to managing the reserves. Best returned and started scoring again. United's performances and league position improved. The damage, though, had been done, and years of instability followed. A story destined to be repeated.

After McGuinness came Frank O'Farrell, who was installed in 1971, but the ex-Leicester City manager could not make a team that was dominated by star names, who still revered the boss on high, dance to his tune. After eighteen months of failure, Busby determined that he, too, had to go. In the dramatic about-turns that had now become the United way, the next manager was as different again.

Where O'Farrell had been quiet, taciturn and methodical, Tommy Docherty, 'Tommy Doc', was colourful, sharp, instinctive, ebullient. United were a team in transition. The old guard of Charlton, Law, Best, had all gone. Their replacements had been unable to recapture the glory days. Tommy Docherty accepted this poisoned chalice in late 1972 and managed to keep the club in the First Division the following year, but their difficulties continued. In April 1974, the unthinkable happened: United were relegated, thanks to a goal from Denis Law, who was now playing for Manchester City.

That last game saw a pitch invasion at Old Trafford, where thousands of fans swarmed onto the turf, prompted by the notion that United might win any replay if the match was abandoned. But as it was, they were wasting their effort. They were consigned to the Second Division, but these rioting, chanting fans set the scene for the coming season in the lower flight.

United became a cause célèbre, as youths joined the 'Red Army', invading places that were not used to sizeable football crowds. Back at Old Trafford, too, the Stretford End became home to a huge, mostly young crowd, intoxicated by the heady atmosphere, but with that came violence and rampant hooliganism. When United played Norwich, fans burned down the main stand. At Millwall, there was a full-scale battle with the home supporters and police. There was a definite 'madness of crowds' element at work. The fans were not protesting against anybody or anything in particular; there was no central objective in their minds – it was violence for violence's sake, for the thrill of punching and kicking and headbutting and running away, trying to avoid arrest. It was a 'sport' alongside sport. If challenged, though, and as their songs made clear, they were doing it 'for United'.

The attraction reached far beyond Manchester. I recall boys at my school, a hundred miles away, making the long journey to follow the Reds on a Saturday. They would return with tales of combat and 'aggro'.

This set the tenor for being 'a Red'. Old Trafford acquired a noise and emotion that had not been there before. To be a Stretford Ender, in the Red Army, meant something. The trips, encounters and run-ins with the opposition, authorities and hapless bar-owners and shopkeepers in small towns the length and breadth of England became the stuff of folklore, retold in graphic detail in books, fanzines, on banners and in song. Other sets of supporters were doing the same but United's followers, as was their wont, saw themselves as first and best, or worst, depending on how you viewed them.

It's no coincidence that some of the key characters involved in orchestrating the protests against the Glazers played instrumental roles in organizing the Red Army. They fought for the soul of United then and, as they saw it, later they were doing the same again.

In 1974–5 United came top of the division, playing a youthful, vibrant style of 'attack attack attack' on the pitch while their fans wrecked grounds and injured people off it as they arrived back in the big time – in their rightful place, as they saw it. Following a United led by the irrepressible Docherty offered an exuberant ride, a foil to the dour, cautious Leeds, which had come top of the First Division in the 1973–4 season.

The revival did not last. A month after United won the FA Cup in 1977, Docherty announced he was in a relationship with Mary, the wife of Laurie Brown, the club physio, and they were setting up home together. Asked how it would affect his position as manager, Docherty replied, 'You'll have to ask the chairman.'

Ten days after the Doc's dramatic announcement, the United board met. The chairman, Louis Edwards, voted for the manager to remain. The majority of directors disagreed, and Docherty was gone.

Louis Edwards was a big man, eighteen stone. He was a wholesale meat supplier, a butcher – a very successful one, but a butcher, nonetheless. He had inherited a food and grocery business, which he built up to be the leading meat supplier in the Manchester area, with a wholesale arm and more than eighty retail shops. The family firm had an annual turnover of £5 million when he floated it on the stock market in 1962.

In 1950, Edwards had met Matt Busby, having been introduced by Tommy Appleby, a theatre impresario. Both Catholics, they also had a family link via Busby's pal Louis Rocca, and they became friends.

Edwards's rise was calculated and assured. He began as Busby's loyal friend, gaining a place on the United board (after Munich, when the directors' line-up needed strengthening), making himself useful to Busby by taking on any task, no matter how small. Then, once his feet were under the table, he started buying out the small shareholders, writing to them and visiting them personally, so that in 1965 he emerged as the club's biggest investor and was installed as chairman.

The majority shareholder and chairman of United throughout much of the 1960s and 1970s, he became nationally and internationally known. His mother's family were Italian silversmiths, which gave him his personal sense of style and appreciation of the finer things in life. Certainly, in his native North-West, 'Champagne Louis', as he was called due to his penchant for champagne and cigars, was a regular on the nightly news and sports bulletins. Edwards was a regional baron; a commanding figure, someone to be feared.

His assiduous courting of even the lowliest of shareholders, aided by a silky-smooth patter inducing them to sell, had been brilliantly finessed. He had the board in his grasp, so that they went along with his share-buying – even though it was clear where it was heading: Edwards, steadily and surely, was wresting control of the club. And for very little money, relatively speaking.

His majority stake cost him somewhere between £31,000 and £41,000 to build. It was a bargain. United's gate receipts alone were £172,000 for the 1963–4 season. The club had paid a British transfer record of £115,000 to Torino for Denis Law in 1962. Yet Edwards had secured control of the whole club for a third of that amount.

It was an audacious stroke, if not immediately financially rewarded. United was still losing money. It wasn't the biggest club either; that was Tottenham, which enjoyed turnover of £328,849 and produced a profit of £125,044. Televised football was in its infancy, with the BBC showing recorded highlights on *Match of the Day* on BBC2, for which it paid the Football League a total of £5,000 a year, with United's share a mere £50 a year.

Today, Edwards's meat business would be regarded as an anachronism, almost comical in the way it went about conducting its affairs.

The meat was generally of cheap, low quality, often from the imported carcasses of animals that had been kept and killed inhumanely. Not that the prices Edwards charged were low. 'Second-class meat at first-class prices' was one saying doing the rounds about Louis C. Edwards & Sons.

Edwards displayed the same methodical approach to selling meat as he did to the buying of United shares. If he wanted a contract – say to supply meat for school meals – he would make it his job to secure it, by all means necessary, including bribing the council officials responsible for awarding the contract. His firm existed on a steady stream of backhanders: 'sweeteners', which were cash handouts, and 'danglers', which were gifts in kind. Its success was based entirely on corrupt means, on cutting corners, making bribes, on nods, winks and brown envelopes.

Gradually, though, the company began to unravel. Edwards himself was devoting more of his time to United affairs and enjoying his status there; those working below him in the meat company were not so zealous when it came to chasing a profit. Britain joined the EU and the rules on meat imports tightened. Councils began to get pickier about the quality of the meat they were serving in their schools and care homes. Edwards's daughter Catherine saw her husband's building firm collapse.

From riding high, Edwards struggled. Fortunately, he had United to fall back upon. Arguably, this would not be the only time a family that enjoyed a chequered history in business would be able to count upon United to keep the money flowing.

In 1978, United made a rights issue to raise £1 million. It was a seminal moment in the history of the club; the moment, arguably, it ceased to be a mere football club devoted to the beautiful game but instead became a business thirsting to make money and using football as the means to do so. Until then, it had trucked along, from one season to the next, riding the highs and the lows. Now, though, just as the Edwards's meat business was suffering, the atmosphere within the club changed. It became more commercially minded, increasingly hard-headed.

Originally, Edwards wanted to increase the number of shares and not raise any new capital. His idea was to sell spare shares to supporters, who would hang the framed share certificates on their walls – he could sell the shares in gift frames for more than their true value. That plan was parked. It was indicative, however, of how Edwards viewed the fans – as folk to be exploited, who would pay for any old rubbish so long as it somehow carried the United name.

Together with United's City of London banker advisors, a rights issue to increase the total number of United shares and raise £1 million in new capital was prepared. The rights issue would be for existing shareholders, who were able to buy 208 new shares at £1 each.

At the same time, Edwards completed some unfinished business. When he'd bought out United's small shareholders previously, he had amassed just enough shares to give him control. It left him on too much of a knife-edge for his own comfort, though, so he set out to gain absolute power. He again started making people offers they could not refuse for their shares, taking the block of Edwards family shares from 47 per cent to 74 per cent. What shareholders had not been told, however, was that a rights issue was in the pipeline. Obviously, if they'd clung on to their shares, they would have substantially increased in value. Edwards, in other words, was insider trading – making a gain out of private, commercial information that he knew but they didn't.

One United director was wholly opposed to what was going on. Busby was furious; he could see the scheme for what it was: a move by Edwards to enrich himself, since he was receiving new shares at £1 each which were worth possibly eight times that on the open market, added to which the dividend payments he received in future would be far higher.

Busby's anger and dismay – he had been responsible for introducing Edwards to the club – was compounded by Edwards's lack of regard for Busby's eldest son. While Edwards was promoting his eldest boy, Martin, and while Martin had a seat on the board, there was nothing for Sandy Busby. As far as Sir Matt Busby was concerned, there had been a tacit understanding that he would one day be United chairman. But now Edwards was chairman and apparently going nowhere, and it had become abundantly clear that he was expecting his son Martin to succeed him.

Busby's isolation was further aggravated by Edwards ignoring a formal proposal for Sandy to be elected to the board, whereas Edwards's younger son, Roger, was elevated. The 'People's Club' was turning into a family money-making machine, a mirror of the Edwardses' meat business, while its great footballing brain, keeper of the Munich flame and the club's legend and romance, Sir Matt Busby, had effectively been sidelined by a coup.

Busby was not alone in being unhappy. There were others at the top of United who were concerned at the turn the club was taking. Les Olive, the company secretary, wrote in the strongest terms to Edwards, warning him to expect 'personal attacks' once word got out about what was planned. Olive tried a threat of his own, saying it would be necessary to reveal details of directors' dealings with the club, including Edwards's sales of meat to United, and Busby's ownership of the club shop – but to no avail.

Naively, he warned Edwards that the proposal could mean the payment of increased dividends to the shareholders, primarily the Edwards family, and payment could be made 'EVERY year', even if it was not in the club's best interests to do so. Years later, in an echo through time, the fans would rage against the Glazers' annual dividend payments.

There was a fan protest of sorts against Edwards's move. It was led by John Fletcher, a millionaire local businessman, who formed the Manchester United Action Group '78 and advertised against Edwards in the local press. He organized a petition which attracted 6,000 signatures. Compared with what came later, this was nothing. Most supporters probably viewed this as boardroom manoeuvrings, financial and distant, and Edwards had control anyway – it was not as if United was changing hands. Also, crucially, Edwards had said the £1 million raised would be spent on players, and in that he was true to his word, as most of it subsequently went on acquiring the England midfielder Ray Wilkins in 1979.

Still, rows about United's finances and an apparent schism between the Edwards and Busby families aroused the interest of investigative journalists, who suspected there was a whiff of scandal around the club. Sure enough, they uncovered improper payments to the families of talented schoolboys to persuade them to sign – United was always proud of its youth policy – and details of how Edwards had gone round encouraging investors to sell their shares cheaply.

Their efforts culminated in a Granada TV *World in Action* programme in January 1980, which did not pull its punches about what was going on at United, whilst also alleging that Edwards had bunged council officials to further his meat business. A month after the show aired, Louis Edwards was dead, having suffered a heart attack while taking a bath. His son, Martin, blamed the media for killing him – his medical notes suggested otherwise; that he'd experienced heart trouble in the past.

A hastily convened meeting which was due to agree the club's official response to the TV disclosures turned into a succession discussion. Martin Edwards was declared chairman, with Busby receiving the honorary, meaningless title of president.

This latest manoeuvre finally did attract the ire of the fans. The young Edwards had defeated Busby, the people's choice, and United and footballing icon. There were rumblings about money mattering more than football, and how Edwards Senior had taken ownership of United by stealth, through the back door, turning up at people's houses and pressuring them to sell their shares.

Supporters, who put football first and finances second, wished Busby to take charge of what they saw as rightfully his. Henceforward Martin Edwards would always struggle to win them over, to turn them round. He was seen as the whippersnapper (at aged thirty-four, he was the second-youngest chairman in the league, after Elton John at Watford), who had been handed the mighty United, their United, on a plate. Manchester liked its sons to earn their fortunes, not to be born with a silver spoon. Try as he might, Edwards Junior could never gain popular acclaim.

'Everyone thinks what the Glazers suffered is new,' says Andy Mitten, the football journalist, editor of the United fanzine *United We Stand*. 'The United fans have hated other owners. Louis and Martin Edwards were hated and abused – and some of the ones before them.'

The young broom, Martin Edwards, carried on where his father left off. He put United on a more business-like, some might say cynical, footing. He cut expenses and introduced a budget for the club. New ventures were launched, including a United basketball team. Edwards wanted United to adopt a more 'Continental' format of a sporting club, laying on various sports, all under one umbrella. So, United bought the established basketball side, Warrington Vikings, to form the Manchester United basketball team. Attendance numbers and interest were low. Undeterred, Edwards acquired Manchester Giants, and merged the two teams. Again, it didn't take off and eventually, after three years dallying with basketball, the franchise was sold to local businessmen and renamed Manchester Eagles.

While the boardroom was aiming to acquire a more serious air, on the pitch, too, the traditional United freedom and abandonment was in short supply. The new manager was Dave Sexton – thoughtful, well-read, a planner and analyst; shy and introverted, he was the complete opposite of Docherty. Unfortunately for Sexton, the team displayed the same attributes, playing a brand of careful, unimaginative, unspontaneous football that ground out draws rather than wins. The joy was draining from Old Trafford. And the attendances dropped. Average crowds in the 1980–1 season were 6,500 down on the previous season.

In the Directors' Box, Edwards did not like what he was seeing. There were plenty of positives about Sexton – as a coach, a man manager, he was second to none. But the numbers, especially the financials, were negative. The board decided he should go. One director voted to keep him. That was Busby, another footballing brain, but Busby did not count any more. Edwards wished Sexton out, and so out he went.

As was becoming the United pattern, his successor was as different again. In 1981, 'Big Ron' Atkinson came in, the club's sixth manager in under ten years. He announced his arrival at 'The Millionaire', a club in the centre of Manchester, a favourite haunt of the Manc money men. He was sipping champagne, naturally.

For all his comedic bonhomie, Atkinson was no slouch. He rebuilt the team, and they were winning again. United were on the up, the fans were flocking back; they were singing once more.

United's success was not going unnoticed elsewhere. In May 1983, they won the FA Cup. Shortly afterwards, Robert Maxwell tried to buy the club. Maxwell offered Edwards £10 million for his shares and was not immediately rebuffed: Edwards was willing to talk.

Maxwell was everything we now know him to have been, but in 1983 we did not know he was a crook. He was a larger-than-life, huge bully of a man. I once interviewed him in his underpants. He was doing a deal that he wanted to tell the media about. I was summoned to see him at his offices in Holborn, central London. It was going on for seven in the evening and I was kept waiting, then told he would see me. I was shown into a room, which was his bedroom. On the bed was a dinner suit. Maxwell was in the en suite. He stood in the doorway, putting on his dress shirt, while barking instructions at me.

His voice boomed as he fiddled with the cufflinks and buttons. What I took away was not the spectacle, terrifying as it was (they were the largest pair of white Y-fronts I'd ever seen), but the memory of his shameless bravura. I could think of no other tycoon who would have done that. Out of decency and respect they would have got dressed first. Maxwell, though, did not care. He was not the same as the others.

He was a preposterous blusterer and self-publicist. While criminal charges had not yet stuck – it was only after his death he was revealed to be a fraudster – there was the sense of something not being quite right about him. In football, he owned Oxford United, his local team, and he had a major portion of neighbouring Reading. No follower of tradition, and showing he cared little for their fans, he'd proposed merging them to form the commercial confection, Thames Valley Royals.

Edwards was anxiously seeking funding for the club, so did not immediately reject Maxwell's offer. Professional football then was not as it is today. TV money had not flooded in, and even in the then League One, the top league at the time, the stadiums were rundown and in need of refurbishment. Equally, there was little glamour in being associated with clubs, the fans of which were intent on fighting each other and the police.

Edwards had approached Irving Scholar, chairman of Tottenham, to quiz him about that club's listing on the London stock market. Tottenham had raised £3.8 million and another £1.1 million in new shares. Edwards and Scholar met at Harry's Bar in London, and over dinner Scholar took him through the intricacies and consequences of the listing.

Edwards requested total secrecy about his meeting with Maxwell. No chance. As ever, Maxwell did what only Maxwell thought best and, sure enough, news that the great man was bidding for Britain's greatest football club soon appeared across all the front pages, notably in the *Daily Mirror*, which he owned.

United were in play, apparently, and those opposed to Maxwell made their voices heard. At Old Trafford, the fans protested. Several climbed on to the roof of the first-aid hut at the Scoreboard End and told everyone to 'sit down against Maxwell'. Andy Walsh, ex-chair of the Independent Manchester United Supporters Association (IMUSA), recalled there was a mass sit-down and the police and stewards struggled to get the crowd standing again. Why the loathing of Maxwell? 'He was just seen as a dodgy bastard,' Walsh recalled.

In the middle of it all, there was even a rival bid – rejected – from a Peter Raymond at a US chemical company.

The sense of craziness was compounded by the meeting Edwards had with Maxwell at Maxwell House in London. Edwards was accompanied by Maurice Watkins, United's legal advisor. They thought it would be a small, private session. Instead, Maxwell was surrounded by PR men. The Soviet leader Yuri Andropov had just died. Maxwell was fielding and making calls, pronouncing on his passing. Watkins described the gathering as 'like a circus'. On the way back, the United pair resolved that Maxwell would not be buying the club.

Maxwell was not finished, though. There was a postscript.

Unknown to Edwards, the tycoon had bought, and kept, a shareholding in United.

Edwards continued to ponder. He was fully aware that United was not in great shape, that the club was making a loss and, in reality, despite Maxwell's move, was worth not much more than £3 million. He even talked to Scholar about the Tottenham man buying a stake. Though Scholar was tempted, he thought the Tottenham fans would react badly and so declined.

Soon after, events conspired to plunge not only United but the whole of English football into darkness. Three tragedies brought home the dire state of the game off the pitch, its crumbling infrastructure, the blind eye turned against appalling behaviour by spectators and the clubs' own treatment of the fans. There was the Bradford City stadium fire in May 1985, which claimed the lives of fifty-six fans and injured more than 260, after a discarded cigarette end set debris alight under the wooden stand. That was followed by events at Heysel Stadium later that same month, when fighting between rival sets of supporters saw some Liverpool fans rush at the Juventus fans who were crushed by a badly built wall collapsing. Thirty-nine people died. English teams were banned from European competitions and, for a period, even TV gave up on the game, not showing matches. Then came Hillsborough in April 1989, when ninety-four Liverpool fans were killed at the FA Cup semi-final in Sheffield. Three more died later of their injuries.

All three tragedies were to do with lack of investment in grounds, the cancer of hooliganism and the clubs' disregard for supporters, treating them as second-class citizens and housing them in dangerous areas.

Lord Justice Taylor's report into Hillsborough precipitated a sea change in safety standards, recommending an end to standing and the introduction of all-seater grounds. From the perspective of the owners, it was a disaster. While they only had themselves to blame, remodelling terracing would cost an estimated £1 billion. This, in a game that had lost its glamour and was not a commercial magnet. English football appeared to be heading in one direction, towards bankruptcy.

It was with this gloomy knowledge that two months after Hillsborough, Edwards agreed to take a call from someone called Michael Knighton. Aged thirty-seven, Knighton was a former teacher who had made a bundle in property and had then seemingly retired. That, anyway, was the story. Knighton was in touch with the former Bolton Wanderers chairman, Barry Chaytow, who said he'd heard Martin Edwards was looking to exit.

Knighton and Edwards met for lunch, and afterwards the United chairman showed him round Old Trafford. They'd started 'filling in' the sides of the stadium, making it a complete oval, but the work had stopped as funding had dried up. With the new rules, the Stretford End as well needed complete reconfiguration. The keen-as-mustard, achingly positive Knighton gushed that with his money, connections and vision, he could ensure it was finished.

Knighton genuinely dreamt of revolutionizing the club. It mattered more to him than any amount of money he stood to make. Knighton had a document drawn up called *Blueprint*, which laid down his ideas. They were ahead of their time and astonishingly prescient. The paper talked about branding rights, using the players as a revenue stream, maximizing the potential from the worldwide interest in the club, even setting up a United TV channel of its own – all of which would eventually come to pass.

Edwards could not believe what he was hearing. Just as top-class football hit rock bottom, here was someone prepared to buy him out *and* redevelop the ground. It seemed too good to be true.

Of course, the old adage has it that if it *seems* too good to be true, that's because it probably is – but no one mentioned that to Edwards. He was enthused by the possibility of sorting out his own personal finances – he was heavily in debt – and leaving United with his head held high, knowing the stadium improvements would be completed. He flew one evening to meet Knighton at Killochan Castle in the Scottish Borders. Over dinner of salmon – 'fished from our very own river, Martin' – and prime Scottish beefsteak, washed down with a fine Bordeaux and a tot or two of Glenfiddich, the deal was done: Knighton could buy Edwards's 50.2 per cent holding in United. The price, agreed at midnight, was £10 million, or £20 a share.

It was a shock on two counts. Edwards had not intimated to any of his colleagues he was that close to selling, and no one, not least those involved in the property business in the area where he claimed to hail from, had heard of Michael Knighton. Edwards had rushed to secure a potential buyer without due diligence.

On 24 August 1989, United were at home to Arsenal, the 1988–9 champions. On to the grass comes a short, stocky man with a moustache. He's wearing the United strip and he proceeds to play keepy-uppy, heading the ball, more to his delight than anyone else's. He's described by the announcer as Michael Knighton, the new owner of Manchester United. The crowd do not know whether to laugh or cry, reflecting perhaps that at least it was not Robert Maxwell. But there was something troubling, apart from the fans' lack of knowledge about him. It was the way Edwards had offloaded the club, their club. The grins and back-slapping and the posed pictures did not disguise the sense of United being a commodity, simply passed from one to the other – without so much as consulting the supporters or anyone else associated with the club.

What did the manager, now Alex Ferguson, think of it? What about the players, the legends, especially Bobby Charlton? The whole show seemed cheap and unseemly, not befitting what many viewed as the greatest of clubs.

As for Edwards himself, he was already overcome with doubt. He claimed later to have watched the giggling ball-header and have felt, 'Horrified. I was sat in the stand, thinking *What the hell have I done?* I couldn't believe what I was seeing. I kept saying to myself, *What the hell have I done?* I realized that I had made a big mistake. The other directors felt the same. They cringed and began to turn on Knighton.'

Odd then that in his autobiography, *Red Glory*, Edwards says he never actually saw Knighton on the pitch. He was entertaining guests in the Directors' Lounge.

When news emerged that Knighton had struck a bet with Ladbrokes that he would play for Manchester United by the time he was fifty, it reinforced the sense of deflation, of United being a plaything rather than a venerated institution. The wager would have netted Knighton, who had played a bit in his youth, £10,000, and if his purchase had gone ahead, he would doubtless have persuaded Ferguson to put him on.

Knighton was wealthy-ish. But he wasn't rich enough to buy United and invest as he had promised in the ground. There followed a period, which only added to the tawdriness of the whole spectacle, during which Knighton began scrambling around to try and raise the cash. Hard to countenance now, given the money that poured into the game, but no bank would lend him the money – such was the depressed condition of football's finances, even at the exalted United level.

In the end, Knighton conceded defeat and gave up. His heart no longer in it, even a last-minute intervention from Philip Green, the fashion retailer, could not persuade him. Green phoned him out of the blue and offered £7 million for Knighton's option to buy. The two men had met briefly while watching football at Spurs and at Old

Trafford. Green was in rant mode, which he thought to be persuasive. Knighton kept a detailed note. 'Michael, listen to me, for fuck's sake listen to me. Don't give him the fucking contract back, Michael, do not give this back to Edwards.'

Green was pumped. 'It's worth a fucking fortune, Michael, and I know that, and you know that, so what the hell are you fucking about at? I can't believe you're thinking of handing that contract back to Edwards. Get some sense into that brain of yours, Michael.'

Knighton was unable to interrupt, as Green poured forth. 'People will give anything to own fucking, gold fucking Old Trafford, and you've got the bleeding contract in your back pocket,' shouted Green. 'Don't be a fucking schmuck, Michael. Just sell the fucking contract to me, now.'

Green would not stop. 'I've got a fucking seven million fucking pounds bankers' draft for you here and now – it's in my fucking hand – it's a bankers' draft, Michael, and it's yours, it's all yours. Just think what you could do with seven million fucking quid in your pocket. And the deal's cost you fuck all at the moment, so that's seven million clear fucking profit. It's here waiting for you, come down to London now, just jump in a fucking taxi and I'll pay for you to get here tonight. St John's Wood, that's where I am, I'm here, Michael, fucking waiting for you to come and take this money from me now. Get that fucking football off your head, Michael, and come and take the money.'

Knighton slept on it and refused. He wanted to be the instigator of change at Old Trafford, the man who turned round the club. Green wasn't promising he could run United. 'It's more than a generous offer, Philip, more than fair, but I'm not here for the money.' Green could not believe it.

'What?'

'I'm sorry, Philip, but it's no deal. Look, I am very grateful for what you have offered me, and thank you for that, but I'm really not in it for the money.'

'Everybody is in it for the money, Michael. Michael, what the fuck is the matter with you?'

Knighton had to endure a pasting by the media, led by Maxwell's *Daily Mirror*. The paper raged against him:

Who is this man?

Where is the colour of his money?

He hasn't got the money, he hasn't got the money, he hasn't got the money.

He is dragging the good name of Manchester United into the gutter.

In the end, the two sides, Knighton and the United board, led by Edwards, met at the Midland Hotel in the middle of Manchester. There were sets of advisors, lawyers and accountants installed in separate suites. It was like a game of chess.

Edwards was well aware of the bashing Knighton had received, but Knighton still possessed the trump card, the legally watertight option to buy that Edwards had handed him. Knighton, for his part, thought that Edwards would be regretting his move, at selling his inheritance short, and in the mood to make concessions. Knighton also knew that he'd failed to raise the cash.

He was at a low ebb but trying to remain cheerful. Edwards, according to Knighton's account, just looked edgy.

That very morning a newspaper had run the headline: BLACKMAIL – KNIGHTON DEMANDS MILLIONS TO GO! That very morning, too, Green had called again. 'Don't give him back the fucking contract, Michael. Give it to me, Michael, give it to me.'

At the showdown, Edwards took charge. Using a phrase befitting *The Godfather*, he pressed: 'We have to find a way, Michael.'

'I know,' Knighton said.

Then, the $64,000, or £10 million, question: 'What is it you really want, Michael?'

'It's not the money, Martin.'

'What is it, then?'

'I think I want to make a difference.'

'Come on to the board, then, Michael, and make your difference.'

Then came the carrot: 'We'll use your plan. Come on board and do what you want.'

It was the clincher moment. What entered Knighton's head was the memory of one of his business associates parking a Rolls-Royce in a street in Eccles, not far from Old Trafford, and how it was mistaken for his own car. Within minutes the car was wrecked by a bunch of local fans turned hooligans. They were chanting: 'Knighton, you fat, greedy bastard. Knighton you fat, greedy bastard.'

He handed back the option to buy.

A joint letter was hastily prepared for the shareholders, confirming Knighton had ended his bid and that he had turned down several offers to buy the club. What it didn't say was that Knighton had been able at any time to sell the option on to a third party, and he could have walked away with millions. It didn't say that, because Edwards's team insisted it didn't.

If it had, the world, the fan base, would have realized just how close United had come to being sold, and that Edwards had been prepared to sign away their club to an unknown, to virtually anyone.

But now, everyone could relax. Except this, a low point surely, was another pivotal moment in the development of football and of United. Whilst the close shave with Maxwell and Knighton's ball-juggling antics are always held up as an example of how close the club came to being sold into oblivion, Knighton did exhibit a love for the club, and an enthusiasm that could be infectious. Knighton had outlined in glowing terms United's future. He was ahead of his time in speaking of United being the greatest sporting leisure brand, a potentially enormous company, there to be exploited.

He told the journalist and author Mihir Bose: 'I had a blueprint to make Manchester United what I believe to be the greatest sporting leisure company . . . This was the greatest brand in the world, which needed to be exploited, not in a pejorative way, but in a positive way to enable the football club to buy any player in the world and to make it profitable.'

Amid the flow of superlatives, Knighton said he'd left Edwards and others with a glimmer of what United was and could become. They took it on board. He lifted them out of the torpor surrounding football and made them look up.

From this moment on, Edwards was serious about the club and its potential. There was precious little evidence of it beforehand, but United, post-Knighton, was an altogether different animal.

As Knighton said to Bose of his period on the board: 'I saw that football club achieve six major trophies: FA Cup, FA League Cup, European Cup Winners' Cup, European Super Cup – even the FA Youth Cup. We'd been to Wembley three or four times, and we'd just missed out on the championship. But more importantly we'd turned the company around and put in the seeds of all those items in my blueprint. I claim no credit whatsoever to say it's all down to Michael Knighton, because that falls straight into the hands of those people that just think I'm some kind of raging egomaniac. What I do say is that Old Trafford on that sunny August afternoon was the new horizon and was the catalyst that made everything that happened subsequently happen.'

Knighton later bought Carlisle United and appointed himself manager, winning only nineteen of the sixty-eight matches he was in charge. He attracted local newspaper headlines by saying that earlier in his life, aliens had spoken to him. As they left their Yorkshire home one afternoon in 1976, he and his wife had apparently watched an alien craft perform a range of 'impossible' aero-acrobatics. As the glowing UFO disappeared, he had received a telepathic message: 'Don't be afraid, Michael.'

After the story was published, he said: 'I made it perfectly clear to the reporter that it was not for publication.' So, the *Evening News and Star* in Carlisle followed up with an 'unreserved' front-page apology and this gem of a sentence: 'Just because Michael Knighton has seen a UFO doesn't disqualify him from being a football club chairman.'

On the pitch at United, things were little better than in the boardroom. The players and the fans were taking a long time to adjust to – and to like – Alex Ferguson.

Nothing was gelling. The team played like a collection of strangers, which is what they were, assembled largely from transfers. Ferguson didn't help matters – in the inevitable post-defeat interviews – by blaming everyone and everything but himself. It was the referee's fault, the linesman, the grass was too long, the pitch was muddy, the other side played dirty. The fanzine, *Red News*, in December 1989, summed it up well: 'What really hurts, Alex, is that under you we've had shit football, shit atmosphere, shit boardroom shenanigans and our support is drifting away.'

Another fanzine, *Red Issue*, also did not hold back. Ferguson's response was all too typical: he banned the fanzine's reporters from the ground. Crowds were down to 33,000 and, to rub it in, the maestro, Georgie Best, went for the jugular. Best said he would not walk round the corner to watch United play. Ouch.

Then, slowly at first, it all began to change. Ferguson struck gold in the transfer market and merged the new players with youthful talent, some of which was homegrown. The team started winning consistently, but not only that, it was playing with abandon and verve again – the sort of football that United had seen in abundance back in Sir Matt's glory days. Ferguson had returned United to the past and, what's more, United were winning in Europe again.

It was as if a cloud had lifted and, in its place, came a feverish exuberance. It was a joy that wasn't confined just to football. In the late 1980s, early 1990s, Manchester had begat Madchester, subsequently recognized on the cover of *Time* magazine as a place for the young, for loved-up ecstasy and smiley faces. Out went hooliganism and in came a much better matchday experience all round, with upgraded seating, improved catering and increased corporate hospitality. The United shop was doing a roaring trade, demand for tickets was soaring – from the people of Manchester, and from far beyond too.

In the middle of the happy delirium, Edwards chose to float the club on the London Stock Exchange. He wanted to sort out his own personal finances, to clear a mortgage and redevelop Old Trafford, which had to keep pace with United's rising popularity. Bose describes his thinking thus, in his book *Manchester Disunited*: 'He could sell off some shares, pay off his bank manager, make vast sums on a scale no previous director of a football club had ever made and still remain in control. He had at last squared the circle.'

Not everyone was enamoured with his move. Ferguson, for one, was unimpressed, believing there will always be a conflict between a PLC and a football club, that the need to pay a dividend will always win through and that harsh, financially driven decisions would end up being taken on the playing side as a result.

The float, on 10 June 1991, valued United at £42 million. For its part, the City was not that interested. The financial institutions stayed away. The big TV money had yet to flood into football. Most of those buying the shares were ordinary fans, who liked the idea of owning part of their club.

It was a fork in the road, though. From now on, United was at the mercy of the market. There was nothing to stop anyone buying the shares. It was another step away from the innocent roots of twenty-two men and a football, playing on a field in Manchester – and a further big stride towards commercialization and globalization.

A sign of how this new world worked came just a few days after the listing. The shares opened at £3.85, then dropped, and were down to £2.60 by the end of the week. In just a few short days, the club had lost a third of its value and was now worth £26 million. Yet nothing had happened on the pitch or in the Old Trafford boardroom or within football to justify such a precipitous fall. It was caused by a fit of pique, an act of revenge, as Robert Maxwell took his 505,000 shares – 4.25 per cent of the total – and dumped them on the market.

THREE

The Leprechaun

In January 1992, United were mounting a title challenge. Alex Ferguson was happy with the team he was assembling, including the blooding of a fast, dazzling young winger called Ryan Giggs. They were about to enter what Ferguson, in his inimitable fashion, called 'squeaky bum time', the latter part of the season when the destination of championships and cups was decided.

In the US, Malcolm Glazer also had reason to be excited. Again, it involved sport. The businessman had taken the plunge and bid for a major American football franchise. He wanted to bring the NFL back to Baltimore. The city had lost its team when the Colts suddenly upped and moved to Indianapolis in 1984. Now there was a possibility of a new team for Baltimore. Glazer faced stiff competition from locals, Leonard 'Boogie' Weinglass, the celebrated attorney, and Tom Clancy, the bestselling novelist.

Glazer, originally from Rochester County, New York, and now living in Palm Beach, Florida, had no links with Baltimore. But if there was the possibility of a potentially lucrative NFL franchise being up for grabs, being the redoubtable businessman he was, he wanted it.

He did not exactly go out of his way to win friends. He claimed to the local paper he could write a check for $150 million to ensure the team was his. Strangely, considering he had that much at his disposal, he wouldn't put up a relatively small $50,000 to help the city and municipal authorities run a PR and marketing campaign for the NFL's return to Baltimore – which would also help his cause. It wasn't in his budget, Glazer said coldly.

While locals Weinglass and Clancy recounted fond memories of the Colts and its star quarterback, Johnny Unitas, before the team decamped for Indianapolis, Glazer liked to focus instead on the financial repercussions of his bid: set-up costs, stadium lease and, if he was successful, profits. In a phrase that left the locals unimpressed he said: 'It's not as good as other investments we've made. But I'd be satisfied.' The divide was clear: Weinglass and Clancy were doing it because they loved the sport; Glazer was motivated by a love of money.

Malcolm Glazer was born in Rochester, New York, on 15 August 1928. His parents were Abraham and Hannah Glazer, and Malcolm was the fifth of seven children (Jerome, Jeanette, Marcia, Rosalind, Evelyn and Dorothea were his siblings) in a Lithuanian, strictly Jewish, family.

His father, Abraham, had emigrated to America in 1912 aged twenty-three. Abraham had been an apprentice watchmaker, and had opened a watch repair business in Utica, New York. He did well and bought a watch parts supplier. The new addition was a disaster, however. 'They cheated him,' said Malcolm. Abraham was devastated and was almost wiped out financially. He spent the rest of his life trying to recover what he'd lost.

Malcolm joined him in the family firm aged eight, selling watch parts and running errands. Then, in 1943, when Malcolm was just fifteen, his father died suddenly.

Abraham had been suffering from cancer, but his death was a shock. It had a profound effect on Malcolm. 'I'm always telling my kids, "Tomorrow the end is coming", said Glazer. 'If you have a father who dies when you are young, you don't trust the future any more. You were cheated once; you'll probably get cheated again.'

Malcolm was haunted by his father's sudden death, and when he became a father himself he made sure that he spent a great deal of time with his own six children (five sons – Avram, Kevin, Bryan, Joel and Edward – and a daughter, Darcie) while they were growing up. He said he wanted to teach them all he could, while he could.

'Death is right around the corner,' he said, 'waiting to grab anyone in this room. Watch out. Walk fast when you go out of the house here, so he doesn't grab you.'

There's no doubt that his father's loss hardened him. 'His death was probably the most tragic thing that ever happened, or would happen, in my life,' said Malcolm. 'But it was good in one way. It made me an adult.'

Abraham left his family all of $300, kept in an old cigar box.

Malcolm, the oldest son, stepped into his shoes. It's remarkable how many successful businessmen I've come across who lost their father at an early age, in their teens, whose education was effectively ended as they had to start work as the main breadwinner. Sir Philip Green, the retailing billionaire, is one such; Lord (Charles) Allen, the former TV chief, is another. They're all driven by necessity and by anger, at losing something their friends have not. It tends to make them insular and driven. They speak of an end to childhood, to innocence. They're forced to become adults early.

So it was with Malcolm Glazer. Two weeks after the funeral, Malcolm, aged just fifteen, set off alone, on a Greyhound bus, selling watch parts out of a suitcase. Around this time, too, he began using what little spare money he earned to invest in shares on the New York stock market.

His formal schooling was virtually over. He was never academic anyway, not destined for college, later openly describing a feeling of inferiority versus the smarter children.

At twenty-one, he got his first real break in business. A friend told him about franchises that were available at the enormous Sampson Air Force base in Geneva, New York. The friend had secured an exclusive photography concession. Glazer negotiated a contract to open a watch repair and jewellery shop on the giant complex. He would make the fifty-five-mile journey to the base and back, seven days a week, for five years.

'It was hard, but I thoroughly enjoyed it,' he said. 'I was making more profit than ever before.'

All his earnings, about $50,000 a year, went to his mother. 'Everything I made I gave to my mother, Hannah. I don't know why I did it . . . I fantasized that I was providing for my mother like her husband, actually. She always said to me, "You're my son, you're my husband, you're my father." '

Another occasion, he said: 'My mother would always say to me, "You are my husband, my son, my everything." My mother had a way of manipulating me.'

He made enough money to start branching out, with his mother as business partner, into real estate. It marked Glazer's discovery of the beauty of using someone else's money to buy something that you then derive the profit from. Everything he had originally came from the profits from his father's watch repair and jewellery business. Once he took charge, Glazer diverted some of the profits to invest in other assets, some of which he put in his name and others he registered in his and his mother's name. They would use as little of their own money as they could get away with as a deposit on a property, and borrow the rest. This method, known technically as a leveraged buyout or LBO, he applied repeatedly in the US. It was what he would much later use to tremendous effect in buying Manchester United.

First though, Glazer used it to acquire unsung duplexes in Rochester, then mobile-home parks. By 1956, Malcolm had left jewellery and watches behind and gone completely into property.

Glazer's business approach was fundamentally harsh and calculated. To put it mildly, he was one unforgiving landlord. At his East Avenue and Forest Lawn mobile-home parks, residents complained repeatedly of unsafe conditions, being hit with improper fees (they were required to pay separately for children and pets, $3 per month for each child and $5 a month for each pet) and rents that were forever increasing. They were instructed to buy heating oil from only one vendor, which had the same address as Glazer's real-estate company, according to the *Rochester Democrat and Chronicle*.

'He could have gone a long way to making amends to these folks rather inexpensively. (But) I think he dug in his heels and said, "If you don't like it, sue me,"' said a Rochester lawyer who represented many of the mobile homeowners, and who confirmed that conditions were as bad as the tenants described. 'They were just awful.'

Many of the residents were elderly retirees who couldn't afford to move, stuck in the mobile-home park and therefore at the mercy of Glazer. According to another lawyer involved, Carl Feinstock: 'They were basically being held hostage. Whatever management wanted to do, management did.'

A lawyer for another group of tenants said: 'Glazer has left a long trail of arrogance.'

Eventually, the local council intervened and forced Glazer to raise standards. He was also required to repay the cash he'd collected in illegal fees.

He went on to amass a hotchpotch portfolio of businesses, including a half-share of a bank in Savannah, New York, mobile-home parks, nursing homes, junk bonds, shopping malls and four TV stations. Many of his investments were in tired assets that had seen better days, which needed a new lease of life that he did not supply. Glazer was a sharp deal-maker, regularly using his preferred LBO route to buy a business. Was he any good at running them, though? If that means nurturing and growing them, then the answer is no.

Nothing was off limits to him, however. His strategy ran counter to most successful business types, who focus on one core activity, learning how to do it frontwards, backwards and sideways, and being on top of it, completely. Glazer wasn't like that; he never seemed concerned if he was entering a field about which he had little knowledge and in which he had zero experience. The one criterion he applied was that whatever he owned had to be capable of producing a steady income stream.

His strange assortment of assets made him rich, but just how rich was never clear. *Forbes* estimated that he was a billionaire, but that was never obvious. Possibly, according to his assets, but at the same time it was impossible to ascertain the depth of his liabilities. Certainly, he proved to be extremely adept at using other people's money to achieve his own ends.

In 1984, he shot to national attention when First Allied Corporation, Glazer's holding company, bid $7.6 billion to buy Conrail, a railway franchise in the North-East US, from the US government. His offer was the highest of the fifteen submitted. But there was a typical twist as he applied that lesson first learned from buying the duplexes in Rochester: his thumping bid included only $100 million in cash from himself – the rest was to come from future Conrail profits. His attempt failed because the government was unconvinced about his financial means. They were worried that so much of it was having to be borrowed.

Undeterred, he pressed on, fast acquiring a name of sorts on Wall Street for being a second- or third-division corporate raider. There were much bigger players who successfully chased the corporate behemoths. Glazer, by contrast, was known to constantly be on the lookout to buy stakes in smaller, underperforming businesses, which he would threaten with takeover (whether he had the money was not obvious) and then back out, making a handy, but not huge, return. He was a 'tyre kicker' – someone who checks a car out, does everything, tests everything, but has no intention of buying. Or in Wall Street investment parlance, he was known as a 'greenmailer'. Adjacent to a blackmailer, a greenmailer's weapon is dollars or greenbacks: you buy a stake, threaten a takeover, the shares go up, the company buys you out at a price higher than the one you paid, and you make a tidy profit. Or similarly, you make a lot of noise about buying the company, the shares go up and you sell, again making a profit. Either way, the trick is to convince the company and the market that you're serious about a takeover when you're not.

He did it with Formica, the kitchen tops firm, making a nice return when he sold his 10 per cent share, and again, with Harley-Davidson. The motorbike company rebuffed him, but Glazer sold his stake in the company for a quick $11 million profit. It wasn't pretty or cosy, more calculating, hard-edged, eyeball-to-eyeball stuff, requiring a certain ruthlessness and unwavering determination.

Malcolm's constant corporate manoeuvrings did prompt one judge to liken him to a 'snake in sheep's clothing rather than a wolf in sheep's clothing'. It was one judge's opinion, Glazer said, with that air of denial and defiance that became a trademark. 'He never met me; he didn't know me.'

Among people who did know him, Glazer was viewed as

notoriously tight with money. 'He's an investor, but not a re-investor,' said Don Nahley, ex-general manager at a television station Glazer owned. 'He doesn't put much money back in.'

Glazer prided himself on driving down costs. It was his one man-agement fallback. If all else failed, hammer expenses. Better still, don't attempt anything else because that might crash and hit your wallet, just keep on murdering outgoings. Emotion was never allowed to impair his judgement, as he would go about cutting jobs and clos-ing product lines he deemed not to be performing adequately.

He had no hobbies – if he had one, it was scanning the papers for a new business opportunity to stalk – and he hardly ever went on holiday. A long-time assistant said he never saw Glazer even read the sports pages.

He was often thought of as shy. Not true, said Tim Reiland, whose Milwaukee stock brokerage worked closely with Glazer. 'There's nothing shy about Malcolm Glazer. He's a pretty serious, cut-to-the-chase businessman . . . and very bottom-line oriented.'

Glazer gained a reputation as a fearsomely hard-nosed operator, someone who was not afraid of relying on litigation – even if it meant going against his own family. When his mother, Hannah, died in 1980, Glazer became embroiled in a bitter dispute over her will with his four older sisters. Hannah's estate was worth $1 million.

Glazer resolved the sisters should not inherit anything. A row ensued at her house while the family was observing the Jewish mourning ritual of *shivah*. It became so heated that physical blows were exchanged between Malcolm and one of his brothers-in-law. Next, the feuding Glazer siblings were reaching for their lawyers.

What followed was sixteen years of punishing legal attrition as Glazer fought his sisters inch-by-inch, never once conceding, in the courts. He went through numerous sets of lawyers and the case was heard over the years by no less than six separate judges.

On the face of it, the row was about the difficulty of obtaining probate on Hannah Glazer's estate. Malcolm insisted part of the estate belonged entirely to him and should not be part of the probate and could not be shared. It was his money; he'd earned it.

He maintained, though, that the real reason had nothing to do with the cash. It was a principle. He believed his sisters were resentful as he was closer to their mother. 'I am very sorry my mother and I had a close relationship like we did,' he said, oozing sarcasm. 'I am not sorry, but we did. In my next life, I am not going to be so close to my mother, and my sisters will be happy. I'm sorry I made my mother wealthy.'

By his account, the trouble began when they were all children. 'I never went anyplace with my sisters. They never took me,' he said. 'My mother would say, "Take him to the movies," and they would say no. My mother would say, "Why not? You're going to sit next to a stranger anyway." They'd say, "We don't care, we're not taking him." '

Said Glazer: 'I thought, "My God, I did all these things for Mother, and she was our mother." Then I began to realize, it was my mother, but I don't know if it was their mother. I don't think they were very happy that Mother got a new Cadillac every year and they had to use an old car.'

Glazer ducked and dived at every turn, probably deliberately prolonging the proceedings to run up huge legal bills on both sides to wipe out the inheritance. Glazer did not care. Indeed, making it as small as possible may well have been part of his thinking.

Glazer blamed the protracted court battle on his four older sisters, to whom he stopped speaking. 'Four greedy people', was what he called them.

Once, following a court order, Glazer delivered an astonishing 103 cardboard boxes filled with bank statements, rent receipts and other records. The files were not arranged in any logical sequence, according to the court report. It took a staff of five office workers about three weeks to put them in order.

During a three-day deposition hearing, in which he was questioned repeatedly about his business dealings with his mother, Glazer was obstructive, answering questions with 'I don't remember', 'I don't know', or 'I don't understand the question' over 300 times.

It did not help either that a witness, who was billed as Glazer's 'accountant' and was supposed to explain the dealings contained in the records, was revealed in the proceedings to be illiterate.

During a break in the deposition, Glazer was left alone with his lawyer and a court stenographer. Unaware he was being recorded, Glazer said: 'We have to keep going until there is no money left in this estate.' (He claimed he was referring to his sisters and it was they who were intent on depleting the estate.)

Judge Raymond E. Cornelius wrote that Glazer, 'beyond a doubt has acted in bad faith' in failing to turn over adequate accounts of businesses owned with his mother.

Subsequently, Judge Lyman H. Smith, cited Glazer's 'intentional and prolonged non-compliance with the court's reasonable orders', and told him to pay various lawyers' fees of $268,299.

Finally, sixteen years after their mother's death, in 1980, settlement was reached. The terms were strictly confidential. Whether there was anything left of the estate after such a prolonged conflict is not known.

Glazer said: 'I think most disputes within families are people getting even with people over things that happened when they were ten years old. I really do.'

None of the Glazer family members I contacted wished to discuss the case. Requests for assistance were met with terse refusals.

One postscript is that one of Malcolm's sisters, Jeanette Goldstein, did something extraordinary. She was moved to take up the full-time study of law, at Syracuse University, aged eighty. In the words of her son, Jeremy, who wrote a book, *Grandma Goes to Law School – Why It's Never Too Late to Live Your Dreams*, Jeanette 'sat down next to the twenty-two- and twenty-three-year-olds, taking notes on constitutional law, civil procedures, and international relations. She had cataracts in her eyes, and she was starting to lose her hearing. She was the mother of eight children and the grandmother of twenty-two. She graduated in May 2004, earning a mention in the *Guinness Book of Records* and the admiration of her professors.'

When Malcolm bought Manchester United, it should perhaps have been no surprise that the only one of all the Glazers to break the fierce omertà surrounding the family was the redoubtable Jeanette. She told a radio station she believed her brother bought the Manchester club because he 'is interested in anything that is a profitable enterprise'.

Said Jeanette: 'I know that whatever he has ever done, he wanted to make it successful. I don't think he would invest the money otherwise.'

His motivation was money, not a love of football, she claimed, saying he was not wedded to sports when they were young. 'He was too busy interested in making money to think about playing in sports.'

She continued: 'He was making money from the time he was eight years old. He was not a student. He was only interested in making money.'

Asked if he was a recluse, she replied: 'He keeps to himself pretty much.'

Jeanette outlived Malcolm. She died in 2016.

In 1988, Glazer moved south, for the sunnier clime of Florida. He paid $2.5 million for a house on the ocean in Palm Beach, and then several million dollars more, having the property rebuilt to encompass seven bedrooms, eight bathrooms, two fireplaces and a tennis court. He had a swimming pool built.

Asked about the house four years later, he said he'd never been for a swim in the sea or the pool. 'Since I do nothing but work, please forgive me – I look at the ocean.'

He joined a country club but went so rarely that when he did turn up the staff did not recognize him as a member. All he would do, occasionally, is go out for dinner with his wife, Linda. Their rich neighbours commented they did not have a chauffeur; they took cabs to the airport. They did not go by private jet but used budget airlines.

A property developer friend from Rochester, Neil Norry, described him as 'very well-known, but nobody knows him'.

Major league sport was seen as the pinnacle of corporate America; the owner of a franchise in baseball, basketball or football was effectively milking a cash cow. In 1990, his sons persuaded Malcolm to go down this route and to pursue a major-league baseball team. The Glazers made a pitch for one of the two franchises that were to be added to the National League.

Their bid was different from the rest. While other investors concentrated on individual cities that lacked a team, talking about how positive it would be for these communities and local economies and so on, the Glazers came up with the notion of having one team located in four hometowns in different parts of the vast country.

'America's team', as Glazer called it.

The idea was that the team would be an owner's dream, earning profits from ticket revenues and broadcast rights across four cities instead of one. Sure, it would mean the team only played a quarter of its home matches in each place, but that did not seem to bother the Glazers. Apparently, they had little truck with the attachment of locals to 'their' team, 'their' players. Local pride, loyalty, love did not come into it as far as they were concerned. It was entirely about maximizing profits: one team, four cities, four stadiums, four sets of fans, four sets of revenue.

The National League was unimpressed. The Glazers were left off the final list of six bidders, cut from eighteen. 'We didn't spend a lot of time on it,' said Douglas Danforth, chairman of the expansion committee.

Glazer did learn a lesson from the experience, however – one he put to good use later. He saw that sports owners liked to deal with single investors, and preferred to deal in cash. 'We learned a guy with the chequebook, a single person, ends up with the team.'

He was now determined to secure a major sports franchise.

'Why buy a pro team? It's vanity, it's ego, it puts you into a higher social network,' said a former senior New York investment banker who has studied the Glazers. 'They specialized in leveraged transactions, in using money that was not theirs. The reason the Glazers can own something is because the banks can finance it. That was always Malcolm Glazer's story. And once you get a franchise, it's like a puffer fish, you expand and appear bigger than you are. All of a sudden, you're more significant – it's why Donald Trump bought the New Jersey Generals in the US Football League.'

The history of the Glazers and sports ownership, he says, 'has an echo in Roman Abramovich. It's why he bought Chelsea, to give himself a strategic market advantage. The Glazers were looking to buy teams in the US but failed. It did not seem to matter where it was, or which sport it was in – there's a clue as to what they were really about. It was about legitimizing them in the marketplace.'

Among those Malcolm looked at were the NFL's New England Patriots, baseball's San Diego Padres and the Pittsburgh Pirates.

In 1995, after five years of trying, Malcolm Glazer submitted the winning bid for the Tampa Bay Buccaneers in the NFL. He offered a league record $192 million for just about the worst-performing team in the NFL; in unfashionable, isolated, tiny Tampa as well, not in one of the major cities in the North-East or West. 'He told me more than once that he was buying the team because the boys loved it,' said Sandra Freedman, who was Tampa's mayor when the purchase went through. 'But you don't go out and spend that kind of money because your boys want a toy. He knew it was going to be a smart business investment.'

Former Tampa mayor Dick Greco said: 'One of the problems with people who don't know him is that you expect a sports figure to be more ego driven, more boisterous, talkative, loud.'

Freedman, another ex-Tampa mayor, said Glazer was, 'Quiet, shy, I think, retiring, whichever word might fit. He didn't say a lot, but you knew he was bright . . . He's definitely not a good ol' boy. I don't know him intimately or anything. I'm not sure anybody in Tampa does.'

Some believed they did when it came to his pursuit of the Bucs. Greco, who helped push through a local tax to build the Bucs a new stadium, said he was sure Glazer 'must have had a tremendous passion for football'.

Greco said he realized that was not the case at the first game he attended with Glazer. 'He didn't get tremendously excited about what was going on. I will never forget the opposing team intercepted a pass and ran about fifty-three yards for a touchdown and it was called back for a penalty. Malcolm Glazer just sat there and said, "Isn't that a shame." He said, "It was such a nice play, they must feel terrible." I thought, "What in the world?" I was used to being with people who would go out the window if something crazy happened like that.'

There were question marks about Glazer. He frequently changed auditors; he engaged in related party transactions, making his companies trade with each other; his company filings were frequently delayed; there were conflicts of interest and issues over governance. But buying the Bucs validated him and gave him a calling card. Said a former New York investment banker: 'Suddenly, buying an NFL team makes Malcolm Glazer more bankable. Any questions people may have about you, cease to be asked. You can continue to grow and to get funding, it's mission accomplished.'

He went on: 'He was commercially challenged on so many fronts, to do with the quality of his assets and how he ran the businesses, about reporting and so on. That's how he was judged, but then acquiring Tampa Bay transcended any economic analysis, it became a legitimizing event.'

He added: 'He was legitimizing himself. Tampa Bay was a bit of a distressed sale. Glazer outbid everyone else, which meant in one sense he wasn't taken seriously. But that was not what he was about – it meant he got his name out there, it would attract attention, it made him a player.'

Strange that for one so low-key and reclusive, so guarded when it comes to his own profile, he bought sports teams, just about the most visible, publicity-attracting assets on the planet.

Sure enough, buying the Bucs meant that Glazer had to make a rare appearance in front of the cameras and a room full of reporters. Short, with his wispy, gingery hair and beard, and pointed features, the then sixty-six-year-old was immediately christened 'The Leprechaun' by the Bucs followers. 'I'm not used to being in front of big crowds like this,' he said in a quavering voice, peering out front. 'You'll have to bear with me.'

Asked what it was like to have paid the highest-ever sum for a franchise, Glazer replied: 'I gulped many times.'

On its face, the Bucs buy was indeed completely out of character for Glazer – paying a record amount did not seem to fit easily with the reputedly parsimonious businessman. But then, was he also staying faithful to his 'first rule', and getting someone or something else, another person or company, to stump up the cash? The oddly named Zapata Corporation provides the clue.

Zapata Corporation was an oil and gas company, founded by the late US President George H. W. Bush. Mention Zapata in some quarters of Washington DC in particular, and eyebrows will shoot upwards and knowing looks will be exchanged. Zapata was almost certainly a commercial front for the CIA for many years.

It was founded in 1953 by Bush, then trying to make his way in the oil business in his native Texas, and an engineer from Massachusetts Institute of Technology called Thomas Devine. A year previously, Devine had been a full-time intelligence operative for the CIA. He resigned to join his Texan friend, Bush, in Zapata, a firm specializing in oil exploration in the Caribbean and Gulf of Mexico. They called it Zapata after the 1952 film *Viva Zapata!* starring Marlon Brando, about the Mexican revolutionary Emiliano Zapata.

CIA internal papers recorded that Devine continued to work for the agency after he'd officially left. He later accompanied Bush on a visit to Vietnam, in 1967, for which he'd been cleared as an asset of the intelligence service and subsequently acted as Bush's unofficial foreign affairs advisor.

Zapata did succeed in locating oil and setting up rigs. It's clear, though, that something else was going on. Soon after Bush became US vice-president in 1983, company records and papers of Zapata covering the period 1960–6 went missing or were destroyed. During the 1961 Bay of Pigs invasion, and the following Cuban missile crisis, Zapata – it transpired – had allowed its rigs to be used as listening posts against Fidel Castro's Cuba.

Zapata did business in Haiti, and here again the company appears to have let its offices be used by CIA agents. Devine died in 2019. He denied to the end that Zapata was used by the CIA, but plenty of evidence suggests otherwise.

For much of its life, Zapata enjoyed a roller-coaster ride, doing well for a period before dipping. In the early 1990s, Glazer's name appeared on its share register. He acquired a 41 per cent stake in the Houston-based corporation. Glazer duly became its chairman and his son, Avram or Avie, the CEO.

At this point Zapata's focus took an unexpected turn. Soon after Glazer bought the Bucs, Zapata – hitherto an oil and gas specialist – agreed to pay $80 million to acquire Houlihan's Restaurant Group, a dull, uninspiring restaurant chain 73 per cent owned by Glazer.

Not surprisingly, Zapata shareholders questioned this abrupt shift into catering and wondered why the company was buying out the chairman's low-rent restaurant business. One investor sued to get the merger blocked, and a Delaware court ruled in his favour. Given that Glazer held substantial holdings in both companies, the court said the deal must win approval from 80 per cent of Zapata shareholders, rather than just 50 per cent. There then came two other legal claims from Zapata shareholders that Glazer was using their company to buy out his other interests and to finance the purchase of the Bucs.

Glazer denied the allegations. He insisted there was no tie between the deals and the Bucs – and that the Houlihan's merger was good for Zapata. The Glazers maintained that it was a strategic shift: they were moving the oil and gas firm into food services. 'We thought there were better opportunities to make money for stockholders,' said Avie, though that rather begged the question why the only companies Zapata appeared seriously interested in acquiring were already controlled by Glazer?

It was agreed that Zapata should pay $8 a share in cash and stock for Houlihan's – more than a 30 per cent premium over the pre-deal price. With 73 per cent of Houlihan's, Glazer stood to make $58.6

million, of which $22 million would be in cash. 'In our view, Glazer is using Zapata to enrich himself,' said Daniel F. Wake, a lawyer for the shareholder suit that won the ruling requiring 80 per cent approval.

In another move, in February 1995, Glazer agreed to sell his 31 per cent stake in Envirodyne Industries, a maker of sausage skins (nothing was off limits to Glazer), to Lazard, the Wall Street investment bank, for $21 million. Two days later, Lazard backed out of the deal. However, Zapata, now under the thumb of Glazer, stepped in to buy the Envirodyne shares instead. His oil-and-gas outfit was now expanding into the sausage-skin business.

Things did not go as smoothly as Glazer liked, however, as at a board meeting his two associates, new board recruits, had the temerity to question the purchase. Shortly afterwards, they were gone. The official reason given was that they'd realized they were too busy to be directors.

They were replaced by W. George Loar, a seventy-two-year-old former general manager of a Glazer-owned TV station, and Robert V. Leffler Jr., whose sports marketing firm worked for the Glazers. Zapata duly agreed to buy the Envirodyne sausage-skins holding for $18.8 million.

Where did that cash go? To pay down a loan, part of $90 million Glazer explained he needed to help pay for the Bucs.

Glazer maintained he didn't have to settle the loan. So, why didn't he keep the Envirodyne stock after Lazard pulled out? Why the rush to sell so quickly? 'What's the difference?' replied Glazer.

Son Avie insisted: 'If we have a sale and we have some loans, we pay off our loans. But they're not tied together.'

Then came another change in direction. Houlihan's agreed, in October 1995, to pay $10 million to one of Glazer's privately held firms for naming rights at the Bucs' Tampa Stadium for the next ten years. This was despite the fact that the chain had just two outlets in the whole of Florida and none around Tampa.

Not all Houlihan's shareholders were enthused. 'I can think of better places they could have called Houlihan's,' said Robert Martorelli, manager of Merrill Lynch's Phoenix Fund, which held 11.5 per cent of Houlihan's. The Glazers argued the deal was similar to those at other stadiums. Yes, but did they go to sponsors who had no interest in the vicinity?

Houlihan's CEO, Frederick R. Hipp, kept his face straight when he said he and his staff examined thirty-two such deals and 'we have felt no pressure to do things to benefit the Glazers solely.'

So why did Zapata tear up its business model and change strategy just as Glazer was buying the Bucs? 'It just did,' Avie said.

The Glazers said they were misunderstood. Prices were rising in the natural gas sector, so they decided to be a seller instead of a buyer. And they simply decided to reinvest the cash in another industry and in companies they knew best.

In October 1996, Zapata, having failed to secure the amounts of votes laid down by the Delaware court, announced that the planned takeover of Houlihan's was off. But the company continued on its zigzag path. The Glazers moved its headquarters from Houston to Rochester and got it out of oil completely, going into natural gas servicing and protein supplements from menhaden fish caught in the Gulf of Mexico. Later, natural gas went as well, and the firm focused entirely on fish proteins.

Then came another radical switch in direction, one that caused further bemusement on Wall Street, as the Glazers sought to exploit the dotcom boom and establish Zapata as a major internet player – even though the Glazers had no apparent internet management experience, and neither did anyone else at the company – under the 'zap.com' banner. To this end they acquired several websites, among them ChatPlanet, TravelPage and DailyStocks, and also took over the company behind Excite.com.

Weirdly (but perhaps not, given the Glazer penchant for adding unrelated businesses), Zapata was by then also making fabric for air bags and cushions. Fish oils, internet portals, air bags and cushions – it's a struggle to see the common link. However, there was one – again, not unfamiliar where the Glazers were concerned: the businesses were not hugely successful.

The Glazers bowed out of Zapata completely in 2009.

At Mount Hope Cemetery in Rochester, New York, there is a memorial to Malcolm Glazer, who died aged eighty-five in 2014.

It's a seventeen-feet-tall granite archway, weighing 150,000 pounds. The imposing mausoleum was designed by one of his sons, Kevin, and daughter, Darcie. The Star of David adorns both sides of the arch.

According to Darcie: 'It is an original, unique in its open design and in the way it greets and welcomes passers-by – the perfect memorial to a civic-minded business leader perhaps best remembered for the way in which he charted his own course.'

Inscribed inside the arch are fourteen of Glazer's favourite sayings. They include:

'A perfect job is never done'

'Some of the best deals I made are the ones I didn't make'

'It's the horse, not the jockey'

'If you want to know the road ahead, ask someone who's been there'.

FOUR

Enter Rupert Murdoch

In July 1998, Manchester United were on their way to football supremacy. The season they were about to embark upon would prove to be the greatest in their history as they set about winning the treble of the Premiership, the FA Cup and the UEFA Champions League. Alex Ferguson would make himself the equal of Busby – soon, he too would be knighted.

In the stands and bars around Old Trafford, wherever fans gathered, there was euphoria. In the boardroom, while there was great satisfaction at what was taking place on the pitch, a drama was beginning that would change the face of United and top-class football for ever.

Six years previously, as United had been getting used to life as a publicly quoted company, Rupert Murdoch's Sky television was revolutionizing the televising of football. Now, in the summer of 1998, Sky wanted to go further. They were about to launch digital channels and they wanted to show all the Premiership matches they did not already televise on pay-per-view. They also wanted to broadcast live matches on a Sunday, thus ending the tradition of the English footballing Saturday.

Martin Edwards and Maurice Watkins, United's legal director, were invited to a meeting at Sky headquarters in Isleworth, just west of London. They assumed it was to discuss Sky's expansionist plans, but over lunch of smoked salmon followed by chicken and rice, Mark Booth, Sky's chief executive, told them straight. The broadcaster had an even bigger agenda: 'We want to buy Manchester United.'

What was driving Booth and his boss, Murdoch, was the thought that the UK competition authorities would rule that collective negotiating of TV rights by the Premier League on behalf of its twenty member clubs was illegal, and that it would be up to each individual club to negotiate their own deals. As the biggest club, United would have the strongest muscle. If Sky owned the club, it would also give the company a major say in European football, the preserve of the rival ITV.

Sky was planting its tank squarely on someone else's lawn – an aggressive, destabilizing move. Murdoch had form for this sort of behaviour – he'd done it before when he bought 20th Century Fox and set about shaking up Hollywood.

Murdoch knew too how to pander to Edwards's ego. The United man was told he could keep his existing job, there wasn't a question of him leaving, Murdoch wanted him as a partner – or at least he said he did. Edwards, meanwhile, was doing the maths, and it soon became clear to him that he stood to gain many tens of millions if Murdoch bought the club.

For Murdoch, he got to keep Edwards's knowledge and contacts in the higher reaches of football, and the United man stood for continuity, which he thought, wrongly, would placate the football community. It was typical left-field, catch-everyone-else-unawares Murdoch.

My own, early introduction to Murdoch and his way of doing business had come years previously when I was a junior business reporter on the Murdoch-owned *Sunday Times*. It had been decided that I was to write that weekend's main editorial, based on an official report castigating Mohamed Al-Fayed over the purchase of House of Fraser, which included Harrods. Fayed, it seems, had been deliberately opaque about the true origins of his funding. We were having a meeting, the paper's much more senior executives and I, about what the leader column should say, when who should walk in but Murdoch. We all leapt up, to attention. He made a gesture for everyone to sit down, then asked what we were discussing.

They said that I was just explaining the importance of the report and that it was going to be the paper's leader.

Murdoch fixed me a stare. 'Son, who cares? Why does it matter?' he said softly and slowly. Nobody else said anything. I was on my own. I was sweating but the room felt chilly. Gulp. I blathered about how we could never be too careful, how it was vital that people didn't lie as to the source of their wealth, how we had anti-money-laundering rules, how organized crime was a growing problem and that we had to be more on top of this sort of thing, and drugs and terrorism . . .

Murdoch looked blank. I could feel the ground opening beneath my feet. Then, a man who was accompanying the press mogul, standing behind him – he was American, tall and wore black, shiny crocodile shoes – said: 'Hey, Rupe, didn't that Fayed take us for 100 mill down in Texas?'

Murdoch turned to him, and said, 'That's right, he did.' He wheeled round to me and said: 'Son, write it as hard as you like.' With that, he and his mystery pal walked off.

The Sky offer was a clear example of just how United's ownership had changed, how the old, cosy private football club had gone for ever, and how it was now a publicly listed corporation like any other, in which 60 per cent of the shares were held by City of London institutions. They would ultimately decide United's future, not Edwards and his executive colleagues, and certainly not the fans, many of whom viewed Murdoch with disdain, as the arch-capitalist who went to war with the trade unions, specifically those in printing, and won.

For now, Edwards and Watkins kept the approach to themselves. They wanted to carry on talking, to gauge Sky's seriousness before telling their board. And anyway, they were already somewhat preoccupied with another secret proposal that could transform United's money-making potential but also risked alienating traditionalist supporters.

For years, the biggest clubs in Europe had seen themselves as increasingly apart from the pack. AC and Inter Milan, Juventus, Ajax, Paris St Germain, Manchester United and a handful of others enjoyed the biggest fan bases, and it was these clubs that regularly won their domestic leagues and European competitions. But prolonged success did not come cheap, and they bore considerable financial risk and substantial fixed costs to maintain their dominance. Meanwhile, they were expected to carry the rest, and to go along with whatever UEFA, the European governing body, decided.

In many respects, they viewed themselves as mightier than their country associations and UEFA. They had higher public profiles, and generated more media interest than the lesser lights. They were the ones who filled their famous, iconic grounds, who employed the superstar players (and paid their stellar wages), and who commanded the largest TV audiences.

The more they moaned to each other, the more the idea of a breakaway European Super League appealed. In short, they desired more of the rewards with attendant spin-offs for themselves. Their new European Super League would be owned by the clubs, not UEFA. They would organize the tournaments and take a greater slice

(UEFA's 45 per cent piece of the cake infuriated them). To be assured of the top clubs' participation, there would be no relegation – the founding members of the rebel league would qualify automatically. While that would make for a stronger competition, with all the best teams represented, a cynic might also say it guaranteed the highest possible income stream.

United was an enthusiastic proponent, sending its senior executives to the clandestine meetings. The list of clubs involved lengthened, the plans hardened. Then, news leaked, and the inevitable storm erupted.

United's position was made worse by a hapless press relations officer, who did not know what was occurring, and who denied the club's involvement. When United's presence was later confirmed, they were accused of trying to cover it up.

UEFA was furious, promising dire consequences, including expulsion from leagues and competitions, for the breakaways.

When the Premiership clubs met and were taken through the scheme, it soon began to wobble further. The rebels had widened their structure, so that half the Premiership clubs would end up playing in Europe in one competition or another. But this did not pacify the clubs, who queried the financial projections and were wishing to stay loyal to their league – to each other, as they saw it – and to the historical English game that was based around promotion and relegation.

The Premier League cleverly sought and secured assurances from the splinter group that, in future, discussions about the European Super League would be conducted through the Premier League. Edwards, without thinking through the implications and wishing to avoid being isolated by the rest of the Premiership, went ahead and gave United's consent.

Meanwhile, alongside Murdoch and Sky, Edwards suspected there might be other bidders waiting in the wings. He'd had an approach from Frank Lowe, the advertising chief, suggesting a multinational could be interested. Edwards thought there might be more.

Martin Stewart, Sky's chief finance officer, was dispatched to discover Edwards's price, the level he thought the board would recommend acceptance to shareholders. The answer was 290 pence a share, more than 130 pence higher than where the United share price stood at the time, equating to a total valuation of £750 million.

It was an astonishing figure. Either it was a try-on, and they were prepared to come down, or it was what they genuinely believed the club was worth, or they were trying to kill off Murdoch's interest by naming a ludicrous amount. Sky thought it was the former, that Edwards was up for selling but that he would reduce his price.

Sky pressed on, drafting in Goldman Sachs as their advisors. Goldman, as is the (invariably male) bankers' almost boyish wont in these situations, insisted on the use of code names for the project, and they chose 'Moore' and 'Best'. Improbably, Moore, the name of the famous England World Cup-winning captain, who was never a United player, was allocated to United; while Best, the United legend, was the name given to BSkyB, Sky's formal company name.

The code, of course, was based on first letters – M for Manchester and B for BSkyB – and was meant as a disguise, but it fuelled the sense that this was a project run by money men, who did not really know their football.

When they got down to the nitty-gritty of agreeing a price, it was clear that United was basing the whopping 290 pence valuation on the European Super League going ahead. Sky argued that this was fanciful. Finally, they settled on 217.5 pence in cash and shares. Edwards agreed to sell his 14 per cent.

On 6 August 1998, at what was meant to be a routine United board meeting, the other directors were told the news. There was shock, although ready acceptance of the reality, that as a stock-market-quoted company, United could fall prey to takeover at any time. They were not so keen to rush; it was felt the board had a duty to test the water, to see if there were other – possibly higher – bidders, and they had to be satisfied that what was being offered was fair. They agreed to hire advisors, HSBC and a firm of media consultants, to assuage their doubts.

Sky continued to press ahead, widening the circle of those who knew, to include PR advisors, because they knew it would be a major news story. United, though, kept it tight. No one was told, not even Ferguson or Bobby Charlton. Possibly this was because they thought that football folk such as Ferguson and Charlton were less versed in the need for confidentiality of price-sensitive information, not so attuned to City protocols. But it reinforced even further the notion that United was just an asset, an investment to be bought and sold, more a City 'bit of business', rather than the great club that could trace its origins back to the former Newton Heath railway workers.

Having settled on a price, United then decided it wanted more money. Another bank, Merrill Lynch, was asked to value the club, and agreed that the proposed share price was not enough. Edwards told Booth he thought the board would agree to 225 pence a share, or £575 million. Edwards's personal portion of that would be £80 million.

At that point, the news leaked, with *The Sunday Telegraph* reporting that BSkyB was making the bid. There was one characteristic Murdoch flick. *The Sunday Telegraph* went to great lengths to hide from the rest of Fleet Street that it had the exclusive on Sky and United. But word got round, and the paper was beaten to the newsstands by the *News of the World* and *The Sunday Times*, both part of the Murdoch media empire. The super-competitive Murdoch could not bear that a rival title had a scoop concerning one of his businesses, so he gave the order for the story to be dropped into his own papers.

The effect of the news was to put United in 'play'. Now, everyone knew the United board was actively considering a sale. At Sky, Booth feared other bidders would be smoked out. To compound his woe, the United board met and formally agreed to reject the 217.5 pence offer – they wanted to see who else was out there and whether they would go higher.

News that Murdoch wanted to buy also galvanized some of the United fans. They were opposed to Murdoch at any price, for his treatment of the unions – of working people, as they saw it – and for his lack of any connection with the club. What riled them most was that their beloved United was being treated as a commodity, to be passed around between rich men.

As well as Murdoch, the other villain in the piece for them was Edwards. There was talk of smashing the windows at his home in Cheshire. Instead, two fan groups came together and conducted a masterclass in peaceful, effective campaigning.

The Independent Manchester United Supporters Association (IMUSA) had been formed in 1997 to provide a voice for supporters. They were fed up with what they regarded as heavy-handed treatment by Old Trafford stewards, ordering people to sit down when they wanted to stand. That and other incidents, they believed, were signs of a club that had grown distant and aloof from its supporter base. The first meeting about the formation of the IMUSA was held in the Free Trade Hall in Manchester, site of the Peterloo massacre. By the time of the Sky takeover, they were well established and well organized.

A second group was formed by Michael Crick, the *BBC Newsnight* journalist and writer. A lifelong United supporter, Crick has a terrier-like determination to never let go, coupled with an ability to drill down and to latch on to embarrassing facts. He's also utterly fearless, and therefore a difficult person to have as an enemy.

His books on Jeffrey Archer and Michael Heseltine were well-researched and critically applauded. In 1990, he'd co-authored *Manchester United: The Betrayal of a Legend*, accusing Edwards and the United board of putting profits above all else. A sale to Rupert Murdoch was, for Crick, vindication of the truth of all that he had argued, a further act of betrayal of his beloved United. Crick and Richard Hytner, an advertising agency chief and old pal of Crick's from their days at Manchester Grammar School, were shareholders in United, and they set up an organization for shareholders opposed to the Sky deal: Shareholders United Against Murdoch or SUAM. IMUSA and SUAM teamed up.

Questions were being asked in the non-Murdoch newspapers about how TV negotiations would work, with United belonging to one of the TV companies. Likely conflicts of interest and competition issues were highlighted. Other Premiership chiefs were quick to voice their opposition.

In Manchester, a public meeting was called at the Bridgewater Hall, the new concert venue in the city centre. One of the shareholders, Jim White, author of *Manchester United – The Biography*, described it as the launch of 'the most sophisticated fan campaign ever seen in English football'. Instead of pockets of angry demonstrators outside Old Trafford shouting 'sack the board' and worse, there was a coming together of those who supported the Reds, with a huge range of support from people who cared. Says White: 'Bankers, trade unionists, political lobbyists, media men, accountants and actuaries working shoulder to shoulder with warehousemen, foremen, dustmen and students. All were bound by their love of the great intangible: Manchester United.'

Andy Walsh, the IT consultant, ex-Militant, chair of the Greater Manchester Poll Tax Federation, was a consummate protestor and organizer (his opposition to the poll tax saw him jailed). He was the leading voice of IMUSA, and he was well-prepared. His organization was already on what he called a 'professional footing'. Ever since United had gone public he had been expecting this day, and had been tracking the United share price looking for any sign of a takeover bid. People in the organization were allocated specific tasks – media workers were asked to prepare releases and second-guess journalists' questions.

With Crick and Walsh at the helm, the joint campaign quickly ran rings around United and Sky. Both men were politically savvy, and they knew which buttons to press and how. What Sky had not appreciated either was the range of United support. Walsh recalled how Sky 'admitted later they thought we were a bunch of ragged-arsed hooligans'. Ordinary fans wanted to help, turning up at Walsh's house to volunteer for the day by folding newsletters and addressing envelopes.

The 217.5 pence offer climbed, as United kept asking for more. The 217.5 pence became 225 pence, then 226 pence, then 230 pence and finally 240 pence, which translated to £623 million.

Even then there was not agreement until Murdoch intervened and forced pens to paper. Still bruised that a competitor had managed to get the original takeover story involving one of his own businesses first, he determined to give the full details to his house journal. He called the editor of *The Sun* and took him through the offer. The front page duly read: 'It's a deal . . . Sky buys Man Utd for £625 million'. And the newspaper's editorial crowed: 'Football is the winner from top to bottom.'

The non-Murdoch press immediately went on the attack. The *Daily Mirror* front page was 'SOLD TO THE RED DEVIL', above a picture of Murdoch coloured red with horns sticking out of his head. That was the front page; the back page targeted someone else:

Edwards. 'Traitor. Martin Edwards is facing a massive Old Trafford revolt after he last night caved into Rupert Murdoch's millions'.

Towards the end of a joint press conference that was called to show how Sky and United were as one, how this agreed takeover was for the benefit of both parties, Sky's chief executive Mark Booth was asked, 'Who plays left back for Manchester United?'

It was agreed that on questions about football, Booth, an American, would refer them to a colleague who would answer, so Booth said: 'Pass. Football is not my area of expertise.'

The next day's *Daily Mirror* front page carried a picture of Booth appearing gormless and the headline: ' "Who plays left back for Manchester United?" Answer: "Pass. Football is not my area of expertise." '

At a meeting at the Stretford Trades and Labour Club, IMUSA pleaded for demonstrations at the forthcoming match against Charlton. At the game, the call was made: 'Stand up if you hate Murdoch.' The Stretford End carried a banner: 'Sold Out. No surrender to the PLC.' The fans' chant, 'There's only one greedy bastard', was directed at Edwards and the Directors' Box.

Alex Ferguson's position drew speculation. Officially the manager was not involved at all, not siding with the club, Sky or the fans. In truth, he was in touch with the latter, urging them to keep the club away from Sky and Murdoch.

He was receiving regular updates about the supporters' campaign. Unknown to them, he had another motive for wanting to be kept apprised: he was trying to put together his own consortium to make a rival bid. His son, Mark, then at Schroders, subsequently at Goldman Sachs, was playing a leading role. Ferguson, it seemed, could call on contacts in high finance when he needed to. The alternative bid never got going, but it showed that Ferguson secretly wanted to be more than a mere manager.

The intended purchaser was Sky, but it might as well have been Murdoch personally. The opponents constantly referenced it as Murdoch's bid and laced their comments with how *The Sun* had denigrated Liverpool fans by suggesting drunken Liverpool fans were responsible for the Hillsborough tragedy.

For many, the threat of being acquired by Murdoch highlighted the two existing United's. There was the one on the pitch, doing well, full of great names, well-marshalled by Ferguson, the latest iteration of a wonderful pedigree. And there was the one that was already exemplified by the matchday experience of being subjected to a hard sell of souvenirs and replica shirts and branded garb and accessories, of going to a stadium that clearly distinguished between the haves and have-nots. The latter were huddled together, often in the cold and wet, but shouting and raucously passionate; the former were in warm, corporate boxes, set up on high, looking down on the ordinary masses and the gladiatorial players.

At every match the fans name-checked, in song, one of their more recent heroes, someone revered for his supreme natural talent and instinct for the game, Eric Cantona. His name and image will always be prominent at Old Trafford, on posters and banners. The fans remembered how, when Cantona provoked genuine grief by retiring suddenly in 1997, he said: 'I gave up early because I don't want to do anything without passion. For me that is part of the emptiness. When I felt I had lost the passion, I couldn't do it any more. I had to stop.'

He accused United of treating him like a commodity. 'When the business is more important than the football, I don't care. I just gave up.'

Cantona, it transpired, had been right all along.

While the United fans simmered with fury at matches home and away, the PR and lobbying campaign moved into a higher gear. Sky published its offer document; Michael Crick, posing as a shareholder, phoned the shareholders' hotline set up to answer their queries. He got the woman on the end of the call to admit it was 'sort of mumbo jumbo'.

Unafraid, Crick took her comments to the Takeover Panel, the august City body that rules on takeovers and mergers, claiming the offer document was confusing and misleading. The panel found for Sky and United, but Crick was garnering headlines and support.

In a twin-pronged attack, Walsh and IMUSA focused on Murdoch and what his concentration of media ownership, with United joining the family, would mean for the sport. They were helped by the government being Labour and pro-football. While Tony Blair had courted favour with Murdoch, that did not extend as far as his back-bench MPs, who could not stand the press baron and hated his newspapers.

The Office of Fair Trading (OFT), which had the power to recommend referral of the deal to the Monopolies and Mergers Commission (MMC) for scrutiny of the competition implications, was flooded with letters opposing the bid. Under severe pressure, Peter Mandelson, the minister responsible, who had zero personal interest in football, accepted the advice of the OFT and referred the takeover to the MMC.

People power had won, although John Bridgeman, the OFT chief, said he was minded to recommend referral from the moment the bid was announced. Murdoch's Sky enjoyed market dominance in pay-per-view and might be able to abuse its position, forcing United fans, if they wanted to watch their favourite team on TV, to switch – and all of it fanned by the backing of his newspapers.

It was a great victory, if not unexpected. Bridgeman said he'd warned the United board that referral was likely, but they'd chosen to plough on – confirming again that issues of fairness among all the Premiership clubs, of access for ordinary fans, many of whom were not blessed with cash, the spirit of the 'People's Game', were of little concern.

The MMC was not due to report back until March 1999. Before then, soon after the referral, United had its own shareholders' Annual General Meeting (AGM) to contend with. United had announced they were redeveloping Old Trafford, enlarging it to seat 67,400. Normally, fans would be appreciative, hearing their ground would be the largest in England after Wembley. But not this year; they had other issues concerning them. Usually, too, the attendance at the AGM would be desultory. This year, there were 1,100 booked in.

The atmosphere was tense and bitter. One shareholder summed up the anger of many when they accused Edwards of trying to sell United three times: to Knighton, to Maxwell and now to Murdoch. 'Martin Edwards, I hope you get to heaven when your time is up. Surely, though, it's three strikes and you're out. Go Martin Edwards, go.'

From the one person who perhaps had the ability to sway the fans either way, there was silence. Ferguson still kept his counsel. Edwards tried to get him to speak out in favour, as did Booth. But there was nothing.

Later, in his first autobiography, *Managing My Life* (1999), Ferguson said this: 'My own feeling is that the club is too important as a sporting institution, too much of a rarity, to be put up for sale.'

In his second autobiography, *My Autobiography* (2013), he was more sanguine: 'From the moment Manchester United became a PLC in 1990, I was certain the club would be bought and taken into private ownership.' He continues: 'With our history and our aura, we were too big a prize to be ignored by individual investors.'

Ferguson was also compromised. While a new owner might have meant more resources to enable him to buy better players, he was also pro-Labour and therefore not given to declaring affection for Murdoch. There is no doubt too that he felt slighted to have been excluded from the talks, to have not been kept fully apprised from the beginning. By refusing to do as Edwards and Booth wanted, he was conducting his own silent protest.

His silence did not stop the anti-Murdoch campaign from using Ferguson's picture and a quote of his in its literature. 'We are United to the core.' The fans were told: 'When Alex says, "We are United to the core", remember so are we and so are you. Show your support for the club as we know it and help to stop this takeover before it makes us into the club we don't know.'

Walsh and Crick pursued a relentless guerrilla war. Constantly, their target was Murdoch, the devil. His television company might have had a cuddly, friendly face but it was Murdoch who was really behind it. If the deal went ahead, it would be Murdoch controlling United. Leaflets were printed, listing all his companies' transgressions worldwide.

They rallied MPs from all sides. No MP, counting on votes, wanted to be seen as anti-football, anti the 'People's Game'. Suddenly, the very future of that game was under threat by a possible purchase of one club. They fell into line and signalled their hostility.

They found skilled lawyers who would argue against Murdoch on competition and public interest grounds. The MMC was fed the idea that Murdoch, having dominated the world's media, now wished to do the same with football. One question from the MMC rocked the Sky camp: 'It has been put to us that if you take over Manchester United, the first thing you will do is buy Ronaldo [the superstar Brazilian striker] and distort the football market?'

Sky could only mutter that it was buying United because it was a good business. Then they were asked if their digital TV business was in trouble, would they sell David Beckham to raise cash? It was a bonkers question – they were separate businesses, and even Beckham's price tag was hardly in the same league as the cost of operating

TV channels. But it showed what they were up against – with these questions, at least, the MMC was reflecting what the court of public opinion, provoked by Walsh and Crick, was thinking.

A stroke of luck for the protesting fans came as well with the shock resignation of Peter Mandelson. He was revealed to have borrowed money from a ministerial colleague, Geoffrey Robinson, to buy a house in Notting Hill, and the loan had not been disclosed. Technically he'd done nothing wrong, but it was smelly. Mandelson, who did not care about football and was a friend of Rupert Murdoch's daughter, Elisabeth, left the government.

Among the Premier League clubs, six – Arsenal, Aston Villa, Leeds, Newcastle, Southampton and Tottenham – supported the bid. The remaining thirteen did not.

When the 254-page MMC report landed, it was unequivocal. The bid should be stopped; nothing could be done to make it acceptable; there were public interest and competition grounds for blocking it. On 9 April 1999, Mandelson's successor as trade secretary, Stephen Byers, duly announced Rupert Murdoch's attempt to buy Manchester United had been blocked.

Of the couple to be married, Sky was the more resigned to being stopped. It had seen this result coming; its corporate antenna had been predicting the outcome. United, however, were taken aback. They clung to the belief that the majority of fans were not bothered as to who owned the club – so long as the team did well, which it most definably was doing. Edwards and his colleagues blamed a minority for whipping up unjustified antagonism.

They were perhaps right to think that most supporters remained unmoved. But the minority had managed to galvanize a huge body of opinion against Sky and Murdoch, and it would be insulting to say this group was easily led – they were people who could make up their own minds. The weight of the football game was opposed to the deal.

The main loser in the whole sorry episode was United. It was now a club that had made itself a fixture on the City pages, that had allowed its finances to be pored over and dissected publicly, that was run by people who were prepared to sell, and – worse – to a company run by someone without a football pedigree, who saw it as a profitable addition to his commercial behemoth.

Like it or not, to everyone involved in the game it seemed that the United directors, led by Edwards, were businessmen, cash-hungry mercenaries, who gave the impression of being in it for the money and not for the love of the famous red shirt, and who kept their brilliant manager in the dark as to what they were doing.

While the fans who campaigned against them were relatively few, against the vast body of United support, it's also fair to say that most United supporters would have loved to be given the chance to sit in the Directors' Box, in the Directors' Lounge, to enjoy the privilege of one-to-ones with Ferguson and his team, to be right at the heart of all things Manchester United. They saw the directors enjoying these incredible privileges, but realized that for them it was nowhere near enough.

The directors were taken aback by the ferocity of the fan opposition to Murdoch. They were out of touch with their own supporters, with Manchester, with the community.

FIVE

'It all started with the horse'

On 18 August 1999, the 3.45 at York was won by Mull of Kintyre. The horse's owner, Susan Magnier, was delighted. The race was the prestigious Gimcrack Stakes, and as well as the prize money and status of landing one of the oldest trophies in racing, the winning owner would get to address the annual Gimcrack Dinner.

Always held in the run-up to Christmas, the Gimcrack Dinner, also at York, is a formal, grand affair attended by the great and good of British horse-racing. The main speech can be an occasion for laughter at the sport's expense, but it may be serious as well, an opportunity to make a point.

While thrilled at winning, Susan did not make public speeches. They were not her schtick. Neither did her husband, John, despite having been a senator in Ireland.

Both the Magniers were known for being publicity shy. A supremely successful businessman, enormously wealthy, reputed to be the richest man in Ireland (he vies for the title along with his friend, fellow Irishman and business partner 'J. P.' McManus), John Magnier is highly personable in private, with a dry, sharp wit. He also takes delight in his public triumphs, of which there were many to do with horse-racing. But put him in the crowd at the races, and he will keep his trademark Panama hat tilted forward over his face, graciously acknowledging any recognition but avoiding any public display.

'John Magnier did an interview in 1977 and he enjoyed it so much that he's not done one since,' said an Irish businessman who knows Magnier.

So, if Susan or John would not give the Gimcrack address, who would?

As a sport, racing struggles to capture widespread interest. To most people it's a closed world, with its own coded language and baffling traditions. Rarely does it make the news; races take place day after day and barely feature in the sports pages of newspapers. Racecourses often face threadbare attendances; there is a shortage of new owners; prize money is lacking. Because of that, those at the top are always looking to make it more popular, to reach a bigger audience, to appeal to folk beyond the narrow racing community.

One tactic is to ensure that well-known faces from other walks of life – pop stars, models, footballers – attend the races and are photographed. Sure enough, Alex Ferguson was one such high-profile figure, who found that being manager of United and genuinely keen on racing secured invitations galore.

Ferguson adored horse-racing. He loved the sport, liked to bet heavily, casting the same gimlet eye over a thoroughbred as he would an up-and-coming footballer, looking for strengths and weaknesses, then thrilling at the chase, bathing in the same mix of sweat, muscle and straining limbs as he did at Old Trafford. Ferguson saw racing as an outlet from the massive pressures of top-league football. He got to know and become firm friends with some of the biggest figures in the sport, including Magnier and McManus.

To them, Ferguson was good company; they would have dinner with him regularly, and he liked to go to Ireland to see the horses.

John Magnier's racehorse breeding centre is at Coolmore in Ireland. Virtually in the geographical middle of the country, Coolmore is a quiet, tranquil place, buried in the rural farmland of County Tipperary. It's here, on 7,000 acres, that Magnier runs the world's most formidable racehorse stud programme.

Blink and you would miss it. There are hardly any road signs, nothing to indicate this stud produces more winning horses than anywhere else on the planet. Turn a bend on a country lane and there it is, a clutch of low-slung, brick buildings set back from the road. From a distance, it looks like a modern municipal golf club. There are clues, though, that this is very far removed from somewhere so mundane.

The car park is well-stocked with top-of-the-range vehicles, alongside 'Coolmore' branded horse boxes. There are cameras discreetly dotted around and there are electric and wire fences, beyond which the most impossibly beautiful, honed, athletic horses are grazing in the lush, vivid green fields. The staff are wearing 'Coolmore' tops. The place is immaculately tidy; nothing has been missed.

Entrance is by appointment only. Inside the front door and along the corridors of the buildings and in all the rooms, there are photographs of horses. Not just any horses, but famous horses that have become household names, like The Minstrel, Sadler's Wells, Danehill, High Chaparral, Istabraq, Galileo, George Washington, Mull of Kintyre, El Gran Senor and Rock of Gibraltar.

Nearby is Ballydoyle, John Magnier's training stables run by Aidan O'Brien. There, in pride of place, is a bronze statue of probably the most famous horse ever, Nijinsky, trained – on this very site – to win the rare Triple Crown of the 2,000 Guineas, the Derby and the St Leger.

Into these twin temples of racing walked Ferguson. He went to Coolmore, and he went to see Aidan O'Brien at Ballydoyle as well. He loved it, loved seeing the famous horses they had.

Ferguson first met Magnier briefly in 1997 at the Cheltenham Festival. He was a guest in the Ladbrokes box, for the Gold Cup. Mike Dillon, a United fan and the betting company's head of public relations, had invited Ferguson and his wife Cathy.

Even as a non-racing person, Cheltenham on Gold Cup day can be intoxicating. For a racing nut as Ferguson was, the occasion must have been mind-blowing. There was the full house, the mix of town and country, English and Irish, lots of Irish, gallons of Guinness, 'the craic', plenty of that, celebrities and royalty and, of course, the horses, the green hills in the distance, the beginning of spring and the promise of summer. At the end of the day, a bowled-over Ferguson suggested to Cathy that they should buy a horse.

Cathy agreed and it quickly became something they could enjoy as a hobby together, on a Sunday morning, to find space well away from football, to visit the trainer and check on the horses. 'I was getting to the time when I was totally obsessed with Manchester United, on the phone from 6 a.m. until 9 p.m. at night. My wife Cathy said, "You are going to kill yourself".'

He turned to the Lancastrian trainer, Jack Berry. 'When I decided to get into the horse-racing game, I wanted a horse in the North, and Jack was having plenty of winners, over a hundred a year', he said.

His first horse was called Queensland Star, named after the ship that Ferguson's father helped to build at the Govan shipyard on the Clyde. 'It was easy for us to get up every Sunday morning and get to Cockerham to see the horse on the gallops and enjoy the hospitality of Jack and his wife Jo. They were a great help to me.'

Queensland Star's first race was at Newmarket in April 1998. Said Berry: 'We went to Newmarket with Queensland Star and Alex had a bet in the first which won at 2–1. He said, "What about the next?" I said, "Keep your powder dry for your horse because I think it will win".'

It did, by nearly two lengths, and then again, second time out, at Chester. Ferguson was smitten, and the Sunday morning trips up the M6 to Cockerham, near Lancaster, to see Berry and the horse, and to wind down, became a regular fixture. Ferguson even referred to Berry's yard as akin to an outdoor 'doctor's waiting room' – as owners, after a tough and stressful working week, could unwind, roaring round the gallops on the back of the trainer's quad bike.

'After a hard game on a Saturday, you are out in the open. No one can get hold of you, mobiles phones are off, you are out in the fresh air. No one can bother you. Perfect. More and more, the horse-racing compensated me for any time we lost – it got any disappointment out of the system. Having another interest, it probably kept me in the job [at Old Trafford] longer. Definitely.'

In July 1999, after United won the Treble, Ferguson was knighted. On the very day he received the honour from the Queen at Buckingham Palace, he had a Berry-trained runner at Yarmouth. Richard Hughes, the then champion jockey, rode Ninety Degrees to victory. Berry made the 550-mile round trip to Yarmouth to watch. Moments after Ninety Degrees crossed the finishing line, Berry's mobile rang. It was Ferguson, from London. 'It was his special day and he wanted to know how his horse had run. That was Alex.'

Ferguson's world was dividing into two, football and racing. That same year, 1999, he'd become so hooked that he persuaded Edwards to endorse the creation of the Manchester United Racing Club. Ferguson's plan was that the club should have 2,000 members, United fans, paying £235 each. That should buy them six horses, which could race in United's colours. Unfortunately, the racing club did not match his own success with Berry. When it was quietly wound up two years later, the United syndicate had 800 members and its horses had won only two out of twenty-seven races and collected just £16,000 in prize money.

With Ferguson a frequent visitor to race meetings, courtesy of Mike Dillon of Ladbrokes and others, it was likely that he would bump into John Magnier again, and he did, later in 1999. On this occasion they had a proper chat. The two men had an easy liking for each other. They had much in common. They'd both reached the summit of their chosen professions from humble beginnings. They were modest about their achievements. They drove themselves hard. They could not stand the racing Establishment.

Their friendship grew. Ferguson was drawn into Magnier's world, and what a world. Not only was there Coolmore and Ballydoyle, and Magnier's business partnership with J. P. McManus, the legendary gambler as well as businessman, but there were other members of a close circle: Irish financier and investor Dermot Desmond, British businessman and bookmaker Michael Tabor and British businessman and currency trader Joe Lewis. All of them were hugely wealthy, all operating at a level far beyond ordinary people, flying on private jets, staying in the Magnier-McManus-owned Sandy Lane resort in Barbados, in palatial villas in Florida. Magnier and McManus shared an office in Geneva, and they were forever travelling between Switzerland, Ireland and the Caribbean.

For relaxation, when not watching horse-racing, the tight group liked to play golf, with each other and their friends, professionals Ernie Els and Tiger Woods. Ferguson was a guest at the glittering J. P. McManus Pro-Am tournament at Limerick. At the charity auction held to coincide with the tournament, Ferguson donated four tickets to a Manchester United home game and drinks with the manager and his squad. It fetched £250,000. That wasn't the biggest amount – Lewis, the billionaire financier, bid £1.4 million for a round of golf with Tiger Woods and Woods's friend Mark O'Meara.

The boy from the tenements in Govan had risen to another tier, one far above even the likes of Edwards and the management at Manchester United.

That's not to say the 'Coolmore Mafia', as they were known in racing, did not follow football as well. It was racing first, then golf, but football was always up there. J. P. was an Arsenal fan, Magnier was not a supporter of any club, but he did admire the best in any sport, and that included United.

They talked about buying into football. Magnier had no interest in investing in football clubs per se, but Manchester United was different. Ferguson encouraged them, and in the summer of 1999, Magnier and McManus met Edwards over dinner with Dermot Desmond. It was more of a social encounter than a serious business discussion, but they said they might be keen to buy into the club.

Nothing came immediately of the dinner, but the Irishmen were left intrigued. What fascinated them was that while on its face football did not look like the sort of investment they would normally make (they felt it was far too risky), they'd noticed that financial institutions they respected were piling in. With their typical preparedness, they asked their advisors to take a close look at United, to carefully study the books.

That same summer, Susan Magnier landed the Gimcrack. Dillon, the PR man and friend to both Magnier and Ferguson, had an idea: that the United manager should make the Gimcrack speech. Dillon said it would be great for racing if someone like Alex Ferguson was involved in owning horses at Ballydoyle. York is as good in a way as Royal Ascot but less formal, and the dinner at the end of the year is well-reported in the racing press. The speaker usually gives an overview of the industry. They thought it would be great if Ferguson would do it.

It was mutually beneficial. Ferguson would cement himself in racing and could use the speech to promote his Manchester United Racing Club. Magnier and McManus would gain the kudos of the association with the United manager; it should help popularize the sport and, who knew, United fans might be persuaded to turn to racing and some might even seek out Ballydoyle as a venue at which to train their horses.

Magnier had a quiet word with the people at York, to see if it was alright if Alex spoke. He said he'd got somebody in his group who was the most successful football manager of all time. Alex Ferguson. He thought it would be a good idea to hear another perspective on the industry.

The York Races Committee, which organizes the dinner, declined the offer. Ferguson was not the owner, he was a football manager – and wasn't he the son of a Glasgow shipyard worker? He was also Labour. They said, 'maybe it is not appropriate' for Ferguson to give the speech. Those were their exact words, 'not appropriate'.

Magnier was dumbfounded. He saw it as an opportunity to raise the profile of the industry, to give the industry more exposure. They would also hear from Ferguson as to the lessons racing could learn from football. And they turned it down. It was madness, and pure snobbishness.

In the end the 1999 Gimcrack speech was delivered by Bob Lanigan, who worked for Coolmore. It was written by Magnier, and saw him both generously offer to sponsor a race at York for £50,000, and to accuse the government of not doing enough to support horse-racing and breeding.

Privately though, Magnier was seething. He could not abide snobs and being patronized, so he determined that Ferguson would make the Gimcrack speech. He turned to Aidan O'Brien and said the next time you have a horse good enough to win the Gimcrack, we will put it in Alex Ferguson's colours, and then they can't refuse.

It sounded light-hearted, but there was a serious point behind it. Nothing was really meant to come of it, beyond allowing Ferguson to deliver an after-dinner speech. However, the Irish sense of mischief, the delight in good craic, as this was, would have profound consequences. As more than one of those around the top of United at the time maintained: 'It all started with the horse.'

The first two horses that the Coolmore-Ballydoyle operation secured for Ferguson, where he was registered as co-owner, were Zentsov Street and Heritage Hall in 1999. Neither proved capable of winning the Gimcrack.

Then came Juniper. This horse had real promise, and Ferguson was again registered as co-owner. Juniper, though, was not an easy, predictable horse to train. Sometimes he could be unresponsive and sluggish, at other times he powered ahead.

Tellingly, when he did not appear to be heading for the Gimcrack in August, the horse's registration document was changed, and Ferguson's name was removed. Then, when he had a good spell, back went Ferguson's name. It was all about getting Ferguson listed as co-owner of a Gimcrack-winning horse – other races did not count, Magnier wanted revenge on the 'blazers' who had snubbed him and his friend.

Sure enough, Juniper eventually made it to the starting line for the Gimcrack in 2000. The horse was ridden by Mick Kinane and it was listed as being owned by Tabor, Susan Magnier and Ferguson. Juniper finished third, only a head and neck off the winner. After that, pretty much, Juniper's racing career was over – he ran a few more races but came nowhere.

There was never any question that Juniper belonged to Alex

Ferguson. It didn't. He didn't own the horse. Sure, he ran in the Gimcrack partly in his name, but Juniper was owned by Tabor and Magnier. Ferguson, despite being registered as co-owner for the Gimcrack, never challenged that position or made any claim to Juniper.

While the quest for a horse that could win the Gimcrack for the United manager intensified, changes were taking place on the United share register. In October 1999, a day after United announced its annual results, Edwards reduced his holding in the club and pocketed £41 million. If the cash he received on flotation is included, Edwards had made almost £80 million from selling shares in United, from an initial outlay of £600,000. What's more, he still had United shares left over, which were worth another £30 million.

In the autumn of 1999, the Irish finished doing their sums. Their advisors gave the thumbs up: United, which had been valued at £1 billion, was now trading at around £250 million; Old Trafford, which then held 67,000, was usually full and the club had a massive following worldwide; the shares, which at one point had been worth £4, were down to £1.20. As they saw it, the only way for the share price was up. In December 1999, Magnier and McManus bought a small stake, so small it did not have to be declared to the Stock Exchange, via a company they owned in the Virgin Islands called Cubic Expression.

Football was a departure for the Irish pair, but those around them insist their investment had nothing to do with Ferguson. It was simply another investment. By their reasoning it was not much money; they'd smelled a bargain, that was all.

In 2001, trainer Aidan O'Brien was having a good season, even by his high standards. He had a bevy of superb young horses, potential stars, of which four stood out: Johannesburg, Hawk Wing, Landseer and Rock of Gibraltar. One, whichever entered the Gimcrack, was earmarked for Ferguson. Landseer, owned by Michael Tabor and Susan Magnier, won the Coventry Stakes at Royal Ascot on 19 June 2001.

Sixth in the same race was Rock of Gibraltar, owned by Susan Magnier. It was a disappointing result since Rock of Gibraltar had won his first race, the 2.15 at The Curragh, on 21 April 2001. He had been fourth at halfway, moved into the lead and won comfortably. It was an impressive performance and there was a buzz at Ballydoyle about the horse, whose father was Danehill, one of the most successful sires of all time, producing horses that between them won eighty-four Grade 1 races.

At Ascot in the Coventry Stakes, Rock of Gibraltar was hampered and could not break clear. Twelve days later, he was entered for the Anheuser-Busch Railway Stakes at The Curragh. This time, Rock of Gibraltar led with one and a half furlongs to go and won easily.

In advance of the Gimcrack, O'Brien did what he usually did; in the first call for entries, he put down the names of several horses. As the date of the race got nearer, he would filter them down to two or three. He selected two: Rock of Gibraltar and Wiseman's Ferry.

On 17 August 2001, five days before the big race, Ferguson was registered by Coolmore-Ballydoyle as the 'first' owner of Rock of Gibraltar. Why first? Because the horse would run in his colours, the same distinctive red and white as the football team he managed, interlaced with red and white stars. Susan Magnier was listed as the other co-owner.

Ferguson, of course, was not really the co-owner. The horse was registered in his name, but it was someone else's property. No money ever changed hands, Alex Ferguson never bought and paid for a share in the horse. Magnier was grateful to Ferguson. He said it was good of him to do it, to put his name on the horse and if it won, make the speech.

The 2001 Scottish Equitable Gimcrack Stakes was run on 22

August. It's a race for colts and geldings, for horses that show great promise. There were nine horses in the field. Rock of Gibraltar, ridden by the Irish champion jockey Mick Kinane, faced stiff competition, but he ran powerfully and smoothly from the off. He kept up with the leaders and was running comfortably. With two furlongs to go, Kinane pushed him to accelerate into the lead and left the rest trailing. Rock of Gibraltar won by three lengths, although that could easily have been much more. Towards the end, Kinane had let up and wasn't pressing him hard.

Ferguson wasn't there in person; he was watching Manchester United at Blackburn Rovers as they drew 2–2.

On the evening of 11 December 2001, the 200 guests in the banqueting suite at the annual Gimcrack Dinner at York Racecourse pushed back their chairs. Some undid their top buttons. The main after-dinner speaker was about to begin his address.

He might have been wearing a dinner suit and black tie, appearing far more dapper than in his day-to-day work tracksuit, but there was no mistaking Sir Alex Ferguson. With the committee men who had previously rejected Ferguson as a speaker looking on, Magnier had made his point.

By the occasion of the speech, Ferguson was so in love with racing and being associated with Rock of Gibraltar that he'd been talking about leaving football, retiring from Manchester United, to focus on owning and breeding racehorses.

He was going to quit at the end of the season and throw himself into his new passion. 'What I hope to do is to venture into the breeding part of racing and hopefully Rock of Gibraltar will be the start of it,' he told the racing journalist Martin Hannan. 'It is something I need to learn about, and indeed I am looking at the catalogues of broodmares at the moment, especially those for the Newmarket and Goffs broodmare sales. I am trying to learn as much as I can because if you are going to get into this game you need to know what you are talking about. Otherwise, you can lose a lot of money.'

He was, he said, with Rock of Gibraltar, going through something which many owners have experienced over the years with champion horses. 'You just spend the winter wondering how it will go. You're dreaming all the time about it.'

Ferguson opened his address with a quip. 'This speech will be delivered in Scottish,' he growled in his native Glaswegian accent.

His audience laughed, and Ferguson was away. Even so, he seemed surprisingly hesitant. Perhaps that was because assembled in front of him were racing's elite – and if he was to be believed, they would be his future colleagues, clients, possible friends and rivals.

He'd planned his speech, and, despite the opening, there were few jokes. It was as if this was Ferguson, the famous football manager, making his case to be allowed to join horse-racing's elite, to come into their world, for him to put down a marker, to show what he could offer, his added value, for them to afford him respect and comradeship.

Their sport, he felt, was too riven by petty jealousies between competing authorities and racing boards. It could be enticing and magnetic enough, but other sports were so far ahead in terms of marketing and capitalizing on their appeal. 'In spite of the unfamiliar look of Manchester United's form line recently, I trust you will not think it inappropriate if I commend the teamwork principle to British racing as a whole. I have never been interested in sending out a collection of brilliant individuals. There is no substitute for talent, but talent without unity of purpose is a hopeless, devalued currency. Togetherness is not just a nice concept that you can take or leave according to your taste. If you don't have it, you are nothing.'

He continued: 'Selfishness, factionalism, cliquishness – all are death to a football team, and their influence could be as destructive for racing. Unless the industry embraces the teamwork principle wholeheartedly, instead of merely paying lip service to it, British racing will never have the success it deserves.

'Racing means so much to me that I am depressed to see its future well-being jeopardized by the competing agendas of sectional interests. Government has rightly decided that it wants to have as little to do with racing as possible, so it is up to those within the sport to shape its destiny. Only teamwork will meet the challenge. Persisting with factional hostilities will be disastrous.'

Said Ferguson: 'Sometimes, racing gives the impression that it is embarrassed by how glamorous and exciting it can be. We should be galvanizing ourselves to reach new audiences, to make racing more appealing to women, to the young and to ethnic minorities. Above all, we need to be more realistic. The internet and the interactive age may have possibilities, but it is folly to imagine they represent a shortcut to riches.

'What matters is what we do to make racing come alive in the public consciousness. There may be no individual who can do for racing what Tiger Woods did for golf, but we should make the most of star performers. And we should maximize the impact of the most thrilling events in the calendar.'

He went on to say that he believed there was scope for a racing equivalent of the Ryder Cup in golf – the American Breeders' Cup race could be staged on either side of the Atlantic. Deliberately pandering to his audience, Ferguson said: 'York – the flattest track in Britain – would be an excellent home. The Breeders' Cup on the Knavesmire [the name for York racecourse] would be a perfect symbol of a forward-looking industry.'

Wearing his football hat, he compared owning Rock of Gibraltar with managing star players. 'Though Rock of Gibraltar may move as gracefully as a Verón or a Beckham, it costs a lot less to keep him happy. And lately he has been more consistent than my Manchester United thoroughbreds!'

Then Ferguson singled out Susan Magnier, his co-owner of Rock of Gibraltar, and her husband, John. 'My deepest gratitude is due to two friends who are not here, to Sue and John Magnier. It is because I have been given the privilege of teaming up with them that I am standing before you this evening. Nobody could be blessed with better partners on the Turf.'

With that, he sat down to warm clapping, congratulatory hand-shakes and pats on the back.

To the wider world, Ferguson was the registered co-owner of Rock of Gibraltar. It was clear that Rocky might have a stellar career ahead of him – three outings had produced two wins, and the wins had been easy. He might be a special horse, and anticipation about him was building.

It would be unseemly if Ferguson, having made the speech, was publicly dropped as co-owner – that was bound to raise eyebrows, with Magnier being accused of using the United manager only to make the speech, which of course he had, with Ferguson's consent. Rock of Gibraltar was going to enter further races, and there was every likelihood he would claim more wins.

So Magnier made him an offer. Magnier said to Ferguson that he had a choice: 10 per cent of the money the horse wins or the cost of one nomination a year (when the mare is introduced and covered by the stallion in the hope the resulting foal also becomes a champion) while it's at stud. When the horse did go to stud a single nomination cost €80,000. So, while it was in its prime, Alex Ferguson could expect to receive €80,000 a year, every year.

Magnier's suggestion was a valuable and generous gift. His advice was to take the nomination, not the prize money, as longer term it was better financially. Ferguson agreed to take the one nomination a year offer. Their pact was verbal; nothing was written down.

When I visited Coolmore, Rock of Gibraltar was at the Magnier family's Castlehyde Stud in Fermoy, County Cork. Rocky was coming to the end of an illustrious stud career, in addition to his time racing. He sired 256 horses that entered races, including seventy-seven worldwide winners and sixteen that won at the highest level. They included Eclipse and Criterium International winner Mount Nelson, Golden Jubilee Stakes and Haydock Sprint Cup winner Society Rock, Irish 1,000 Guineas winner Samitar, and Hong Kong Cup winner and Epsom Derby runner-up Eagle Mountain. He was also a broodmare sire for the 2020 and 2021 Guineas' winners, Kameko and Poetic Flare.

A nomination for Rocky was down to €5,000. So, Ferguson would still have got €5,000 even then, after all that time.

It's not clear how much of the conversation with Magnier Ferguson understood. The nuances of horse-breeding and ownership were still new to Ferguson. Did he realize fully the implications of what was being suggested? Also, did Magnier hear that Ferguson had accepted? Was the United manager clear in his agreement?

As far as Magnier was concerned, there was no problem – he'd sorted out Rock of Gibraltar's future earnings with Ferguson. Everyone was happy. Everything was great. As a two-year-old, Rock of Gibraltar was superb, then as a three-year-old he was superb again. After the Gimcrack he kept winning – seven Group One races in total.

The Irish and Ferguson were basking in their friendship and success. Meanwhile Magnier and McManus had upped their stake in Ferguson's club, paying more than £15 million to almost double their holding, which also now had to be publicly declared. They duly became the second largest shareholder, via Cubic Expression, just behind BSkyB which had 9.9 per cent, a hangover from its failed takeover.

The Irish pair attempted to calm talk of a bid, issuing a statement saying they had been investors in United for some time and they were taking advantage of weakness in the share price to increase their joint holdings.

Few were convinced. The thought was that they were readying to mount a takeover with their friend Ferguson, who had a long-held ambition to one day own the club. They tried to insist their move had nothing to do with Ferguson and was pure opportunism but barely anyone believed them. Rock of Gibraltar, for a start, was public proof of their closeness.

The United board was unimpressed. Ferguson, with the super-rich second-biggest investors seemingly in his pocket, now apparently had an all-powerful role in the club. His position was unassailable.

Back on the racecourse, Rocky continued to run and win top races in spectacular fashion – Grand Criterium, Dewhurst Stakes, 2,000 Guineas, Irish 2,000 Guineas, St James's Palace Stakes were all claimed, one after the other. His success reached far beyond the confines of racing and the regular betting community. He was being talked up constantly, and the tabloid papers were running features on him; when he ran, pubgoers would ask the bar staff to switch over the TV so they could watch the race. He was European Horse of the Year in 2002 and European Champion three-year-old colt in the same year. And always, everywhere, he was referred to as 'Alex's horse', running in United red.

No one could have predicted this. They knew the horse was good, but they did not know how good. What was meant to happen was that he would win the Gimcrack, Ferguson would make the speech, and he and Magnier would have cocked a snook at the Bufton Tuftons on the York committee. Ferguson could – and perhaps should have – given him back, but he didn't, and to be fair, he wasn't asked to. Instead, Magnier had made him that verbal offer, and he'd agreed.

It suited Ferguson to keep quiet about the horse being free. Perhaps his pride meant he did not like to admit the horse was a gift; that he'd never bought the horse and its success was not down to him.

It suited Magnier and his associates, too, that Ferguson did not admit it was a gift. The Irishmen were no fools and they realized how it would seem if they were shown to have handed a share in the horse to Ferguson. They were now locked in a pact of silence, both living a lie, Magnier and Ferguson both.

There was also the possible impact on the United situation. Whilst Magnier and McManus repeatedly stressed they weren't plotting a bid for the club, Ferguson's position at the club meant he had the power to influence the outcome of a takeover. If it came to light that they had gifted him Rock of Gibraltar, it might look as though the Irish businessmen had 'bought' him in some way.

Ferguson, however, was under pressure, being asked over and over by excited punters and press to explain how he had alighted on such a terrific animal. His story shifted almost inexorably; he began to move from being tight-lipped that it was a freebie to maintaining publicly that he'd purchased his share. He began telling people that he purchased his half-share after the Coventry Stakes at Royal Ascot in June 2001. This in itself is slightly odd because that was the race when Rock of Gibraltar finished sixth with Landseer victorious. Rocky was hampered, but according to his telling, Ferguson had seen enough to convince himself that this was a horse worth buying.

Then he wrote a first-person piece for the *Observer*: 'My first real memory of Rock of Gibraltar was at the Gimcrack Stakes at York in August of last year [2001]. I had bought him a couple of months earlier, and he had already won once. But it was exciting to watch him there, and the way he won it I didn't expect, though John Magnier had said he had a good chance. So, when it won, I was excited. But I don't think any of us, including John, expected it to turn out the way it has.'

Ferguson also wrote: 'John [Magnier] knew that I'd had one or two successes with the horses, and he said, "We'll try and get you a Group One winner." And I said, how's that? And he said, "Well, we'll offer you the chance to buy one of our horses." '

Examining what Ferguson says here raises some questions. His 'first real memory' of Rock was seeing him win the Gimcrack. Surely, his first real memory was whatever it was that made him fork out what would have been a considerable sum to buy a share in him?

He says Magnier offered him 'the chance to buy one of our horses'. Not a share, note, but a horse. And which horse, how was it decided? Would Coolmore simply hand over a brilliant horse, a future horse of the year and, as it transpired, the best in the world, just like that? If it was potluck, Ferguson had hit the jackpot with Rocky. According to Ferguson's account, the breeders had said goodbye to a half-share in one of the greatest racehorses of all time, which at stud would command huge fees potentially worth tens of millions of pounds. It was an odd way to run a business, and their track record suggested that is not what they did, ever.

Despite the *Observer* piece, Ferguson was not entirely confident in relaying his version of events. When asked about his ownership in public, he would usually mutter that he bought Rocky after the Coventry Stakes. Details about the purchase, how much he paid, were always thin. The press reported he'd paid £173,000, but the figure was not attributed directly to him.

He told the racing journalist, Martin Hannan, that Magnier had 'offered me a half-share in it [Rock of Gibraltar] before it even saw the track'. So that was before the Coventry Stakes, not after, as he'd said elsewhere, but that might tie in with his other claim, that his first real memory of the horse was seeing him win the Gimcrack.

Magnier's associates noticed as well that, despite the acclaim and hoo-ha surrounding Rocky, Ferguson appeared uncharacteristically disinclined to put himself forward. As they saw it, it was a valuable and generous gift he got, and he knew that. But when Rock of Gibraltar won the 2,000 Guineas (in May 2002), they noticed how reluctant he was to get the trophy.

But as far as the breeders were concerned, the private verbal agreement stood, and if Ferguson wanted to give another side of events, to maintain his pride, they did not especially mind.

Whatever, the story hardened, and it was accepted almost everywhere that Alex Ferguson had struck gold when his friend John Magnier had allowed him to buy a share in a Coolmore horse and he chose the brilliant Rock of Gibraltar. He even made the *Sunday Times Rich List* on the strength of his half-share in Rocky.

There, it could have ended, and no one would have been any the wiser. Certainly, if it had stayed there, events at Manchester United would have taken a very different course.

One person who is a friend to both Magnier and Ferguson is Brough Scott, the former jockey turned racing journalist. He recalls that critically, the exact relationship between Ferguson and Magnier was not put into writing. 'Somehow, somewhere this was either overlooked or not acted upon, and the exact expectations not clarified. Somehow Ferguson's team had forgotten racing's oldest adage: that it is not enough to look a gift horse in the mouth, it is necessary to listen very carefully to what its owner has to say.'

SIX

The Glazers make their appearance

According to those who worked for them, Avie Glazer and his younger brother, Joel, claim to have held lifelong interests in football, or soccer as it is known in the US.

'They used to watch the North American soccer leagues. Rochester had a team of sorts, and they would talk about how it was always getting smashed by teams containing European stars at the end of their careers, like George Best and Johan Cruyff,' said one ex-Glazer worker.

Joel would later give a rare interview to United's own TV channel, MUTV: 'My family have always been very passionate about two sports, American football and British football. And it's because in the town I grew up, Rochester New York, we had the North American Soccer League. And in Rochester we had the worst team in the league. But week in and week out I was there to support my club . . .'

The Glazers' former public relations advisor, Tehsin Nayani (his brief appears to have been more reactive than proactive), recalls Joel saying, 'Of course I love football, I've followed the game for as long as I can remember. I got into the Premier League when I roomed with an English friend at college. He may have loved Tottenham but for me it was all about Manchester United and Fergie.'

Joel Glazer was born in 1967. He went to the American University in Washington DC when he was eighteen, which would have been in 1985. The Premiership did not begin until the 1992–3 season. As for Ferguson, he was United's manager from 1986, but his first few seasons in charge were marked by failure, so much so that a banner was unfurled at Old Trafford: 'Three years of excuses and it's still crap . . . ta-ra Fergie.'

Given Ferguson did not secure his first major trophy with United until they won the FA Cup in 1990, it's difficult to conceive of him and the Reds captivating a student from across the Atlantic. Indeed, Joel's college days coincided with an especially dull period in United's playing history.

Still, let's cut them some slack and allow Joel and Avie to be keen on football from some moment in their lives and, with that, United. Those who have been to Joel's office in Maryland outside Washington certainly swear it's a veritable shrine to all things United. 'It's a mecca, like a museum at Old Trafford,' said one former Glazer staffer. 'It's a Manchester United temple.'

While their father cared little for sports, the two brothers seemingly followed the NFL and soccer. Later, they would claim that it was their plan, one day, to own United. 'They always said they wanted to buy United, they said they were always destined to try and buy United,' said the former executive. 'I must admit, I never saw any evidence for that.'

He shrugged. 'But then United was listed, so it was available, so it was possible they thought like that.' He added, pointedly: 'Martin Edwards had made it saleable by listing it.'

This former senior colleague of the Glazers said he had no doubt 'they did a lot of analysis themselves, they're a debate-oriented family.' He described them as 'middle-class billionaires. They have no trappings of wealth. For them, it's all about work and family. They're very serious people – they would have spent hours analysing United.'

The first indication the Glazers might be interested in investing in football was in the summer of 2002, when Avie visited the New York offices of Allen & Overy (A&O), the City of London law firm. He was meeting Andrew Ballheimer, one of A&O's partners in New York. Avie had been talking to other NFL leaders, including Bill Parcells, former head coach of the New York Giants.

The US major league owners were waking up to a new prospect across the Atlantic. While they enjoyed reaping the benefits of holding sports franchises, they were being told that baseball, basketball and American football were all going to be eclipsed by European football, that the money from TV rights in Europe was going to be huge. Avie wanted to know from Ballheimer the ins and outs of investing in soccer in Europe. The conversation was said to be general, not tied to a specific club and certainly not at that stage to Manchester United.

Over in England, at Goodwood, on 31 July 2002 Rock of Gibraltar won the Sussex Stakes, equalling Mill Reef's record of six successive Group One victories.

Mick Kinane, his jockey, said afterwards: 'That was a great performance. He is the ultimate racehorse.' That was followed by the Prix du Moulin at Longchamps on 8 September. With 200 yards to go, Rocky was trailing Banks Hill and Proudwings. Then Kinane launched Rocky's trademark last-minute surge. Rocky was struck by a whip in the face but brushed it off with ease. Suddenly, he'd caught and moved half a length clear. Mill Reef's record had been broken; Rock of Gibraltar was a world record holder.

Banks Hill's jockey, Richard Hughes, summed it up for many

when he said: 'We were beaten by a wonder horse – the best horse in the world.'

Rocky fever was rampant. The horse was featured everywhere and, with him, Rocky's football manager co-owner. Even the governor of Gibraltar issued a statement saying how delighted the people of Gibraltar were to be associated with such a great horse, adding, 'And then there is the connection through Sir Alex Ferguson to Manchester United, which is famous around the world.'

His next race was to be the Breeders' Cup in Arlington, Chicago, at the end of October 2002. Win that and Rocky would have won eight successive Group One races, a record that would surely stand for a long time.

For once, though, Rocky's run did not go to plan. Just as he made his customary charge for the front, he was blocked by another Magnier horse, Landseer, making a sudden unexpected sideways move. It wasn't normal, and Landseer's jockey pulled him up. Rocky's acceleration had been checked, though, and he had to readjust, losing seconds of pace. Despite a typically powerful final quarter-mile, he could not make up the lost ground and finished second to Domedriver.

Racing was in shock. Rocky had not won and, at the same time, Landseer had sustained a fractured cannon bone in his near foreleg. The end for Landseer was quick and merciful, but deeply distressing for all, with the horse lying in grievous pain on the track, the curtains going up, then the grief-stricken trainer and grooms walking away.

Magnier might have been ruthless in business, but he could not bear what he had witnessed. He was traumatized and, having lost Landseer, understandably could not bear to lose Rocky. The decision was taken to retire him to stud at Coolmore. The Press Association carried a valedictory statement from Ferguson:

'As a relative newcomer into ownership I cannot adequately

express the pleasure I have derived from the association with such a great horse. I owe an eternal debt of thanks to everyone associated with Ballydoyle. Whilst I will be saddened not to see Rock of Gibraltar in action on the racecourse, I look forward to the future with keen anticipation, and I have every confidence that he will transmit his amazing talent and courage to his offspring.'

Attention soon switched to the stud fees and the fortune awaiting Ferguson. He was portrayed as incredibly lucky. An Irish priest, Father Sean Healy, a poverty campaigner, was quoted in the *Daily Mirror*: 'That horse will make a ten-million-euro profit a year and he will get half of that, but Ferguson will not pay a cent of tax in Ireland. I believe five million euro is a bit too much to go untaxed. Even a modest levy would bring money into the Exchequer and still leave him with an enormous amount of money in his pocket.'

The first hint that all might not be as it seemed surfaced in print in the Peterborough diary in *The Daily Telegraph*. Its author, Charlie Methven, wrote about how Ferguson's entry into owning racehorses 'has been the stuff of dreams'. He went on, 'but will the canny Scotsman ever really cash in on his prized asset? Fergie owns a 50 per cent stake in "the Rock", entitling him to half of its £1.2 million career earnings. But the real cash cow, so to speak, will be the horse's breeding rights – estimated at a whopping £50 million.'

Then he wrote: 'Rumours circulating in racing circles have it that they are secretly retained by John Magnier, the Irish bloodstock baron whose wife Sue owns the remaining share in the horse.' Methven quoted a racing source: 'No one knows whether he has a share. Magnier's whole operation is opaque and they're suspiciously hazy on this detail.'

The United fanzine *Red Issue* also reported: 'Much has been made in the press about Fergie's foresight in investing in such a promising prospect, but could it be right he only bought into a share of the steed's prize winnings and not its stud rights, where potentially the real millions are?'

Yet there was evidence to the contrary. 'Friends' of Ferguson and 'insiders' would pop up, saying there was no issue with the breeding income; that he'd bought a half-share and that meant he was entitled to half of whatever the horse earned.

Coolmore got on with the business of preparing the horse for breeding. They registered the horse with Weatherbys Ireland, official keepers of the Irish stud book. And then there it was, in black and white, that the owner of Rock of Gibraltar at stud was 'Rock of Gibraltar syndicate' – in other words, no longer Mrs John Magnier and Sir Alex Ferguson as it had been during his racing career.

The change did not necessarily mean that Ferguson was not co-owner – he could have been part of the syndicate – and the press did not pick it up. But it's quite likely that Ferguson did see the entry and it set him thinking. Certainly, at that time in February 2003, he was talking among his circle about the mountainous fees that would be coming to him from Rocky. He was jumping the gun: in racehorse breeding the owner of the stallion only gets paid months after the mare is in foal. The horse was just covering his first mares; it was far too soon to be discussing what he might be owed.

Ferguson plainly did not know that, or he chose to ignore it. Coolmore received a phone call. It was the first inkling they had that something was untoward. It was a call to a Coolmore executive. Alex Ferguson would like to come over with his tax advisors to discuss how best to deal with the breeding rights in Rock of Gibraltar and his half-share. They were baffled and could not think where he'd got that notion from.

A senior Coolmore executive called Ferguson back and told him he was mistaken; he did not own a half-share. Could Ferguson have been mistaken about the offer Magnier had made him, the one he'd accepted? As far as Magnier was concerned, there was no doubt Alex Ferguson knew exactly what the deal was. It was, though, all word of mouth, there was no written agreement.

The problem only arose with Rock of Gibraltar, because the horse was so good, so valuable. Other Coolmore horses ran in Ferguson's name and he never paid for them, and he obtained no money from breeding.

Coolmore did not offer Ferguson half the prize money as a sop. He never received half the winnings. He had the verbal agreement with Magnier and that was it. But by now Ferguson appeared to have convinced himself he was due several tens of millions from owning a half-share in Rock of Gibraltar.

On Saturday 15 February 2003, Manchester United lost 2–0 to Arsenal. Ferguson was down, snarly and grumpy. This wasn't wholly unusual after a loss, but this was worse than normal. In the dressing room he gave the players his usual 'hairdryer' treatment when they had played badly, but on this day he went further. He lashed out. He kicked at a football boot lying on the floor and, as bad luck would have it, the shoe flew across the room and hit David Beckham full in the face, above the left eye. Beckham, the captain of England, tried to retaliate and had to be held back.

Stories about Beckham's exploits, good or bad, always made headlines. This one was no different. 'FERGIE DECKS BECKS' ran *The Sun*. Beckham seemed to milk the incident PR-wise, turning up at training with a plaster on his left eyebrow, slowing his car and not shielding his face so the photographers could get the picture. Amid the furore, there was comment and speculation that Ferguson had not only gone too far but that he seemed wound up about something that possibly was other than the match. It was noted that it couldn't be money worries, since he was about to earn a fortune from the stud fees due to him for Rock of Gibraltar.

This was, of course, precisely the time that the realization he might not collect that fortune was gnawing away at him.

Hostilities between Magnier and Ferguson developed the week after the Beckham boot episode, with a piece in the *Daily Mail* saying that Ferguson is 'not reinvesting in another horse with the Coolmore team this year, reasoning that lightning is unlikely to strike twice. Rock of Gibraltar is now earning him around £6 million a year from stud fees.'

There was another story in the *Racing Post* saying that Henry Ponsonby, who ran the United Racing Club for Ferguson, had formed a syndicate with the football manager and their horses would be trained by Mick Channon, the ex-England footballer. There was no mention of Coolmore-Ballydoyle, and Coolmore-Ballydoyle would certainly have picked up on the piece.

Magnier and McManus hit back, in considerable style and with guile. On 6 March 2003, they spent £14 million to take Cubic Expression's holding in United to 10.37 per cent, making it the club's biggest shareholder. Ferguson found himself with two shareholders with whom he was in dispute. Except that was not known – to the media, the public, or the United fans. So far as they were concerned, Magnier, McManus and Ferguson were all still besties.

Bid speculation was rife. A *Manchester Evening News* columnist suggested it would be good for United if the duo took over – they had sporting backgrounds and they were friends with Ferguson.

This prompted a salvo from the United board, in which they referred dismissively and snobbily to Magnier and McManus as 'two Irish racehorse owners', rather than as hugely successful businessmen with numerous, varied interests. It contained this plea, to 'rank-and-file supporters' of the club: 'Would you like your club to be under the control of two Irish racehorse owners who know absolutely nothing about running a football business or would you prefer the club to remain in the hands of a PLC board with a track record in all fields, which speaks for itself?'

For all its public bravado, behind the scenes the United board was growing increasingly anxious. They really could not stomach the club being owned by Ferguson's two Irish pals.

Other investors had also been buying shares. They thought the club was undervalued as well, the shares underpriced. United's coming interim results were thought to be good. Among those attracted to the shares were John de Mol, the Dutch media tycoon behind the creation of Big Brother, and Malcolm Glazer, owner of the Tampa Bay Buccaneers. They each spent £8.6 million to acquire 2.9 per cent, just short of the publicly declarable threshold. Joel and Avie had persuaded their father to take a punt on United shares and see where it led.

At first, the board was not unduly bothered by the new American investor. The main attention was still focused on Magnier and McManus. Paddy Harverson, then United's communications director, recalls being asked for a rundown of the shareholders. 'The Glazers were into lots of things, like fish oil and shopping malls. They had the Tampa Bay Buccaneers, which was a newer NFL franchise. We concluded they were "not that rich". The Irish didn't know anything about football, but they did know racing and they were friends of Fergie. We saw them as strengthening Fergie's hand.'

Harverson took a call from an Irish journalist about Magnier and McManus. 'I am being serious – whatever you do, don't mess with them.' It was an echo of something I'd heard a friend of John Magnier's say: 'The softest thing about John is his teeth.'

Harverson laughs. 'It was funny. We had the new American shareholders who were a mystery; and we had the Irish shareholders, and they were a mystery. We didn't know what any of their intentions were, why they'd bought the shares.'

There was little real concern about Glazer, though. He was the owner of the Tampa Bay Buccaneers, so dipping his toe in English football was a logical move. What was provoking more angst was the sudden presence on the share register of Dermot Desmond. A member of the Coolmore Mafia, Desmond was a director of Celtic in Glasgow and that club's biggest shareholder. He was also another person close to Ferguson, closer to him than Magnier or McManus.

Ferguson had talked about retiring but then reneged. He'd had a large pay rise, now it appeared, thanks to his super-rich Irish mates, as though he was on the verge of adding to his status by becoming some sort of owner of the club.

On the pitch, United were riding high. They were right at the top of the Premiership with a team built around homegrown stars: Paul Scholes, the Neville brothers and Ryan Giggs. In the European Champions League, they almost did enough to beat Real Madrid and advance to the semi-final.

I was at the second leg against Real Madrid, at Old Trafford, on 23 April 2003, as a guest in a corporate box. It was a dizzying occasion, matched by a thriller of a game, with brilliant attacking skill and the genius of two men: the great Brazilian, Ronaldo, who scored a hat-trick; and David Beckham, who came on as a substitute to claim two late goals.

Much of the chatter among those watching that evening was about Beckham and his poor relationship with Ferguson. After the boot incident, there was a general feeling that the star had become too big for the manager's liking, with a popstar wife and jet-set life-style. He'd not been picked to start and had been dropped in favour of Juan Sebastián Verón.

Beckham, though, seemed to embody what was happening with football. Money was pouring in; T V rights were taking off; the game was advancing across the world; brands were queuing up to associate themselves with elite clubs, of which United was one, and star players, like Beckham.

After the match, we decamped to the Malmaison Hotel bar in the middle of Manchester – a cool hotel chain, then in its relative infancy, beloved of celebrities and media, and symbolizing Manchester's cultural and economic renaissance. While we were in the bar, joshing and basking in the privilege of having witnessed great actors on a great stage, none of us noticed Beckham enter the hotel lobby and slip upstairs. He was meeting officials from Real Madrid to discuss his transfer to the Spanish side.

The sense of a gold rush was compounded when Roman Abramovich bought Chelsea that summer of 2003. His wealth dwarfed anyone else's, but he'd chosen to buy Chelsea, a smaller club than United, with nothing like the history or romance. This only seemed to affirm United's position as best in class on the pitch, and off it as well.

Meanwhile Cubic Expression was flexing its financial muscle and unnerving the United board. The club put out a statement that fooled no one and did nothing to calm the takeover talk: 'The prevailing view has been that they are not preparing for a takeover and even though they have become the largest single stakeholders there is still no reason to change that view.'

Running alongside, however, but hidden from plain sight, was the simmering feud between Magnier and Ferguson. Magnier attempted to calm the row. He, at least, was prepared to compromise. The Coolmore chief contacted Ferguson and offered him four nominations a year, two in Ireland and two in Australia, at Coolmore's operation there. Rocky was due to go there for part of the year. Ferguson did not bite.

He tried again, offering Ferguson £300,000 a year or a 'take it or leave it' sum of £7 million. That was a generous sum, not least because

Ferguson had paid nothing for his share of the horse. Again, it was rejected.

The view over in Ireland was that Ferguson was being persuaded by his sons, Mark and Jason, and that they were saying it was not enough. They believed that Ferguson's sons were telling him 'Rock of Gibraltar is a 20–1 shot, 20–1 that you will get what you ask for, it's worth trying.' He was taking advantage of there not being a written contract and a recording of his conversations with them. That made it not black and white, and he could play on that.

Mark Ferguson was a Goldman Sachs banker and his brother Jason a football agent. They were both in the money business and Ferguson would listen to them.

But there was a clear sense that Ferguson was trying it on. There was absolutely no way Coolmore would give a share in a horse like that away for free. Aidan O'Brien has a few hundred horses at Ballydoyle, and they're lucky if three or four in any one year are good. Aidan was telling them this was one of those three or four. There was no way they would give anyone a share in a good horse free of charge. They gave a lot of bad horses away, but none were as good as Rock of Gibraltar.

What grated as well was the claim they'd heard being made in the Ferguson camp that the football manager's 'ownership' somehow added to the success of the horse and that he was 'owed'. It's true that Rocky seized the popular imagination, and the media gave him tons of coverage because he was seen as 'Alex's horse'. But that did not make any difference to his racing – he was a brilliant horse, with an excellent team behind him, including Mick Kinane, his jockey.

It could be claimed that Coolmore could not live with the fact they'd made a mistake, that Ferguson was listed as co-owner and they were trying to wriggle out of their obligations, and it was their fault for not formalizing the contract. Such an argument could only serve to annoy Magnier further, since he was a firm believer in his word being his bond. To his mind, a handshake was all that was required, not a legal document. That had always stood him in good stead, and he did not appreciate now having his word impugned.

They had made improved offers to Ferguson; there was no doubting their generosity. He was abusing it and, over the water, the breeders were inflamed. They could not believe that someone could go there and be friendly, and then do that. It was hard to understand. They saw Ferguson as mean; he saw an opportunity. Perhaps it was pride that made him do it, that he could never admit it was a gift and he'd said it wasn't, but also he had to be as tough as nails to do what he did.

The shutters came down between the two sides. Talking was over. Magnier said he'd made his final offer; from now on, at Coolmore-Ballydoyle, Ferguson was off limits. There was one more gesture to be made: as before, Cubic Expression went into the market and bought more shares, spending another £5 million to reach 11.4 per cent. Cue another round of stories about Ferguson's friends stalking United and working with its manager. Cue Ferguson being made to feel awkward, uncertain and on edge once again.

Possibly, the two sides should have tried to maintain some sort of dialogue, but it was not to be. War was formally declared on 17 November 2003, with Ferguson appointing a Dublin barrister and beginning legal proceedings.

What had been known to little more than a handful of people now burst into the open. *The Sunday Telegraph* reported a source close to Coolmore as saying: 'There is a major fight going on between Magnier and Ferguson ... they have fallen out over breeding rights to the Rock. I understand that Ferguson believes he is entitled to 50 per cent, but Magnier is adamant that it should be much less – if anything at all.'

The *Daily Mail* said Ferguson was 'very disappointed at the behaviour of John Magnier and the Coolmore team'. The *News of the World* quoted a 'friend' of Ferguson: 'He doesn't want to say anything at this stage as this is likely to be settled in court. The Magniers have offered him a one-off settlement of £10 million if he walks away. But compared to Rock of Gibraltar's stud earnings potential it's a pittance. All Sir Alex wants is a fair deal. He is half owner of the horse and should at least get half the stud fees.'

By the time a writ was served on Magnier by Ferguson, the Irish racehorse breeder and business tycoon and his partner J. P. McManus had taken their holding in United to 23 per cent. They'd bought Rupert Murdoch's shares and added some more.

Magnier and McManus were not alone in targeting United shares. Malcolm Glazer had made three separate purchases, raising his stake to 9.66 per cent. On 28 November, eleven days after the formal outbreak of war between United's biggest shareholder, Cubic Expression, and effectively its chief operating officer, Ferguson, Glazer bought again, taking his holding up to 14.31 percent.

Glazer's move was measured and calculating. Slowly, steadily buying small amounts, which were all adding up. In a club rocked by turmoil, Glazer had positioned himself nicely on the rails as its second biggest investor. It was where he liked to be and followed his modus operandi of holding strategic positions. He could be kingmaker or, who knows, he could even be king.

By issuing a writ, Ferguson might have applauded himself for turning up the heat on his opponents. In truth, he probably had no choice; he'd run out of road, as Magnier had closed him down. At first, he looked to be in the ascendant as the press portrayed him as the victim. But the statement of claim was not quite the all-gunsblazing document that the media had been led to believe. Instead of saying he'd bought Rocky, it spoke of how he'd added value to the horse by having his name attached to it. The document did make plain, though, that Ferguson was demanding half the horse's value.

If Ferguson thought the writ would have the effect of forcing his opponents to capitulate, he'd horribly miscalculated. Magnier responded to the attack the only way he knew, by going on the offensive himself.

The United shareholders' Annual General Meeting was attended by the usual crowd, plus a group of new shareholders who, when questioned, turned out to be actors. It was never clear who hired them. The assumption was the Irish contingent, but an undercover T V programme-maker tried to maintain it had retained them for a documentary it was preparing on AGMs. Given that they tried to raise embarrassing questions for Ferguson about player transfers, the hand of Magnier seemed more likely.

Magnier and his team also proved to be no slouches when it came to manipulating the press in London and elsewhere, and getting their version of events across. The media turned, challenging Ferguson and accusing him of not having paid anything for what he maintained was his half-share.

Questions were asked as well as to whether it was right and proper that the United manager should be gifted a share in Rock of Gibraltar by the club's biggest shareholders. Ferguson's supporters insisted the United board knew of the arrangement. It was stated that he might have been given the half-share of Rocky, but he'd not benefited financially.

As well as ensuring journalists were briefed and fully apprised that Ferguson had been given his half-share, they were also told he had shares in other Coolmore-Ballydoyle horses, four in total, for which he'd paid nothing.

A story reappeared in the newspapers that Ferguson had been paid a five-figure sum to attend a charity dinner in memory of John Durkan, the young Irishman who had found Istabraq for McManus but then died of leukaemia when he was thirty. It was a

Coolmore-sponsored evening, in Dublin, and several United players were in attendance, along with the likes of sports legends Lester Piggott and Eddie Jordan. Ferguson's pals leapt to his defence, pointing out it was part of his testimonial and that's why the players were there, and he had donated half the takings to the John Durkan Leukaemia Trust.

Magnier and McManus employ their own researchers, and they had heard rumours about Ferguson. They knew about his gambling ('ferocious' was how one of their associates described it), and they were aware of allegations made in Tom Bower's book, *Broken Dreams: Vanity, Greed and the Souring of British Football*, and elsewhere, of Ferguson's habit of inserting himself into transfer deals, and the frequent involvement of his son, Jason, as well.

Magnier ratcheted up the heat and hired Kroll, the international private intelligence agency, to take a closer look. It was a hugely aggressive, heat-raising, significant step, one that showed just what Ferguson was up against. It said clearly: Magnier and McManus were fighting to win. Or worse. 'For John it was not about winning, it was about crushing,' said a business friend of Magnier's.

'What do they say, all square in love and war? Well, if Ferguson wants to act the prick with us, we will act the prick with him,' said the Magnier friend.

At various moments it looked as though there might be some rapprochement. The Irish businessmen appealed to the United board to order to get Ferguson to back off, but word came back that the directors were behind their manager.

So, Magnier and McManus went for the jugular. On 16 January 2004, they sent a 'strictly private & confidential' letter to Sir Roy Gardner, the Centrica chief and by now United's chairman. It contained sixty-six questions – ninety-nine if subheadings are included – that the board should answer.

This was Magnier and McManus showing in the most vivid way possible they were more than mere 'racehorse owners' – a description that had hurt them deeply. That hurt had been compounded by a visit made to Old Trafford by their representatives for a United Champions League game. One of the United directors, keen to emphasize how well-connected the club was, how it operated in the world of big business and high finance, unlike these hicks from Tipperary, said he'd noticed how they did not have copies of the *Racing Post* in the offices of the Bank of England. Then, instead of being seated in the Directors' Box with the United hierarchy, their tickets had been left for them in an envelope by the main entrance. The seats they'd been allocated were right next to the Deportivo supporters. They were sat next to them, with their drums. They found the experience awful.

Over eight pages, the letter covered the gamut of United activities, from the 'presentation of statements in the annual accounts' to 'conduct of player transfers by the company' to 'commissions paid in large transactions' to 'conflicts of interest' to 'internal audit'.

It was obvious they had all the answers to the questions they were raising, but it was intended to make United and Ferguson squirm. One section detailed several player purchases and sales, and asked when these deals had first been brought to the attention of the board? How long did the board have to consider these transactions? Did the board make any changes to the transaction from the terms initially presented to them?

Magnier and McManus knew – as did the United board and Ferguson – that by citing these particular deals, they were highlighting the involvement of the Elite agency, run by Ferguson's son, Jason. They were pointing out how transfers were being arranged by Ferguson and his son, and commission fees were being privately agreed and paid.

Kroll had been busy. They struck once, and then they struck again.

No sooner had that bomb landed than they dropped another: sending a follow-up letter inquiring about Ferguson's contract extension and his age and health issues.

As United's lawyers struggled to respond, they tightened the screw, releasing the '99 Questions' to the press. 'It was no use them fighting Ferguson on the sports pages, where they would not get a fair hearing and would lose. This was about them moving the fight to the business pages and attacking the board as well as him,' said a public relations pal of Magnier's. 'In that they were helped by the board – Roy Gardner was as much use to Alex Ferguson as a chocolate fireguard.'

In private, Ferguson was despondent. These were wounding personal attacks, directed at him and his family. He was not used to this level of public scrutiny. Publicly, he came out fighting, saying he'd never abused his position in his seventeen years at the club, and claiming he and his family were being targeted, that Jason's rubbish bins had even been searched.

The veteran warrior knew his audience well. He was not appealing to the media – he'd always had a love–hate relationship with them. He was reaching out to the United fans. He was saying, 'This is personal, they're after me; they're threatening your team, your manager. I've never let you down, please help.'

It worked. What had begun as a sideshow, a dispute over a horse, and had then gone into the boardroom, did not overly concern the fans. This was an attack on their hero, and that might impair his ability to manage the team and therefore the performances, and they were not going to stand for it. Magnier and McManus had overplayed their hand; they hadn't factored in the bond between supporter and manager, that the supporters related to the manager as one of them, as opposed to the suits upstairs. It was evident at every home match, when Ferguson would walk purposefully along the touchline, waving and smiling to the fans. It was a familiar spectacle; one he'd made his own.

This was Ferguson, man of the people, Labour, son of a shipyard worker, being got at by wealthy types. So, what if he made a pound or two? He'd delivered glory to United. He'd made thousands, millions, of followers proud and happy. The stuffed shirts on the York Races Committee, those smooth folk in the Directors' Box, the smarty-pants in the Winners' Enclosure, they didn't matter. They weren't his or their sort.

Manchester's manager, 'The Boss', required assistance; the Mancs would do what they'd always done. They would rise up; they would take direct action.

SEVEN

The Leprechaun rises

The first sign of the trouble that was brewing was when chanting began at Old Trafford directed against Magnier and McManus. Banners started appearing attacking them. A protest movement of sorts was taking shape.

Shareholders United, the leading supporters' group, formally declared it was staying out of it, but a new outfit sprang up with the sinister title of the 'Manchester Education Committee' (MEC). They dressed in combat gear and remained anonymous. Their name had a class war, revolutionary tone, suggesting that these unnamed people were custodians of something precious, the soul of Manchester, and they were going to teach these billionaire interlopers a lesson.

Another group formed, with the more obvious name: United 4 Action. There was a terrorist flavour to the way both groups organized. Members' lists were not available, no minutes of their meetings were preserved, they had cell-like structures, so one lot of members did not know the others – as had been developed by the Irish

Republican Army (IRA). Their nearest legitimate equivalents were the animal rights and hunt saboteur groups.

The way they organized was deliberately made to suggest determination and force – these were not polite, respectful lads who would air their views around a table.

Fans arriving at Old Trafford were greeted by men, their faces covered, handing out leaflets urging protest. They contained no identifying names and addresses as to who had written and published them, but they did give out Coolmore's phone numbers and addresses, inviting fans to harass the people who were making life for their hero, Sir Alex, such a misery.

They discovered that Kroll had an office in Manchester. A pantomime horse turned up and tried to kick the doors in, while protestors held up placards: 'Stop the horseplay, Coolmore.'

Not to be outdone, Shareholders United launched its own campaign to try and get enough supporters to sign up and buy shares, to stop United being taken over and going private. A 10 per cent block would be enough.

Then the temperature rose again. A Magnier house in Ireland was daubed with graffiti. Then a hardcore group decided to attack Magnier and McManus on their own territory, at the racecourses, where their horses were running. The first demonstration was at Hereford on Friday 6 February 2004. It was small – no more than thirty protestors involved – but nevertheless disruptive. They ran onto the track before the 4.20 p.m. race, which included McManus's horse, Majestic Moonbeam, and draped banners over a fence. The race was held up for twenty minutes.

The protestors did not stop there. They threw glass into the paddocks that could seriously injure the horses. It was getting very nasty, with the Manchester Education Committee the worst.

The racing authorities were horrified. Even more so when United 4 Action made it known their next target was to be Cheltenham and the annual festival, striking at the heart of what Irish racegoers held dearest; their Mecca, their Vatican, a trip that was the highlight of the year for many thousands of racing enthusiasts.

United 4 Action members had bought tickets and the plan was for 150 demonstrators to enter, climb over the barriers and invade the track. There were serious concerns that the ingredients were there for significant disruption and violence.

Magnier and McManus were certain that the protestors were doing Ferguson's bidding; that he was either goading them on, or at least must have been aware of what was planned; that he was doing nothing to stop them, and by doing nothing was implicitly encouraging them. The men managed to get a message to the protest groups that they believed this to be the case.

Still, the campaigners would not back down, so Magnier and McManus let it be known that should the demonstrations go ahead, and Cheltenham Festival be stopped, they would demand the board remove Ferguson, blaming him as the person whose actions led to the protests. Alternatively they would call an Extraordinary General Meeting of United shareholders, at which their ninety-nine questions and more would receive a public airing.

Ferguson was very popular with the supporter groups, he played to them. The board feared him. Magnier and McManus's crime was to go against the Great One. But, as they felt, it was difficult for them as major shareholders having learned so much about him. He was the club's best asset, but they should also fire him. Imagine the fun and games that would have resulted then.

As it was, Ferguson blinked. He issued a statement calling on the protestors to stand down: 'The reputation of Manchester United is paramount to my thinking. The private dispute I have is just that and

I don't want to exacerbate the whole thing. Cheltenham is such a great festival, and I don't want it marred in any way. There is a lot of concern about what could happen, and I would ask supporters to refrain from any form of protest. I am strongly opposed to any violent, unlawful or disruptive behaviour which may reflect badly on the club and its supporters in general.'

His statement was followed by one from the United board: 'Sir Alex also knows that this is the view of the Manchester United board, who have previously urged fans not to participate in any disruptive or criminal activities.'

Ferguson's climbdown was uncharacteristic, and the protestors were dismayed – angry even. The Manchester Education Committee issued one of its own, typically oblique authoritarian statements, asking Sir Alex 'to refrain from giving his name to any form of statement opposing action by United supporters'.

United 4 Action did call off the planned Cheltenham disruption, however. It was so out of the blue and untypical of Ferguson that fans were set thinking. Some began to believe his accusers and to take the ninety-nine questions seriously rather than dismissing them.

A United 4 Action leader said: 'The planned protest at Cheltenham was an action formed out of anger towards the powers-that-be at Cubic Expression. We felt that these people were bullying our manager and destabilizing our football club. We had to act and act in a big way.' The aim, he said, was to embarrass Magnier and McManus and force them out of the club.

The United 4 Action leader said that from the start of the protest he'd been contacted by 'people involved within the different fan groups in Manchester. These were people I had never met but grew to trust and befriend ... These people were connected, seriously connected at Old Trafford all the way to the top. They advised me and guided me on many issues around the protest, including media relations. I was advised that Sir Alex was grateful for our help, and I was assured that he would not make public any call for the protest to be stopped. I believed this.'

Then, just before Cheltenham, Ferguson himself called. 'Sir Alex contacted me after being given my contact details through a fan representative (one of the connected people) and we discussed the protest and my plans for Cheltenham. We also discussed other issues around the Rock case, and he assured me that the case was nearly at an end and that he felt the pressure on the club would end thereafter. He then dropped the bombshell that the protest must be cancelled.'

The United 4 Action leader was 'gutted'. Ferguson 'let me down – he revealed that he had spoken to me after we agreed we would do no such thing. I hadn't even spoken to other members of United 4 Action and they felt betrayed by me. I was not popular in Manchester and had "friendly" warnings to stay away.'

Then he said, 'Maybe, looking back, I was naive. After all, look how he treated his so-called "son" David Beckham. Other fans and I are left wondering who really destabilized Old Trafford, who really brought the club into the war over the Rock, and who was letting the fans down.

'Quite simply, one great racehorse, two powerful men, one massive mess. And who suffered most of all during this period? The millions of Manchester United fans worldwide, me included.'

For the first time, the United fans doubted their manager. Events had moved against Ferguson and he had to close it down, fast.

Ferguson had a meeting with Dermot Desmond, who volunteered to act as intermediary. Desmond saw his Irish pals and, in March 2004, a settlement was reached. In return for a payment of £2.5 million tax-free, Ferguson would drop all claims over Rock of Gibraltar. He also admitted there had been a 'misunderstanding'.

Against what Ferguson was originally seeking, Magnier had won.

The sum was even smaller than the amount he'd been originally offered by Magnier. But it was still £2.5 million, when Ferguson had paid nothing at all. By anyone's calculation that was a smart result.

Coolmore maintained he did not merit being paid anything, but that was not strictly true either. Without doubt, his presence as co-owner had fired the public imagination, and Coolmore-Ballydoyle basked in the extra adulation the horse received. Ferguson's involvement was good for Coolmore, for their industry. For that and for being an 'ambassador' for their operation, they owed him something. They had also kept quiet about the real ownership situation and did not correct him, either in public or in private.

There was an element, too, about their response that had little to do with Ferguson. They were fired up by how they had been treated by the United board, which in their eyes was nothing short of pure racism. Ferguson was not part of that – indeed, the way the board belittled Magnier and McManus gave some idea, perhaps, of what the manager, a paid 'below-stairs' employee, had himself gone through over the years. It might also help explain his desire to one day own the club rather than be its servant.

Meanwhile, another investor was remaining squarely in his preferred stamping ground. Malcolm Glazer was watching and waiting, and scarcely able to believe his growing good fortune.

At the United shareholders' AGM on 14 November 2003, the one that was infiltrated by actors and actresses asking questions about player transfers, David Gill, the United chief executive, was asked about Malcolm Glazer.

The little-known owner of the Tampa Bay Buccaneers was sitting on 14.3 per cent of United's shares. Gill said that United had not managed to meet Glazer, but he intended to see him soon. The club was keen to understand his intentions, as they were of all the major investors.

While Gill and the then United chairman, Sir Roy Gardner, were brimming with confidence in public, their mood was very different in private. They and the rest of the United directors were very worried about Magnier and McManus buying the club, the same people who had once been friends of Ferguson but clearly weren't any more. They had to find a friendly 'white knight' investor, someone who could come to their rescue and take out Magnier and McManus, and they had come to believe that saviour was Glazer.

Perhaps for the first time in his life, thanks to a row about a racehorse, Glazer found himself in the position of being wanted. A company board in England, unaware of his reputation on Wall Street, was crying out for him to get involved.

Soon after the AGM, Gill flew to Florida to see Malcolm, Joel and Avie. The Glazers were left with the impression of a board that was exhausted and desperate to find a solution to the Rock of Gibraltar dispute without throwing the club into even more turmoil.

The Glazers were told that the board thought an offer of £3 a share to the Irish shareholders would be enough to persuade Magnier and McManus to sell. And the board would love the Glazers to bits.

There was no talk about the Glazers going for ownership of the whole club; it did not cross the directors' minds. The feeling was that they were investors looking for a handy return, that they were not interested in owning and running the entire organization, with all the attendant stress and publicity that went with it. It was assumed that, as Americans, they would not care enough about association football or the club to make a full bid.

The Glazers, though, seemed quite taken with the image of themselves as white knights, saviours of Manchester United.

United's public line about the trip to meet the Glazers was that it was nothing special, a meeting of the sort that chief executives had all the time with major shareholders. Said Gill: 'We had an excellent meeting with Malcolm and his sons. He sees the shares as a good investment and that was the end of the discussion.'

Gill was attending the launch at Claridge's Hotel in London on 1 December 2003; the event was to mark United's new shirt sponsorship deal with Vodafone. He was asked if he was worried about Malcolm Glazer and he replied: 'I am not worried.'

Two months later, on 12 February 2004, the Glazers raised their holding to 16.3 per cent.

There was a difference with this purchase: they had used Commerzbank to buy the shares. It felt as if a quantum shift had taken place; they were using external, well-connected and powerful assistance. That meant they were spending additional money, which suggested they were serious – that something else really was afoot more than merely building a sound investment.

The *Financial Times* reported they'd met Keith Harris, the former Football League chairman, head of Seymour Pierce, the small investment bank and a specialist in brokering football takeovers. Three days after they'd increased their stake, on 15 February 2004, *The Sunday Times* ran this headline: 'The Leprechaun – will this man buy United?' For United supporters it was their first introduction to the retiring figure of Malcolm Glazer, nicknamed for his short stature and ginger beard by the Tampa Bay fans.

The piece repeated the tale told to the New York newspaper, *Village Voice*, by Malcolm, about how his son Bryan wore $200 Hugo Boss trousers while he wore trousers costing $19.95. 'And you know something? I like my pants more than he likes his pants.'

For the first time in the British press, the Glazers' background story was set out; of how Malcolm's parents were Orthodox Jews from Lithuania who settled in the US and ran a jewellery and watch repair business. How Malcolm had inherited the firm from his father and built it up into a substantial enterprise, buying trailer parks and shopping malls and the Tampa Bay Buccaneers. Home was now a $25 million mansion in West Palm Beach and he had another residence in New York.

It was unlikely, said *The Sunday Times*, that the Glazers had the money or the stomach to buy United. Oliver Houston of Shareholders United was quoted as saying: 'Someone like Malcolm Glazer is not going to want to take on 35,000 pesky fans who are all asking questions.' He was described as 'small potatoes' versus Roman Abramovich. 'There are also question marks over whether he truly has the resources to mount a full bid.' A City insider said: 'He simply hasn't got Abramovich's wealth, Abramovich can buy £110 million of playing talent with loose change. Glazer would struggle to spend £10 million after buying United.' The piece concluded: 'Perhaps the story about the cheap pants doesn't look so ridiculous after all.'

What the paper failed to mention was that Glazer had already proved himself a master of the leveraged buyout, using other people's money to buy businesses, and that he was also a corporate raider who would buy a stake, threaten takeover, then exit with a tidy profit. Nevertheless, it was enough to send a signal, to immediately set the fans against him. He was a money man, many concluded, interested only in what he could extract from their club.

That view hardened when Malcolm's sister Jeanette was asked what she thought about his interest in United. 'He's centred on one thing. He's like a machine – money, money, money. There's no other dimension. He's always striving for more which, I suppose, is why he wants your soccer team.'

Glazer's stewardship of the Tampa Bay Buccaneers did not impress, either. There, after renaming the stadium after a restaurant chain that he owned, he held the local city council to ransom. Glazer said he would move the franchise to Baltimore unless they built him a new stadium. While that might have looked like a positive for the fans, they were not fooled: here was a businessman who cared so little for them that he would take their team to Baltimore. To top it all, fans saw him subsequently renege on his part of the bargain to pay half the building costs.

Despite all this, the Bucs won the 2003 Superbowl. While the rest of the NFL and the other owners were full of praise for Glazer, for having taken the bottom team and propelled it to the top, not all supporters were so impressed. The NFL draft system meant the Bucs benefited from being a lowly ranked side and so had first pick of the college leavers, but Glazer was accused of not investing enough in the team overall. What also inflamed the Florida supporters was that, under Glazer, their ticket prices seemed to be on an ever-upwards curve.

Back in the UK, the United fans could see Glazer's record and their minds were already hardening. In London, in the City, the Glazers' share-buying was also causing consternation. The United share price had been pushed up to 290 pence on talk that a takeover bid was imminent, and the official watchdog, the Takeover Panel, demanded to know the Glazers' intentions. The Glazers said they'd not made up their minds: they might buy the club, they might not. They did appoint an investment bank advisor, though, J.P. Morgan, and a City PR firm, Brunswick.

No sooner did the protests against Magnier and McManus quieten down with the March 2004 settlement between them and Ferguson, than those against the Glazers began to take off. The fans had a new target in their sights.

A 'Not For Sale' coalition was formed, comprising the Independent Manchester United Supporters Association, Shareholders United, and the three fanzines, *Red Issue*, *Red News* and *United We Stand*. It was against anyone trying to take over the club, while at the same time urging supporters to purchase shares to build the 10 per cent block to stop a would-be buyer.

The Glazers continued regardless, in their deliberate, slow, relentless way. In April 2004, they took their holding to 18.25 per cent; in June they bought more shares to reach 19.1 per cent. The United board were becoming freaked out by the steady increase in the Glazers' shareholdings. From having privately recommended a price of £3 to buy out the Irish shareholders, the directors changed tack and now avoided mentioning the Glazers in public. They were scared on two counts: afraid of the Glazers' intentions and mindful that the fans were opposed as well, and likely to turn on the board for being in cahoots with the mysterious, unlikely US raider.

In September 2004, the board attempted to smoke out the Glazers' plans. That's when I was flown up from the *London Evening Standard* for the United v. Liverpool game, along with Peter Thal Larsen from the *Financial Times*. The idea was for us to meet David Gill and Sir Roy Gardner, the United CEO and chairman. Weirdly and embarrassingly, neither man was present.

David Gill and Nick Humby, the finance director, had flown to Florida for a 'cards on the table' meeting with the Glazers. Gardner was otherwise undisposed. We were treated to a surreal evening where the elephant in the Directors' Lounge was the Glazers. United was defeating their arch-rival on the pitch and the fans were going delirious, but upstairs, amid back-slapping and smiles among the remaining directors and their guests, there was also an underlying anxiety. We were repeatedly asked if we knew the Glazers and what we thought of them.

Officially, the reason for the Florida meeting was the same as the previous one – for the United executives to brief a major shareholder on the latest happenings at the club and their plans. But it was really an attempt by Gill and Humby to get to the bottom of the Glazers' intentions. According to Mark Rawlinson, a partner at Freshfields, the law firm that was advising United, David Gill and Nick Humby were there to convey a message from the board that 'first of all, they needed to sort it out.'

United had hit the wrong note. The Glazers, having previously been welcomed by the club at the last meeting, thought the warm atmosphere would continue. Instead, here were these two representatives, striking a very different, much frostier pose. The Glazers wanted the unequivocal backing of the board – but the board, mindful of the fans' likely reaction – would not give it. Instead, they told the Glazers to talk to Magnier and McManus. 'We said, don't come back to us until you've got the Irish,' said Rawlinson.

The United directors were hoping that the Glazers would stick around as shareholders for a while, then vanish, based on their observation of Malcolm Glazer's record in the past, of taking strategic stakes, then selling out. The United board was still working on the basis that the Glazers were simply looking to make a quick profit on their shares.

Attempts by the Glazers to engage with Magnier and McManus, to get them on side, came to naught. In response, the Glazers increased their holding, from 19 per cent to 25.5 per cent. The United board and its advisor, Rawlinson, gave them a nickname, 'the Terminator', after the Arnold Schwarzenegger character who gets blasted to bits, but simply puts himself back together and keeps on coming. Said Rawlinson: 'The Glazers just carried on, whatever happened. We realized they weren't going to go away; they were seriously there.'

Details emerged in the press that Malcolm Glazer was indeed considering a full bid. It would be a leveraged buyout; he would borrow the money needed to buy United, the loans would be flipped on to the club, and they would be repaid out of the club's profits. 'Profits which could be ramped up by increased ticket prices,' said John-Paul

'JP' O'Neill, lifelong fan and at that time a writer for *Red Issue*. 'The plan was fraught with danger due to the crippling interest rates chargeable on some of the loans. With United as the ultimate security against the loans, in the event of any default on payments, there was a risk of the club being taken over by hedge funds and possibly even Old Trafford itself being sold off, a humiliating and needless prospect for a club that, in 2004, boasted of being the richest in the world.'

This was the blue touchpaper for the supporters. They were outraged. Six months after the protests against Magnier and McManus had died down, the same protestors, fans who cared for the soul and identity of their club, mobilized once more. But there were more of them this time, and there was ever greater urgency, as the secretive Glazers really did seem intent on owning their club.

The Manchester United diaspora came into its own – alongside the fans protesting locally at Old Trafford, Reds who lived in London and elsewhere in the country – and even those living and working abroad – all made telling contributions.

'Within hours of anyone appearing in the media acting in any capacity for the Glazers, their name, email address, employer, phone number and even their home address would be splashed on internet forums, leaving them at the mercy of the mob,' said O'Neill.

Brunswick's offices at the end of a Georgian terraced row in discreet, quiet Lincoln's Inn Fields in London were targeted. Skips piled high with stinking rubbish were deposited outside. The PR firm found itself having to accept deliveries of loads of pizzas and parcels containing used condoms and tampons. Taxis would just turn up at the doors saying they'd been booked. Attempts were made to penetrate the agency's computer system.

Brunswick had made its name advising on numerous takeover battles, most of them involving far bigger organizations than a football club in Manchester, but they had not experienced anything like this. They had to take their website offline, delete all staff contact details, and tell their switchboard not to divulge the names of anyone working on the Glazer account.

However, leading players in the protests, like JP O'Neill, found themselves receiving tips from United fans from within the City, so they were able to stay one step ahead. Maurice Watkins, the United director, had his car covered in paint by the Manchester Education Committee after he was found to have sold 1 million shares to the Glazers. The fans were furnished with Malcolm Glazer's home address in Florida, accompanied by the detail that 'his neighbours include Rod Stewart and Donald Trump'.

On 7 October 2004, at Altrincham's Moss Lane football ground, twenty men in balaclavas ran on to the pitch and disrupted a Manchester United reserve game that was being broadcast live on the MUTV channel. The Manchester Education Committee released a statement:

'For far too long the wishes of Manchester United fans, and football fans in general, have been ignored as clubs sacrifice everything at the altar of commercialism.

'The Manchester Education Committee would like to stress that in the event of the wishes of Manchester United supporters being ignored in any takeover situation, we intend to initiate a civil war effectively setting the football club – the supporters – against the company. In such a situation it is our intention to render the club ungovernable and actively disrupt all manner of commercial activity associated with Manchester United.

'The club's sponsors and commercial partners should note that the Manchester Education Committee will view them as legitimate targets.'

The club condemned the protest and pleaded for calm. It fell on deaf ears.

The next home game was against Arsenal, champions and 'Invincibles', who were arriving at Old Trafford having gone forty-nine games unbeaten. It was always a major occasion anyway, but now there was also the backdrop of a supporters' rebellion. The scene was set before the match. At a protestor meeting, said JP O'Neill: 'I suggested that fans had to take the [Manchester Education Committee's] promise into their own hands by targeting the club's sponsors, and that the best way to do so was via the Old Trafford Megastore, owned and operated by the kit suppliers Nike.'

A large group flash-mobbed the shop, forcing its closure, 'which left legions of tat-tourists disappointed. It wasn't quite Jesus driving the moneylenders out of the temple but the symbolism was there for many of the more traditional fans involved.'

Inside the ground, the atmosphere was sulphurous. At half-time, an effigy of Malcolm Glazer was hung from the Stretford End in front of a flag bearing skull and crossbones, and the words: 'WARNING – USING MUFC MAY RESULT IN SERIOUS DAMAGE TO YOUR HEALTH'.

Throughout the match, the chant went up, 'United, United, not for sale'. Fittingly, as a reminder perhaps of what United really stood for, the Reds won the game 2–0, with goals from Wayne Rooney and Ruud van Nistelrooy, ending Arsenal's historic run of victories.

From their seat on the sidelines, the Irish shareholders mischievously re-entered the fray. Ever since the settlement with Ferguson, the heat had been off them. The protests stopped immediately. Now, they told an emissary from the supporters that they would sell their holding to the fans. This would enable the Glazers to be blocked. But Cubic Expression wanted around £250 million. That was a sum that ordinary supporters could not possibly raise. In stepped Keith Harris, the City financier. He had been talking to Nomura, the giant Japanese investment bank, about putting together a £200 million financing package which would allow the fans to hold a blocking stake. The plan was to partly repay the loan through future ticket sales or TV rights.

It was never going to fly, since Malcolm Glazer held more than 25 per cent (for good measure he'd bought more shares, to go to 28.1 per cent), which effectively gave him a veto on any move, such as Nomura's, which would require 75 per cent shareholders' approval.

United turned the screw. Glazer had always said he would only make an agreed bid. Staging an opposed, full takeover was not his usual tactic. Going hostile was more expensive, riskier and, as the fight progressed, would leave him open to all sorts of accusations about his past business dealings. He wished to be wanted, for his bid to be recommended to shareholders.

For the avoidance of doubt, United said it 'would regard an offer which it believes to be overly leveraged as not in the best interests of the company'. So, no 'welcome mat' there.

Gill explained: 'The club has 126 years of history and is recognized as one of the most successful football clubs in the world. I don't think any sensible person would think we could recommend a proposal that could jeopardize something that has been built up over so many years.'

Edwards's decision to publicly list the club's shares, which had made the share-trading and the Glazers' stake-building possible in the first place, was conveniently forgotten, as were United's early overtures to the American family, when relations between the Coolmore team and Ferguson soured.

Ferguson also broke his silence, putting a statement up on the United website:

'I have always tried to be the bridge between the club and the fans. I have tried to support the fans in a lot of their pleas and causes. It's important for the club to recognize the fans. We are a special club in that respect.

'When the PLC started, there were grave doubts about it – I had them myself – but I think the supporters have come round to that. There's a stronger rapport between the club and fans than there's ever been. We are both of a common denominator: we don't want the club to be in anyone else's hands.'

Similarly, Ferguson chose to omit any mention of the dispute between himself and Magnier and McManus that had allowed the Glazers in.

Undeterred, and living up to their Terminator billing, the Glazers just kept on coming.

They'd not formally made an approach for the club, although that was how it was being reported and how the United board were allowing it to be said. They'd spent about £160 million, and while Joel and Avie in particular were sure United would be a golden buy, their father Malcolm always needed reassuring. What they wanted was the cooperation of the United board to make it easier, to smooth the path towards their goal of owning the club. They needed access to the financial books – that would help them structure the funding of their bid as, so far, they'd talked only about possible financing arrangements.

The three brothers most closely involved – Joel, Avie and Bryan – decided to target the forthcoming annual United shareholders' meeting. Their lawyers from Allen & Overy would turn up and act as their representatives and vote by proxy, using their 28.1 per cent holding.

United were told to prepare themselves for their arrival, and the probability arose of the usually staid shareholder gathering turning into a full-scale riot, as United fans realized there were Glazer representatives sitting in the room. They were alarmed, too, as to what it was the Glazers were hoping to achieve – what resolutions were they going to vote against?

J.P. Morgan and Brunswick, reeling from the fan protests, strongly advised the Glazers to tread carefully, to avoid whipping up hostility among the fans present and with the board. The Glazers saw it differently, though. They were in no mood to instruct their lawyers to back off; they were determined the United board should stop dismissing them and begin taking them seriously. They could show willing by granting them access to the company's numbers.

Amid tight security, the lawyers arrived at the annual shareholders' meeting in an unmarked Mercedes with blackened windows, a whole three hours before the meeting was due to begin in the Manchester Suite at Old Trafford. They were not spotted and were whisked upstairs.

During the meeting, the Glazer legal team sat off to the side, near the exit, and kept their heads down, which was wise, said Rawlinson: 'Because there might well have been some people who might have attacked them physically . . . There were thousands of people very pumped up, very hostile people with big biceps and tattoos, wearing Manchester United shirts and shouting, "Would the Glazers stand up!" Even one elderly man said, "I'll take my coat off and let's go outside." There was quite a lot of hostility to the Glazer representatives and a lot of speeches were directed at the Glazers.'

Sir Roy Gardner, the United chairman, did not escape the vitriol. He might have had a distinguished corporate career, but he was a West Londoner, who spoke with a London twang. Oh dear. Asked a question by a shareholder he said, 'Sorry, I did not quite catch that.' To which the shareholder responded: 'If you could understand my accent then maybe you would have understood it. Perhaps you should fuck off back to London, you're just a City fat cat.'

Manchester United team, *c.* 1923. United were in the Second Division, and the average home attendance at Old Trafford was 21,951.

Manchester United line up for a group photo before a match, *c.* 1930. While back in the First Division, the 1930–1 season saw them concede twenty-five goals in the first five games as they went on to lose twelve successive matches, the worst run in the club's history.

First goal at FA Cup final, Wembley, 1948. United beat Blackpool 4–2, coming up against Stanley Matthews and Stan Mortensen. The victory parade in Manchester saw a turnout of 300,000, and they diverted the bus to visit the home of the United chairman, James Gibson, who was convalescing after illness.

Rescue workers at the wreckage of the Munich air disaster in February 1958. Twenty-three people died, including eight United players, among them the young star Duncan Edwards. This was the lowest point in United's story and there were doubts as to whether the club would ever recover.

United's George Best holds the trophy at the European Cup final, Wembley, 1968. Bounce back United did, in great style, with Matt Busby, who nearly died at Munich, in charge and a team of greats, not least the Holy Trinity of Best, Denis Law and Bobby Charlton, also a Munich survivor. United's rebirth culminated in the defeat of Benfica 4–1 to become the first English club to lift the European Cup.

Manchester United players after winning the UEFA Champions League final in 1999. United's greatest-ever season, with Alex Ferguson, who was knighted shortly afterwards, leading them to the treble of champions at home, in Europe and as FA Cup winners. The squad was largely built around the Class of '92: homegrown stars such as David Beckham, Ryan Giggs and Gary Neville.

Racehorse owners Susan Magnier and Sir Alex Ferguson to the left of Rock of Gibraltar, Irish jockey Mick Kinane, Cathy Ferguson and John Magnier, 2001. Ferguson was gifted a half-share in the horse by John Magnier. Rock of Gibraltar proved to be the finest racehorse in the world, winning seven successive top Group One races. Ferguson and Magnier, a shareholder in United, fell out over the horse, paving the way for Malcolm Glazer to take over the club.

Malcolm Glazer during a Super Bowl victory parade in Tampa, Florida, 2003. Businessman Glazer bought the NFL's Tampa Bay Buccaneers in 1995 for a then record $192 million. This experience spurred Glazer and his children, principally Joel and Avram, on to buy Manchester United.

A fan wears a T-shirt warning shareholder John Magnier that United are not for sale before the FA Barclaycard Premiership match, 2004. United supporters demonstrated against Magnier and his business partner, J. P. McManus, because they were in dispute with the fans' hero, the manager Sir Alex Ferguson. They were fearful Magnier and McManus would prevail and Ferguson would be forced to leave the club.

Leading racehorse owner John Magnier at York Racecourse on the day he sold his shares in Manchester United Football Club, 12 May 2005. Magnier and J. P. McManus were the subject of sustained abuse from United fans, who threatened their racehorse interests. In the end, they disposed of their shares, allowing the Glazer family to purchase the whole club.

Above: Joel Glazer (*left*), Avram Glazer (*second right*) and Bryan Glazer (*right*), sons of new Manchester United owner Malcolm Glazer, with Sir Bobby Charlton at Old Trafford, 30 June 2005. They had come to inspect their new acquisition – Malcolm never did go – and to meet the club officials and media. They were met by hostility from fans who questioned their motives and whether they had sufficient funding.

Left: Manchester United owners Joe Glazer (*left*) and Avie Glazer on the eve of the UEFA Champions League final football match, 2011. The brothers made one of their infrequent appearances at a United match, only to see their team lose 3–1 to a Lionel Messi-inspired Barcelona at Wembley.

Joel Glazer (*centre*) and Avie Glazer (*centre, left*) prepare to ring the opening bell at the New York Stock Exchange, 2012. After rejecting Hong Kong and Singapore, the Glazers settled on floating the club in New York. In a highly controversial move, they only offered class A shares for sale, each of which carried one-tenth of the voting power of the class B shares which they retained. The NYSE was carpeted in green Astroturf and the traders wore United shirts embroidered with 'MANU' – United's ticker symbol.

INEOS founder and chairman Sir Jim Ratcliffe (*left*) and Toto Wolff, team principal and CEO of the Mercedes team, at a press conference, 2020. Ratcliffe sponsored the Mercedes F1 team and liked it so much that he became a co-owner. Unfortunately, his commitment was not met with success on the track. Mercedes joined a list of Ratcliffe sports investments that struggled after he bought in. Undeterred, he was keen to buy United when the Glazers put the club up for sale after seventeen years of ownership in November 2022.

Sheikh Jassim bin Hamad Al Thani, chairman of Qatar Islamic Bank and son of the former PM Sheikh Hamad. Inspired by Qatar's successful hosting of the World Cup in 2022, a bid was put together for United, fronted by Sheikh Jassim. With Sir Jim Ratcliffe, he was the co-frontrunner to take over United from the Glazers. Sheikh Jassim said he would buy 100 per cent of the club outright, whereas Ratcliffe would purchase only enough of the Glazers' holding to give him control and buy the rest of the club's shares in stages, while keeping the Glazers involved.

Fans of Manchester United protest against the club's owners, the Glazers, in April 2023. Ever since they bought the club in 2005, the Glazers were subjected to opposition, much of it organized by United supporters. The level of abuse was often highly personal and vicious. Not once did the Glazers exhibit any sign of being swayed by it. Stubborn to the end, they only put the club up for sale when they saw the price paid for Chelsea in 2022.

Every so often the shout would go up: 'Mr Glazer's representatives, we understand they are here, please get up and identify yourselves.' There were cries of, 'If you hate the Glazers stand up!'

Eventually, after two hours, the meeting drew to a close. The Allen & Overy lawyers were able to slip through the side 'Exit' door and skedaddle back to London. They'd voted against three United directors seeking re-election, including Watkins.

Immediately afterwards, the United board hit back at the Glazers' actions, saying the Glazers were taking a cheap shot in retaliation for not being allowed access to the club's accounts.

J.P. Morgan and Brunswick had had enough. They both resigned, prompting the *Financial Times* to accuse Malcolm Glazer of 'scoring an own goal'. It reported that the Glazers' planned takeover of Manchester United 'appeared to be in tatters on Friday after J.P. Morgan, the investment bank, prepared to fund most of the US sports tycoon's planned £700 million-plus bid, abruptly resigned. The departure was swiftly followed by the resignation of Brunswick, Mr Glazer's public relations advisor, and came after a turbulent annual shareholders' meeting in Manchester.'

It seemed all over for the Glazers. They'd been too aggressive and lost their heavyweight financial advisor. Writing in the *Independent*, Jason Nisse said of Malcolm: 'He might be able to find another bank, but the chances are pretty slim . . . investment banks don't like clients they can't control.'

But he'd neglected to remember the Terminator's calling card: 'I'll be back.'

EIGHT

'A wound that will never heal'

The fans were cock-a-hoop. Malcolm Glazer and his sons had been seen off; their swanky, uncaring City of London advisors had also gone.

Quite what would happen to United was not known, but for now at least, the club was safe. That was how the fans saw it. To reinforce that belief, the United board had turned 180 degrees, and was giving its backing to the supporters – to them, the ordinary people.

David Gill attended a protestors' meeting where he declared the Glazers' plan 'unworkable' and pronounced that 'debt was the road to ruin'. He followed that up with the claim: 'If I wasn't in the position I'm in now, I would be behind the barricades with you.'

This was, of course, the same Gill who had fervently wanted the Glazers in the first place, who, on behalf of the board, saw them as saviours, and had encouraged them to buy United shares to defeat Magnier and McManus. Clearly, that was then and this was now.

If the fans had been a fly on the wall at Donald Trump's gaudy pleasure palace at Mar-a-Lago in Palm Beach in the first week of January 2005, they might not have been so ecstatic. The Florida club was still cleaning up after the traditional New Year's Eve extravaganza when a poolside table was taken for a lunch party comprising three bankers from the UK and the Glazers, led by Joel.

Mar-a-Lago might have seemed an unlikely choice of venue for the low-key, low-spending Glazers, but they were local, and while other members used it for more lavish purposes, to them it was a neighbourhood restaurant, albeit one with high security, which they also appreciated.

The visiting trio, Robert Leitão, Majid Ishaq and Richard Bailey, were all from Rothschild. The first two worked in the investment bank's London office, while Bailey was based at its Manchester outpost. Leitão was the most senior, head of the bank's Mergers and Acquisitions department.

Rothschild had originally been asked by lawyers Allen & Overy if they would be interested in assisting the Glazers. Then the job went to the American bank J.P. Morgan. Now, the Glazers had turned to Rothschild & Co., which was smaller, but still had a successful track record when it came to deal-making.

Over the meal, Joel vented his frustration. They discussed how at first the Glazers had been desperately courted as a buffer to Magnier and McManus, how the United board had exhorted them to buy shares, and then how the directors had turned against them. Now they were also subject to protests, although they insisted it was only a minority of fans who were causing the trouble.

The Glazers were left sitting on 28.1 per cent of the shares. They could fold, which they did not want to do; they could stick at 28.1; or they could twist. But if they went even a smidgeon higher – above 29 per cent, according to the takeover rules – they would have to bid for the whole lot.

There must be something in the air at Mar-a-Lago, part of the DNA of its brash, always bullish proprietor, because as the lunch wore on, they resolved to go for it. Effectively, they were playing double or quits, they would buy out the Irish and then table a formal bid.

It was a slam-dunk strategy – with theirs and the Irish stake they would be sitting on so many shares that the rest of the United shareholders would effectively have no choice other than to cave in. The fans would be powerless to resist. The supporters did not possess enough shares themselves to block the move. They could lash out as much as they wanted, but once Magnier and McManus had sold, it would effectively be game over.

The Glazer-Rothschild thinking was that the Irish businessmen did not love United, they were not emotionally attached to the club, quite the reverse. Make them an offer and follow it through with hard cash and the shares, and the club would be theirs.

As Magnier and McManus saw it, the fans had chosen to support Ferguson over Rock of Gibraltar; as a result, they had been abused and vilified and forced to endure a vicious campaign that even encroached on their beloved horses and racing. So, on their heads be it – they would happily extract their revenge by selling out and enabling a new owner, who the fans loathed, to come in. But they did want hard cash.

First, though, the Glazers had to conduct due diligence; they had to see United's books. They'd asked before and been rebuffed. News they were trying again, that they'd not gone away, that they were back, leaked on 6 February 2005. It was a very sombre day for United fans, the anniversary of Munich. The coincidence – some fans thought it deliberate – served only to refuel their ire.

It also transpired that J.P. Morgan had not vanished either; that the US investment bank had also returned and was working closely with Rothschild, helping put together the funding package for the

Glazers. Leading for J.P. Morgan was a go-getter former accountant and tax advisor turned banker called Ed Woodward.

Had the supporters known, too, that the project to buy their club had the codename 'Hampstead', the howls of anguish might have been louder still. United was called 'Mercury' and the buyer 'Red Football'. But Hampstead, for the acquisition of Manchester's finest? Naming it after one of London's most expensive suburbs seemed like someone was determined to add insult to injury.

After a lull, the fans immediately kicked off again. This time, United followers were exhorted to 'go straight from work to Old Trafford . . . take your car/van/lorry if you have one . . . we want to see cars parked on the car park opposite the Megastore with your lights on full beam and your horn sounding. Make sure they know we will not accept Glazer.'

One Saturday, seventeen fans managed to enter the Rothschild offices in Manchester. The place was empty and they got stuck in a lift, and would have been there the entire weekend, but for someone hearing the alarm.

Then on Saturday 12 February, a large group of Reds invaded stores belonging to the United sponsors Vodafone and Ladbrokes in the centre of Manchester, and effectively forced them to temporarily close.

Behind the scenes, a leading protestor quietly met Ferguson and asked if he would side with the supporters and resign in protest, but he refused to do so. The manager's reasoning was that he was coming towards the end of his career anyway, and he would not leave his colleagues and staff exposed. Ferguson's refusal to come out in support was a blow to the protestors, who seemed to be running out of road. He was seen as the one influential figure who had the ability to put a brake on the Glazers. To make matters worse, the protestors were arguing among themselves, unable to agree on the best way forward.

One faction decided to do something quite unexpected. They would form their own Manchester United.

Except it could not be called Manchester United, it would not be allowed. But it would be the next best thing, with an identifiably associated name, and it would be owned by the fans and pursue those values the protestors believed the main club had lost over the years. It would be called FC United of Manchester.

All credit to them for remaining true to their principles, but the establishment of a 'new United' was never going to derail the Glazers and the institutions that were massing. To them, FC United was a minor diversion, a point of focus for some of the fans, but little more. They were engaged in taking over the biggest club in the world, not starting a new one.

Even the supporters themselves could not agree on the merits of the enterprise. They still can't. 'Big Tony' – also called O'Neill – is a legend among Stretford Enders. Tony O'Neill was a leader of the 'Red Army' of United hooligans; he's got convictions for football violence and was once shot in a pub in Manchester. A large, muscly, outspoken character, as you might expect, today he runs a popular fan podcast and helps 'Gary' – Gary Neville – with his security. We met in the basement of Hotel Football, the hotel that Neville and Ryan Giggs built on just about the one piece of land around Old Trafford that is not owned by the football club. In a clever PR move, they turned the otherwise redundant basement bar over to the Old Trafford Supporters Club as a clubroom and meeting place.

At the very beginning of my meeting with him I committed a cardinal sin. I said, 'Man U'. Tony reared up. 'What did you say?' he roared. 'Say it again'. Man U. 'No Manchester United supporter ever says, "Man U". It's always Manchester United or United, never ever Man U.'

Phew. Lesson learned. Except two minutes later I said it again.

And again, he reacted. It was scary. All I could do was smile and apologize.

We talked about the Glazers buying the club and the protests. Then he said: 'You know what the trouble is with Manchester United? Our support is too big. There are too many protestor groups. There's FC United, the Green & Gold [the people who wear the old Newton Heath colours], the 1858, loads. They all sell scarves and memorabilia. Do you know why they can never agree, can't combine?'

He rubbed the fingers on one hand together. 'It's this. Money. It's not in their interests to have one group. Don't get me started on FC United.'

He put his hand over his heart. 'Cradle to grave, that's what it is. Manchester United. Cradle to grave. No genuine football fan sets up another club. Never.'

The takeover was moving inexorably forward. The Glazers finally managed to look at United's finances. They, J.P. Morgan and three US hedge funds – Citadel, Perry and Och-Ziff – were putting up the money and were allowed to examine the players' and manager's contracts and other details about the club, in strict secrecy at Freshfields' offices in London.

To the anger of the fans, the United board never came out and said they were opposed to the Glazer bid. If they had done, they could have stopped the Glazers. They could have said the price was nowhere near high enough and rejected it outright. The Glazers would have been forced to launch a hostile bid and the Glazers did not want that. The board were afraid, though, of what the response would be from Magnier, McManus and Dermot Desmond to them blocking the Glazer bid, and of the prospect of a court action; that having said they thought £3 a share was a good price, they could hardly now turn round and reject it.

There was another scenario in which the bid could have been

thwarted. J.P. Morgan and Cazenove, United's advisor, had merged. If
the Glazers had gone hostile, J.P. Morgan would have been presented
with a clear conflict of interest and would have been forced to stand
down – and the Glazers would not have had their funding.

The Glazers' offer was for £790 million. The Glazer family had
spent £222 million so far in acquiring the shares and they were prepared to put in another £50 million. The rest was coming from J.P.
Morgan and the hedge funds. The latter had a clause in their agree-
ments: if the hedge funds were not paid back within sixty-three
months of the takeover, the hedge funds got 30 per cent of the club.

In the trade, the hedge fund debt was known as 'fingers crossed'
debt or 'payment in kind' (PIK). They received higher interest, which
accrued over the term of the loan, and they were paid back at the end,
not during the term. In United's case, the hedge funds were thought
to be accumulating interest at 20 per cent or up to £54 million a year.
If Red Football, the name given to the Glazer vehicle making the bid,
failed to hit 85 per cent of its target operating profit in the first three
years, the hedge funds received 'extraordinary powers', including the
right to appoint 25 per cent of Red Football directors.

As details filtered out, fan incredulity and rage grew even further.
As they saw it, their club had gone from being debt-free, in sound
financial shape, to being in hock to a bunch of American financiers
who shared none of their feelings for Manchester United, who were
out to make a fast, fat buck at the Reds' expense. The Glazers did not
have the money, but they had swooped in and borrowed and borrowed, using the club as security. Others, with similar degrees of
chutzpah and access to the City and Wall Street, could have done the
same.

On 12 May 2005, Magnier and McManus sold their shares to the
Glazers, their dalliance with United finished. They'd made nearly
£100 million profit on their United stake. They were seen as enemies

of a man who was regarded as untouchable. There was no hatred because they were shareholders, it was all because of Rock of Gibraltar.

J. P. McManus said: 'It was part of my life for a while, but for something that was meant to be a bit of pleasure at the start, it ended not being so pleasurable. I couldn't get far enough away from it quickly enough.' The clincher, he said, was, 'When the fans stopped the racing that day in Hereford. I said, "I've had enough."'

If he meets Ferguson today, McManus will say hello. 'Life's too short.'

When the news broke, a thousand fans gathered outside Old Trafford. They burned an effigy of Malcolm Glazer and the police made five arrests. Another faction visited Rio Ferdinand's home in leafy Alderley Edge in Cheshire, demanding to know if the star, who was in contract talks with the club, would sign a new deal.

In *The Daily Telegraph*, the authoritative football writer Henry Winter wrote: 'The battle is over, but the resistance begins. As the Theatre of Dreams becomes Sold Trafford, Manchester United's irate fans will rally to defy the American carpetbagger, Malcolm Glazer . . . Glazer is a predator that all of English football must resist. This man will damage our national game.'

There was a nasty undercurrent to some of the coverage and the abuse. The *Daily Mirror* published a cartoon of Malcolm Glazer, with an exaggerated hooked nose and sharpened teeth, raiding the safe of Manchester United. It looked like a piece of Nazi anti-Jewish propaganda.

As much as the supporters howled, it got them nowhere. The Glazers carried on, mopping up the remaining shares. To them it was an automatic process, but not to the fans whose shares they were buying.

It was once pointed out to Joel, by a fan who resented being bought out, that he had loved owning his few shares in the club, and he was heartbroken to see them go. 'They'd no financial value to me, it was about the emotional value they provided,' he told Joel, who looked nonplussed, as if it had never occurred to him that people could own shares out of sentiment rather than the return they might provide.

On 6 June 2005, the Glazers seized full control of the club. Joel, Avie and Bryan joined the board and the non-executive directors, including Gardner, all departed.

Defending themselves against criticism, the Glazers claimed that they had put in north of £200 million of their own money. That, by anyone's standards, was a substantial amount, and seemed to go against the grain of previous Glazer acquisitions – Malcolm generally preferred using other people's money rather than his own. Did the Glazers use their own money, though? There is strong evidence that a large part of the Glazers' contribution was itself borrowed; that they did not stump up their own cash at all.

Among their myriad businesses, the Glazers had a real-estate operation, First Allied Corporation. It owned and rented out shopping malls across the US. These were not prime, indoor, ultra-smart, top retail centres attracting the best brands, with palm trees, play areas and air con, but rows of humdrum shops and car parks in the suburbs.

A leading London investment analyst and United follower, Andy Green, took it upon himself to ferret around in Allied. Green is sharp and clever, an experienced operator who knows his numbers and the markets. He's head of investment at Rockpool, a private equity firm. 'In my spare time I'm proud to be the finance director of the Manchester United Supporters Trust.' He's been involved with the trust since January 2023.

Back then, he was just a United supporter with a sceptical, curious brain. 'I was suspicious of the Glazers. They'd used all the mechanisms of debt; they were masters at borrowing. They'd used different types of debt to buy United, and I also wondered if they weren't secretly using another, borrowing against their own equity elsewhere.'

Green looked around their businesses. The only area he could identify that could feasibly be used to raise the sort of sum they were putting up for United, and claiming was their own cash, was real estate, the shopping malls. 'Having sold all their other substantial business assets (nursing homes, trailer parks, radio stations and controlling stakes in listed companies), First Allied was the third major leg of the Glazer family's empire alongside the two famous sports clubs.'

First Allied was registered in New York and secretive Delaware, where private companies do not have to make their accounts public. But Green found sixty-three of the sixty-four shopping centres that First Allied listed on its website had taken out publicly listed mortgages. He was able to examine the public filings for these mortgages and assess the state of the Glazers' real-estate business. His conclusion? It was not pretty.

The portfolio was 'hugely over-leveraged', with half the centres at risk of going bust and four already foreclosed. The majority of First Allied's properties were in negative equity, leaving the family little or no wriggle room. It shattered 'their self-professed reputation as savvy businesspeople'.

It was a rare glimpse into the inner workings of the Glazers' business empire. Usually because most of what they held was via private corporations, and Malcolm and his children were not forthcoming with any detail about anything, it was impossible to get any detail. But First Allied had failed to keep up the mortgage payments on its Crosswoods Commons shopping centre in Columbus, Ohio. As part of the foreclosing process, the mortgage documents were required to be placed on the public record.

These showed that the mortgage it received from Lehman Brothers had been 'securitized' and wrapped up into a Collateralized Mortgage-Backed Security or 'CMBS' investment instrument. It was precisely defaults on mortgages such as these that led to the credit crunch and the collapse of the CMBS market. The Glazers were riding the same wave of aggressive, reckless lending that saw Lehman and other banks crash.

'When I started to look at which other First Allied shopping centres had mortgages in a CMBS, I was amazed to find that loans on sixty-three of the sixty-four properties listed on the company's website had been securitized.' (The final one was remortgaged in January 2008, but was not securitized, because by then the credit crunch had caused the market in CMBS to dry up.)

Says Green: 'Because CMBS's are freely traded, mortgage holders whose loans are in such vehicles must report regularly on the financial performance of the property on which the mortgage is secured.' He found that First Allied had mortgage liabilities totalling $570 million, secured on properties worth only $566 million. He estimated that 'thirty-one properties, virtually half the portfolio', were in negative equity.

Despite generating rental income of over $76 million and cash flow before interest of about $47 million, the debt burden of interest and repayments was so severe that the whole portfolio of sixty-four shopping malls was currently only producing $9.7 million of surplus cash per annum before tax. This was 'a tiny sum for what was supposed to be a large and successful real-estate business and totally inadequate to even cover the interest accruing on Red Football Payment in Kind notes or to invest in the Bucs playing squad.'

An additional three centres had already gone bust. Green says 'the only explanation for the Glazers' failure to inject further equity into the businesses was obvious. The family did not have the money.'

The vast majority of First Allied's mortgages (fifty-eight from sixty-three) were taken out with Lehman Brothers, 'perhaps the greatest symbol of the excesses of the credit boom in the United States.'

The Glazers had burdened the centres with loans they could not repay. 'An incredible 44 per cent (twenty-eight) of First Allied's shopping centres had been placed on a "watchlist" by the trustee banks of the relevant CMBS, indicating they believed there was a significant risk of default on their loans.'

More than one in four properties (seventeen) had a 'debt service coverage ratio' below times one, in other words, 'income did not cover mortgage payments. Unless occupancy rates pick up sharply, these centres were likely to go into foreclosure in the next few months as reserves were depleted.'

Concluded Green: 'Unless someone can point to other assets acquired at the time, the £272 million of "equity" the Glazers contributed to the acquisition of Manchester United was at least in part really debt secured on First Allied's shopping centres.'

As there was also 'strong anecdotal evidence that loans secured on shares in Zapata were also part of this "equity" element, we were left wondering how much, if any, true equity the Glazers ever put in . . .'

There was another conclusion: the Glazers are not business geniuses. Adding United's debt (including the PIKs) to *Forbes* magazine's estimate of the Bucs' borrowing, the mortgages on the malls, and estimates for the family's residential mortgages, Green came to a figure of at least $1.8 billion of total Glazer family debt.

He made a case study of Centre Court Shopping Center in Sandy Springs in the northern suburbs of Atlanta, Georgia. It had sixteen stores, which combined provide a similar amount of retail space as a

Tesco Extra superstore in the UK, and a large car park. The Glazers bought it in 2002 for $6.85 million.

Edward Glazer, president of First Allied, said: 'We love the Atlanta metro area and plan on acquiring more centres in the area very soon.' To buy Centre Court, the Glazers used $1.55 million of their own money and borrowed $5.3 million from Lehman Brothers.

In 2005, they remortgaged it. They'd had the centre independently valued and now it was worth $9.7 million. They borrowed $8.245 million, or 85 per cent of its value, again from Lehman, who put the mortgage into a CMBS. The Glazers still owed $5.1 million on the original mortgage, but now they'd raised another $3 million. 'This is a textbook example of how leveraged real-estate investing is meant to work. Not bad at all for two years of doing nothing more than banking rent cheques and very handy if you wanted to buy a football club,' says Green.

Then recession hit, and four lots at Centre Court fell empty. The Glazers did not have enough rental income to cover the mortgage payments. 'Like many other property speculators, they were too used to the constant game of remortgaging off ever higher property prices. The first Centre Court mortgage was barely in place for three years. In the boom years, it was common to remortgage just before one interest-only period ended and to start another mortgage. The capital never needed to be repaid. Perhaps they also thought rents would rise with the buoyant economy. Perhaps they didn't think.'

Green said: 'What Centre Court needs is an injection of new equity to reduce the mortgage burden . . . As First Allied have demonstrated with Hebron Heights, The Shops at Cumberland Place and The Crossings at Roswell and . . . with Crosswoods Commons in Ohio, they have no money to support centres as they run into financial trouble.

'The centres coming off interest-only periods this year were collectively valued at $393 million when the Glazers took out $313 million of mortgages against them in 2005. All of the $80 million of equity value they had is now in danger of being wiped out. Savvy businessmen, you say?'

Green could 'only assume that David Gill and Sir Alex Ferguson had no idea about the true state of the Glazers' finances and believed they really were wealthy and successful'.

He wrote to Gill to ask whether he felt United supporters should worry about the family's ability to repay the PIKs in the light of his analysis.

NFL commissioner Roger Goodell had made a stout defence of the Glazers when he said, 'I talk to the Glazers on a regular basis. I will tell you that they are sound owners. They are terrific for the NFL and we have not seen that there is any stress that would affect the way they operate any of their professional teams, much less the Tampa Bay Buccaneers.' But as with United's management, Green assumed this assessment 'was a product of not knowing the truth about the situation'. Green called upon the NFL Finance Committee to look into their affairs more closely.

What especially bothered him, Green says, was that the story of First Allied he uncovered had 'some chilling parallels'. First Allied Corp was not a property development company, it was 'a property speculator, using high levels of debt to try to ride the real-estate cycle and enrich its owners'.

In the same way the Glazers brought debt, risk and huge costs to United, they also added nothing to their portfolio of shopping centres, built nothing, created nothing. 'This would be of less concern if the management of First Allied had proved themselves adept at timing the market, but sadly the opposite is true. Not only did the Glazers borrow too much, but they did so at precisely the wrong time and at unsustainable, inflated valuations.'

His overall conclusion is damning. 'The more I discovered about the Glazer family, the more they seemed to be an unappetizing morality tale. Their story was one that took in financial "innovation" by out-of-control banks like Lehman Brothers, which in turn allowed pointless real-estate speculation and created the mirage of wealth creation, before the whole facade starts to crumble.'

On 27 June 2005, United shares were delisted from the stock market. It was a private business once again, now under the control of its new owners, the Glazer family.

Three brothers, Joel, Avie and Bryan, flew to London and that night held a party for their advisors at Nobu, the ultra-smart Japanese restaurant in Park Lane. There was no Malcolm. Their PRs were charged with imparting the message that 'these three would be running United, that the takeover was largely their doing, although Malcolm's status as family patriarch was decisive in all business affairs.'

The following day they met the Premier League for lunch and the Football Association for afternoon tea at their offices, and the government in the form of the sports minister, Richard Caborn, for dinner at the House of Commons. The only thing missing was a reception at Buckingham Palace – otherwise the full panoply of official British red carpet was laid before them.

We do it very well, supplanting suspicion and wariness with copious cups of tea. Underneath it all is a message: that the outsider can become one of us, provided they play by the same rules and don't do anything to upset the status quo.

What was striking about the Glazers was just how low-key they were. The fans were portraying them as monsters and criminals when they appeared anything but. Similarly, they were not brash or flash or overbearing, as we're conditioned to expect US billionaires to be. They were more normal, bloke-next-door. Perhaps there was another reason for their understated manner – that they were not billionaires at all.

The same questions came up at the three meetings: how could they repay the debts and what made them buy United? The Premier League was concerned, as well it might, that the only way they could meet their borrowings was to break the collective selling of TV rights and raise more by United going it alone. No, the brothers claimed, that was not their plan.

The next day was altogether different. After seeing Vodafone, the club's sponsors, they headed north, to Old Trafford and the fans.

Joel, Avie and Bryan duly posed for pictures on the hallowed turf. They appeared humbled by what was now theirs, not larking around or posing, but standing taking in the vast stands, and with them, the proud history. They seemed genuinely moved and honoured to be the new owners. Again, perhaps they could scarcely believe their luck and were having to pinch themselves, that people like them were not meant to own something like this. 'What struck me then about the Glazers,' wrote the watching Nayani, their new PR advisor, whose agency Smithfield had taken over from Brunswick, 'was their sometimes awkward and unassuming body language.'

Then, they had a rude awakening. All day, fans had been texting and emailing each other to say the Glazers would be at Old Trafford. This was the moment to let them know what true, local Reds really thought.

While the brothers were inside, crowds gathered outside, and kept on gathering. The police were blindsided, policing a match at the neighbouring cricket ground. Cries of 'die Glazer, die Glazer!' rang out around the United stadium. There was the possibility of a serious incident and harm coming to them.

Eventually, the Glazers left at 11 p.m. in the back of a police van. They might have spent £800 million on buying Manchester United, but here they were, being told they were not wanted in the most unpleasant and demeaning terms imaginable.

Yet, remembers Nayani, the following morning the three 'seemed completely unruffled by the preceding night's events'. It's as if they decided the rioters were just a tiny minority of the club's total support, and that the majority, who would fill the giant venue and beyond, would not be so opposed. Or was it stoicism that took over; that their faith taught them to persevere and to suffer, for the good will come, and that throughout they kept their eyes on the longer game?

Certainly, the morning after the night before, the three brothers received a more reassuring greeting from the staff at Old Trafford. Joel did the talking, wearing a buttoned-up blue blazer and striking a humble note, emphasizing their conservatism and love for United's traditions and their 'business as usual' ethos. The accompanying Nayani thought his speech was 'received very positively and served to diffuse much of the tension in the air'.

The Glazers were introduced to Sir Bobby Charlton. 'They hung on every word the football legend had to say as he eulogized about the club he had served with distinction for the best part of half a century.'

Joel then did an interview with MUTV. For many years, this interview remained the Glazers' only direct communication about the club.

One by one, Joel rebutted some of the charges and rumours that had built up during the takeover. They were wholly behind Ferguson; he promised 'resources to compete on the field at the highest possible level'; Charlton would not be removed from the board; they would not pull out of the Premier League's collective TV agreement; the club crest would not be changed; Old Trafford would not be sold and leased. He did admit that ticket prices could rise, although not unreasonably. He stressed his family's respect for the club's traditions. He even apologized for the turmoil that the Glazers had created.

It cut little ice – the media remained hostile. The size of the debt imposed on the club was the overriding issue. Henry Winter in *The Daily Telegraph* wrote: 'Manchester United supporters demonstrating outside Old Trafford have every right to make life uncomfortable for the profiteers from Florida who have taken over their beloved club.'

A *Telegraph* headline underscored the reality: 'A wound that will never heal'.

The press too was cynical that the Glazers had given their only interview to a TV station that they now controlled. It did repair some of the damage, though, as *The Guardian* reported: 'In a piece of textbook if somewhat schmaltzy PR which saw him press every diplomatic button, Joel disarmed the doubters by presenting his family as change-resistant, caring capitalists who, far from regarding history as bunk, are enthralled by United's heritage.'

Only some bought it. The stickers that appeared among Manchester supporters everywhere read: 'Love United, Hate Glazer'.

NINE

The Black Box

Malcolm Glazer only ever said thirty-three words in public about Manchester United. In early April 2006, he said: 'We are enjoying it [owning United] greatly, it is a wonderful franchise, we just love it. I just want to say hello to the fans. It is a great franchise. It will just do great.'

There you are, you've bought the biggest football club, one that has a pedigree like no other, whose players and former players are household names, which fills its colossal stadium with devoted followers and has millions more all over the world, for whom the club, the team, is everything, and that is all you can manage? Worse, he used the word 'great' three times and 'franchise' twice. That's all he could think to say. Even allowing for the ill-preparedness of having a microphone thrust in his face and Glazer not being the most naturally articulate of people, it's terrible. There's no humility, no passion, no connection. Instead, it's banal and empty. There's nothing there, except reliance on a commercial term, a word from US major league sports, that football fans might well find offensive.

America does 'franchises'. It sells the rights to a name that can then be moved around and sold again. There's no root, no bond. It's meaningless, a commercial device to play sport and sell advertising, sponsorship, TV rights and 'merch' against. Glazer himself had already shown in the States that he could not see what was wrong with extending the idea of a city-based franchise and playing across four locations far apart; indeed, because it might well make him more money, it must therefore be right.

In his one quote about Manchester United he avoids saying anything at all about the future of the club, or indeed its illustrious past; there is no detail, no sense of a basic understanding of the club's legacy and importance to soothe fans' fears. When United fans are asked what it is about the Glazers they can't abide, they say the lack of interest, the sense, as one said to me, that 'the Glazers don't give a shit'.

But this does not square with the claim made by those who have been allowed inside, who say that Joel Glazer's office, for one, is a veritable shrine to Manchester United. Does that mean he is content surrounding himself with souvenirs and watching games on TV, rather than experiencing the real thing, live, from the vantage point of the Directors' Box? Or is it that the memorabilia represent more than a romantic attachment and equates to fond reminders of commercial exploitation, something at which Joel and his family have excelled? Malcolm himself never went to Old Trafford, while those around the Glazers say that the rest of the family stopped going to the stadium because of the protests.

The fans point to Abramovich, who attended Chelsea matches regularly, and John Henry, likewise, at Liverpool. Distance is no excuse. My friend, Paul Casson, who owned Barrow, would regularly fly from Dallas, where he lives, to Heathrow, and take the train from

Euston to Barrow in Cumbria, in the far North-West of England, then do the whole journey in reverse after having been heckled by the Barrow fans for not spending enough of his own money (Glazers take note) on their club. Unlike Casson, who is wealthy but not that wealthy, the Glazers had access to private jets, and the various family members could have taken turns in going. But they were never willing to make that commitment, that connection.

It can be strong, the bond between the fans and the owner. At Fulham, if Mohamed Al-Fayed was there – and he usually was – the fans would seek a wave. It's about a shared experience, knowing that the owners feel your joy and yes, the pain; that the team that matters so much to you also matters to them. Of course, that affection only extended so far as he continued to lavish cash on the team – football fans are extremely fickle.

The present owners of Fulham, the Pakistani-American businessmen Shahid and Tony Khan, are less in evidence, but Tony Khan does go and his father, Shahid, now and again. They certainly attend matches more often than the Glazers.

The Glazers' reign went sour from the outset. They don't do communication. There they were, having bought the club and loaded it with a whole lot of debt that was not there before, but they resolutely refused to explain themselves.

It's worth stressing that, while the fans gnashed their teeth, the Glazers did not technically do anything wrong. Perhaps there should be a debate about debt in football, maybe the rules should change. It's as much a regulatory environment question as anything. The Glazers did not break the law or any rules. Their communications strategy was not much different to Roman Abramovich's at Chelsea, but he was perceived as having saved the club and put his own money in, and he didn't load it with debt.

It's also forgotten that the Glazers put in more than £200 million in equity. Although that was almost certainly also borrowed. Strictly, though, how they got it also does not matter.

The name 'Glazer' resonated with J.P. Morgan in the summer of 2004, when they had started buying shares in United. Woodward was working for the investment bank, which was on the Glazer ticket. From a sports perspective, as fas as the bank was concerned they made a good fit with United. Key to the Glazers' standing inside and outside the club was Alex Ferguson. He was supportive of anybody taking out the Irish. Then, he wanted them to be supportive of what he was trying to do, and they were. The first sign of that was when Ferguson wanted to buy Wayne Rooney in August 2004. United phoned the Glazers and said they were thinking of buying Wayne Rooney, what did the Glazers think? The Glazers immediately said to go for it.

Woodward joined the club in late 2005. He left J.P. Morgan and was given the title at United of 'chief of staff', a post he held for the next seven and a half years. His main job was to be a conduit between the Glazers and the people on the ground. Inevitably, this made him deeply unpopular with those most opposed to the Glazers. Along with the family, Woodward or 'Woodentop', as one leading protestor named him, became a hate figure.

Those who know him well say he's a good-humoured, self-deprecating, self-confident man. He's not a growling ogre, nor is he a baleful, sinister character like his namesake, the actor who played *Callan* and *The Equalizer*. He brought with him the J.P. Morgan 'can do, will do' giant US bank attitude. Instantly, he set about applying the same standard of money management to United. It's what he knew, so he did it. Again, the romantic idea of the core purpose of a football club being twenty-two men chasing a football around a field went out the window. Manchester United was a business now, which is how the Glazers and their ambitious US banking recruit saw it. Under the Glazers, Gill and Woodward, Manchester United turned into a monied behemoth, albeit a debt-ridden one whose voracious appetite always required more feeding. Partly that achievement was down to the Glazers being American and having a different approach; partly it was down to Gill and Woodward, their recruit from the Wall Street bank, a Brit who nevertheless spoke their language and shared their vision.

Woodward identified things that were wrong with the back-office operation. Data from the United call centre showed that 50 per cent of telephone calls were dropping, callers kept waiting for so long that they rang off in frustration. This was stopped straightaway.

There was no separate sales team for the corporate boxes. The same people who were selling parent-and-child seats and dealing with fans wanting away tickets, were also expected to schmooze global marketing and sales directors and persuade them to take a box with all the trimmings. That changed; hospitality got its own dedicated salesforce.

Ticket prices went up. Having been vague when asked about ticket prices, Joel soon moved to increase them. Gill was in agreement; others were opposed. But the proprietor and CEO wanted it, so the prices went up.

The calculation Gill and the Glazers made, as their former PR advisor Nayani describes, was that ticket receipts were 'strong and a waiting list augured well for a full uptake of the 8,000 new seats in the corner quadrants of the enlarged Old Trafford. Factor in the UK economy – which continued to bask in a period of uninterrupted growth, providing for very low unemployment – and add to this the loyalty of Manchester United supporters, and any potential rise would likely have had a negligible effect on demand, thus enabling revenues to be recouped.'

So, to put that another way, the loyalty of United supporters could be taken for granted and they would pay more, and if they didn't there was always the waiting list. The tickets went up an average of 12 per cent.

'The ticket price rise was a big mistake, United prices were nineteenth in the Premiership, which was impossible to argue against, then they put them up,' said a former United insider. And for the next few years they carried on putting them up. The protestors maintained the prices had had to increase to service the debt. Not true, said the club.

This, though, was a running sore in their relations with the fans and with their PR. The perception was that United had substantial borrowings when others didn't, and that cash that could otherwise have gone on buying players was being used to pay the debt – notwithstanding that for a period the team was still doing well, still winning trophies. The fans' hard-earned money was going towards servicing the debt – debt that had been taken out to enable the Glazers to buy the club. And then the Glazers stayed away and did not engage with the fans. There was always, too, the comparison with Abramovich.

An alternative argument, one the Glazers tried to promote, was that the debt was not the fans' concern. If the family could meet the interest payments, which they could, there was nothing to worry about. Paying the borrowings did not encroach on the club's activities, they maintained, it did not affect the team's ability to win matches or impact on the fans' matchday experience.

But the Glazer debt was not like a normal mortgage where the borrower has the same rights to their home as the person next door who paid straight cash for theirs. The Glazers were operating on a twenty times multiple, once the fixed costs of players' wages and energy bills and so on were paid. That's considerably higher than the mortgage standard of up to three times salary.

This did not include, either, the Glazers' separate borrowings on their shopping malls. Even compared with other leveraged buyouts in that crazy, fin-de-siècle, pre-the-2008 banking crash period, twenty times was still quite exceptional. And this was lending, let us not forget, against football, the beautiful game, not an ever-constant, money-spewing utility.

It was not a concern, maintains Nayani. 'Yet, unlike other highly leveraged buyouts that went on to encourage significant trouble, the Glazers were prudent and oversaw a more than doubling in operating profits. This was thanks in part to a sharp lift in media and expanded stadium revenues (which they were not directly responsible for but had the sense to factor in) but also to the strong rise in highly profitable commercial revenue, which they were to personally drive.'

Woodward, the lending banker who did very well while at J.P. Morgan from arranging the Glazers' funding, became the person charged by the Glazers with ramping up that commercial revenue to meet the borrowing he'd arranged.

First though, Woodward made it a priority to refinance the debt of £558 million, to make it easier to manage. Around half were the bank loans syndicated by him while at J.P. Morgan; half were the PIK notes.

TV rights were due to rise, with a new broadcaster entrant, Setanta, competing for games alongside Sky. United had sealed a British record shirt sponsorship deal with AIG, the giant US insurer. It was worth £56.5 million over four years, more if United sold AIG financial products, such as credit cards.

The casual nature of what had gone before was highlighted: in the past, United threw in for free the right for the shirt sponsor to advertise their wares on hoardings on the East Stand. Not any more, that was now extra.

Joel and the brothers were delighted. The AIG tie-up had symmetry: an American corporate colossus known the world over, coming together with a globally recognized football club. It gave a sense of how they saw the future. United was to operate on a higher level, playing football of course, in England, but thinking worldwide in other respects. Both AIG and United were targeting Asia, for instance. That made them perfect for each other.

Symbolically, Woodward did not base himself in Old Trafford or at Carrington, United's training ground outside Manchester. He was chief of staff, but his office, his life, was in London, initially in Belgravia, bang in the middle of hedge-fund land. Nor did it seem like a football office behind a stand, usually relying on cheap plastic furniture and pictures of players. His lair had a mosaic-tiled floor in the lobby and lots of polished wood, and a Chesterfield sofa. He used a whiteboard to explain the club's financial arrangements. 'He delivered these briefings with as much aplomb and didactic fervour as a star university finance lecturer, sketching out the many permutations that a refinancing could involve,' remembers Nayani.

The aim of the refinancing was to lower the annual interest bill of £30 million in cash plus the PIKs' theoretical £60 million on top. News of what Woodward was doing leaked, prompting speculation he would throw in anything commercially if the price was right, including the naming of Old Trafford.

He managed to reduce the interest payments, but the borrowings actually rose as he borrowed more so he could take advantage of falling rates and use the money to pay back half the PIKs plus interest. It was a clever plan but, as far as the protestors were concerned, completely unsatisfactory: the debt hanging over their club had climbed even higher.

None of this would work, indeed the entire Project Hampstead would founder, unless the club's revenues were driven sharply upwards. Joel liked to say that the average spend per head at a US major league sports game was $35, while at a Manchester United match it was less than a fiver.

At English football matches, Joel discovered to his horror, you can't drink alcohol in sight of the pitch, the food is poor, there's no popcorn, no people going up and down the aisles selling beer and candy, the fans prefer to drink and eat at their regular haunts away from the ground and there's no post-match entertainment, so everyone rushes for the exit as soon as the final whistle blows.

There was little the Glazers could do to change that – it was a mixture of rules and tradition embedded in the fabric of the game, so they instructed Woodward to attack other potential revenue sources.

He used the same techniques he was familiar with at J.P. Morgan, putting more structure around everything. It was like being in mergers and acquisitions in the bank, with a cast of thousands and everyone having to know their place and take responsibility for their role. Except this was not M&A in a US investment bank; it was a football club.

In another sign of a shift, Woodward expanded the London office, setting up an entire commercial team in the capital. Old Trafford and Carrington had environments that felt like being in one big family. In a 140-year-old club there were lots of traditions and values. He wanted a different, possibly more demanding way of working, so he set up in London.

He also wanted loyalty, no distractions, for the London workforce. It's a moot point as to what was more important to the Glazers and the future well-being of their club: Old Trafford and Carrington or the London outpost.

Woodward's operation moved from Belgravia to nearby St James's, to 50 Pall Mall, around the corner from the Carlton Club, the Tory Party citadel, opposite St James's Palace and the Oxford and

Cambridge Club. As London addresses go, there are none smarter, none so internationally known.

Old Trafford and Carrington comprised the United heartbeat, but 50 Pall Mall was its new money-making hub. As for The Cliff, it remains on the United books, as a facility for youngsters, but the place in Salford that nurtured so many of the club's stars and was the site of the great rebirth after Munich, as well as being the training ground that delivered the Treble, was largely ignored, wearing an air of abandonment as its buildings were neglected and fell into disrepair. As Andy Mitten, editor of *United We Stand*, says: 'All they had to do was to spend £300,000 on doing up The Cliff, then it would not look so shabby, but they were not prepared to.'

There was another difference between Manchester and the London operation. Carrington and Old Trafford had security, but they were still open, signposted, publicly visible places; 50 Pall Mall was highly secretive, tightly guarded, entirely anonymous. There was no Manchester United name on a brass plate outside, nothing at all to indicate who was working there. Within the club it became known as the 'Black Box'.

This was entirely new for football. Nobody else was doing it. United got to one hundred people working for them in London. Prior to the Glazers and Woodward, the United sales team comprised two people, based in Manchester.

Other clubs, once they'd gleaned what United were doing, followed suit. Today, twelve CEOs from twenty Premiership clubs are now based in London; almost every big club has an office in London. Liverpool, Manchester City – they have offices in London. It's the football business city.

To that end, 50 Pall Mall was fitted out to as high a specification as possible. The Glazers wanted the office to 'reflect the allure of Manchester United to any visitor and potential sponsor', recalls Nayani. 'In place of a humdrum (albeit well-appointed) London office, they were keen to project a sophisticated ambience akin to a Ralph Lauren-styled clubhouse.'

The main flooring was replaced with dark parquet, red leather armchairs were installed, the lobby was oak panelled. In the London 'boardroom', they erected a podium, upon which they placed the 'Manchester United Opus', an 'exquisitely produced tome containing hundreds of silver-leaf-edged pages of exclusive photos and articles. It would have been the ultimate coffee-table book, had it not been too heavy for such a table. On the wall, behind the Opus, was a large United crest, resplendent in silver, in between two alcoves housing full-sized replica trophies.'

The boardroom itself was cream-carpeted and accessed through sliding wooden doors. Its long oak table was accompanied with 'delicately crafted chairs covered in the softest of suedes, projecting an intimate warmth and sense of tradition'. The room was equipped with a state-of-the-art sound-and-vision system, with a large flat-screen on one wall, showing reels of United triumphs.

All this was done in total secrecy. Said Nayani: 'There was significant journalist interest in 50 Pall Mall, the existence of which I would barely admit to, and would never elaborate upon. I got used to reading snide speculation about the "secretive" London office, which only served to bond the tightly knit workforce that was in the employ of one of the most famous companies on earth, but that had to work amid such cloak-and-dagger secrecy.'

It helps explain why the fans' sustained protests had such little bearing, that while they were picketing the Megastore and spray-painting in Manchester, the Glazers' real business and interest lay 200 miles away in the hushed confines of London's St James's.

It shows too the mindset of the Glazers. This was not an accident; it was pure calculation, more Blofeld-style global commercial aggrandizement than mere soccer. It's hard to conceive of anything so removed from the soul of the game.

To ensure there was linkage between the two, the Glazers upgraded the executive suite at Old Trafford behind the East Stand. The thinking was, according to Nayani, 'that the Manchester United sales team, having taken part in initial discussions with marketing directors in the Pall Mall boardroom, could now host them in similarly luxurious surroundings at Old Trafford on a match day.' The suite was fitted out with the same soft cream furnishings as London and inlaid with similar wooden panelling.

The view of the pitch was stunning. The visiting dignitaries could watch the game from the comfort of the suite, through a huge window that could be lowered at the press of a button, to allow in the noise and atmosphere. Finally, the business types got within shouting distance of the real fans. Unfortunately, this was one aspect even the Glazers could not control and the window would be raised again if their swearing and abuse got too much.

The operation at 50 Pall Mall put paid to any idea that the Glazers were only at United for the short-term, that they'd stumbled upon the club by chance and would soon be off. They held deep ambitions, and they were clearly there to stay, regardless of any protests.

For those that cared to notice, from day one their intentions were clear. When the new owners were asked what they intended to do with United: 'Asia', replied Joel. Not keep winning competitions, playing the most attractive, brilliant football; not pleasing the loyal fans and putting something back into Manchester; not continuing the great line from Sir Matt to Munich to the Holy Trinity of Best, Charlton and Law, to Sir Alex and the Class of '92.

But Asia.

What mattered most now was where the Glazers saw the growth potential. 'The club has barely scratched the surface over there,' Joel continued, 'Manchester United is already huge there but it could be so much bigger.'

They committed £40 million to transforming the marketing strategy. One comparison that Joel clung to was with their Tampa Bay Bucs. Under NFL rules, the owners effectively have a seventy-five-mile exclusive marketing zone around their home base. That's fine if you're located in New York or Los Angeles. Not so good if all you have to exploit is Tampa. But even with that constraint, the Bucs was pulling in more in sponsorship packages than United.

Soon after they took over United, the Glazers commissioned a major study from the market research firm, TNS. Everyone said the Reds had global reach and their fans were worldwide, but they'd never bothered to find out how true that was or to attempt to put some hard numbers on that support. In their calculating manner, the Glazers sought certainty.

TNS went far and wide, conducting thousands of interviews across continents and in countries identified as crucial: USA, China, South Africa, UAE, UK. They went down another tier and looked at a hundred or so other countries.

The results were astounding: one in twenty of the world's population cited United as their favourite team, that was 333 million people. Of that total, some 139 million went further and described themselves as 'active' fans. Opponents of the Glazers, of United, greet these figures with incredulity. Certainly, they do seem incredibly high, off-the-scale, but that, apparently, was the finding and United stuck to it.

The Black Box had its ammunition. Woodward's department was fired up. Until then, most football clubs relied upon sponsors knocking on the door, asking if they could back the team. For the Glazers and Woodward, that was not nearly scientific enough; they would leave no stone unturned in their quest for sponsors; they would go out and find them.

Similarly, at most football clubs, endorsements were confined to the shirts and some hoardings around the ground. In contrast, United put everything up for sale; things that had never been considered before.

Richard Arnold, Woodward's then deputy, says: 'You don't set off on a journey without an understanding of where you are trying to go.' The club's management, the Glazers, he said, looked at the world 'like a Risk board', referring to the game which has world domination as its goal. 'The early months of what we did was spent in very high-depth strategy discussions [with] multiple, multiple iterations. Even now, two days a month is spent iterating all those strategies.'

The Black Box brainstorming sessions yielded a search for an official club wine partner, a courier partner, office equipment provider. Match shirts were sponsored, but why not the shirts worn in training? Put them on the list.

Mobile phone companies were special targets. There are the global networks, but they operate on a country-by-country basis. So, instead of doing a tie-in with one operator globally, United would pick off countries individually and earn even more.

In all, across the Glazer years, United ended up with more than thirty corporate partners. They included Hublot, the Swiss watch-maker, Russia's Aeroflot, Diageo, DHL, Aon, Budweiser, Seoul Metropolitan Government, Nike, Turkish Airlines, Singha Thai beer, Indonesia's Bank Danamon, South Korea's Shinhan Bank, Malaysia's Public Bank – and even Mister Potato. The latter Malaysian brand signed as United's official 'savoury snack partner'.

Pierre Pang, deputy general manager for sales and marketing at Mamee-Double Decker, which owns Mister Potato, was asked why. 'Three hundred and thirty-three million fans globally, with close to two-thirds coming from Asia,' he said, repeating the Glazer-Woodward script. 'That's basically along the lines of where our strategy is: the vision of being Asian number one for the potato snack segment.'

How they secured the wine partner was typical. Out of the blue, a parcel arrived at the head office of Concha y Toro, the 127-year-old winemaker in Santiago, Chile. It was addressed to the marketing director. Inside was an ornate box lined with black silk, holding a leather football. The Concha y Toro insignia was embossed on the ball, next to that of Manchester United.

Accompanying the gift was a book explaining the advantages of a partnership between the football club and the winemaker. Within thirty-six hours, United executives were on the phone with their counterparts at Concha y Toro, working on the outlines of a deal. That was followed by an official ceremony at Old Trafford. Under the terms, the executive boxes and lounges at the stadium were to serve only Concha y Toro's Casillero del Diablo wines, and the company's adverts were to appear on the digital billboards around the ground.

Something similar happened with the shirts. In the banking crash, the same one that brought down Lehman, AIG hit the buffers. AIG indicated to United it would not be renewing, so Woodward and co went to work. As Nayani tells it, they drew up a long list of potential successors, including those that were already backing other clubs. The Glazers told them to inject a 'wow' factor, as they did with Concha y Toro and the silk box and the special football.

Every company on the list had an XL Nike United shirt mocked up with their brand across the chest. Why XL? Because the CEOs and marketing directors who were to receive it were more likely to be at the heavier end of the weight spectrum. The shirt was folded and packed into a black box, embossed with a silver logo and marked 'Shirt Sponsorship'.

Alongside the shirt in the box was a hardback book of pictures of United players wearing their branded shirt and the accompanying message: 'No need to imagine what it would be like for Rooney to wear your company's shirt . . . we've done it for you.'

As promotional material went, the packaging was incredibly luxurious and bespoke and not something you would normally associate with a football club.

After the mail-outs, Woodward and his team waited a while, then began working the phones, setting up meetings with those who expressed interest. The United sales executives would fly out to meet them, and straight out of the J.P. Morgan how-to-win-business manual, they were instructed that even if the result was a 'no' to the shirts, they were to explore how else the company and United might do business together.

Meanwhile all over the world, company fat cats were proudly sporting XL United shirts displaying their branding.

Aon, the large US-based global financial services firm, won the shirt contest. Its new marketing head, Phil Clement, had received – unsolicited – the box with the shirt and book. The United sales team in London followed up and soon they were discussing how the football club could help Aon. They were furnished with tickets for United's 2009 Champions League final against Barcelona, in Rome, which is where the sponsorship was signed.

Clement said he saw the marriage as an opportunity to unite Aon's then 36,000 strong workforce, located around the word, under the single United 'umbrella'. Another international financial corporation, Standard Chartered, had been in the running to back United, but the bank was insisting on performance targets and the Glazers refused; they would only operate on their own terms.

Another deal was put in place for the training kit. Without asking, DHL executives were sent iPads showing the United players in training wearing DHL-branded tops. The courier service signed a four-year deal worth £40 million, a higher sum than all but four

Premiership teams secured for their main shirt sponsorships. Then again, United secures more media coverage of its players on the training pitch than most other clubs get for their matches.

United used their former players and star players as sellers, ambassadors, encouraging them to meet potential sponsors. Bobby Charlton was wheeled out, as a touchstone. The Glazer–Woodward attitude was that they'd got this great club, now they had a commercial rocket ship attached to it. Theirs was a circular strategy: you can't sell sponsorship without access to players, but you need sponsorship to get the players.

At the same time, ticket prices and matchday revenues continued to rise. There was, though, a growing issue: Old Trafford was getting quieter. Ferguson said as much when after one match he complained: 'The crowd was dead. That was the quietest I have heard them. We needed them in this game . . . The players need the crowd to respond and vice versa but it was like a funeral it was so quiet and I don't think that helped us. We need them to motivate us.'

Prior to that game he'd written in his programme notes: 'At a number of clubs there have been problems with friction between managers and owners. But you can see how smoothly the United ship is running as far as that is concerned, despite early hostility over the Glazer family's ownership, those protests were unfair because they weren't given a chance but the Glazers kept their cool and our owners have been nothing but supportive. Good teamwork starts at the top and I am happy to say that is what we have at Old Trafford.'

This and his complaint about the lack of noise was seized upon as proof that Ferguson was out of touch and that the reason Old Trafford was so silent was because the 'real' fans had been priced out of attending. Writing in *The Daily Telegraph*, Henry Winter did not hold back: 'For such an intelligent man, Sir Alex Ferguson should really see the link between the loss of noise at Old Trafford and the increase in ticket prices forced on Manchester United by the Glazer family.

188 | THE WORLD'S BIGGEST CASH MACHINE

Strangely, United's august manager decries supporters while also praising the Glazers . . . The astonishing greed-driven hike in ticket prices at Old Trafford has disenfranchised some of United's traditional support, the Salford lads who sing and chant. This is not rocket science. Sir Alex . . . needs to call on the Glazers to re-think a pricing strategy which is damaging Old Trafford's atmosphere. No chance.'

The Glazers realized that it wasn't only the team who got a lift from a noisy Old Trafford; it helped on the revenue side as well. In their eyes, the objectives of the stadium, within the bounds of health and safety, were to be full and noisy. United were attracting 74,000 to Old Trafford, while an average of 50 million people would be watching the game on TV. Old Trafford being full and noisy was essential to their product.

By having a fantastic atmosphere, United could charge more for corporate hospitality and gain a bigger TV audience, enabling it to make even more money. As they saw it, Old Trafford was a theatre, and the show was the players and the fans. The prawn sandwich brigade came for the whole spectacle – they wanted the game but they also wanted the noise and the singing.

Get that spectacle right, and United could sell hospitality tickets for thousands of pounds per game.

To do that, they reasoned, they had to have the loudest people in the cheapest seats, behind the goals. In one sense, they were of limited commercial value. They turned up one minute before kick-off, didn't shop in the Megastore because that was for the tourists, didn't eat and they didn't stay for a drink and food afterwards, but went home. But those fans were also doing something they loved and they were prepared to sing about it. And that made them extremely valuable in terms of creating an atmosphere that could then be sold to others. One suggestion was to give them all voice meters, on lanyards round their necks, and provided they sang for a certain length of time they'd get in for free.

According to the sums, United would make so much more from the increased price of hospitality that it would cancel out the cost of allowing the fans behind the goals in for nothing.

The ends would be free and rewarded in some way. There were 74,000 in Old Trafford but there were 50 million watching on TV. So, was it a stadium product or a TV product? If TV, they needed vibrant, noisy fans, they need to be able to make that connection.

Some United fans might see themselves as little more than performing seals, there to entertain the high rollers on instruction; others might have been prepared to go along with the money-spinning vision, to sing in return for getting in free. Quite how they proposed monitoring what the supporters sang, whether they were anti-Glazer lyrics or ones full of obscenities – or both – was not clear.

TEN

Charge of the Red Knights

A s much as the Glazers and Woodward harboured ambitions of United's commercial domination, there was always the decidedly non-sexy, thorny issue of the debt to be attended to.

It hung over the club, reputationally and financially. It was the albatross that blighted the relationship with the fans and skewed the media coverage. Always, whatever United did, however the team performed on the pitch, or whoever joined the club, or whichever new marketing coup Woodward deployed, the debt was there, lurking like a dark shadow in the background.

One of Woodward's very first acts on joining from J.P. Morgan in 2005 was to refinance the borrowings. The Glazers had another go in 2007 but that failed. In 2009, with the credit and banking crisis of 2007–8 receding, they decided to try again and secure a more manageable package.

This time, instead of going cap in hand to the banks, they went down another route, of raising a Manchester United bond. It had merit, in that the Glazers would not be subject to onerous conditions laid down by a lending bank, but the downside was they would have to sell the bond to the international corporate debt market, and that would entail a presentational roadshow and disclosure of details about the club's finances – anathema to the secretive Glazers.

As ever in the male-dominated world of high finance, they gave it a codename: 'Project Free Kick'.

The pinstripe-suited protagonists were far removed from Manchester and from the simple game of football. Allen & Overy in the City were handling the legal side, while J.P. Morgan, Woodward's former Wall Street employer, were back, advising on the selling exercise.

Then, the news broke that ostensibly super-rich Dubai was in crisis over its own debt burden, and the global markets, including bonds, plunged. 'Project Free Kick' was put on hold.

But not for long. At the end of that year, 2009, the Glazers were planning on trying again. The news leaked to *The Sunday Times*: 'Sources familiar with the situation say the amount that Manchester United will seek to raise depends on the appetite shown by investors. At present, the figure is between £500 million and £600 million. If demand is strong, the club could seek more. It is unclear whether the proceeds of a bond issue would be used to repay the controversial PIK debt or the £520 million that is secured against the club.'

That same day, in January 2010, United lost to traditional arch-rivals Leeds United in the FA Cup. After having suffered a torrid spell regarding their own funding that saw them shed players, Leeds had hurtled down two divisions. Defeat to them was doubly humiliating for United, the reigning Premier League champions.

Whenever United did well on the pitch, the ferocity of the fan protests receded. There was still the same kernel of demonstrators, but they were not joined by the mass of followers who were mollified by seeing their team winning. But when they lost, and they had just lost in the most embarrassing fashion, then the full-on, bloodcurdling cries rang out again. Losing to Leeds, *and* just when the issue of the Glazer's borrowing had resurfaced again, and the unhealed wound reopened, raw and vicious, same as ever.

The Manchester United Supporters Trust said it was time for the Glazers to go: 'We warned from the beginning that the Glazer takeover would saddle the club with huge debts and now we can see them biting. If it were a race, then United are dragging their owners behind them like a tractor, while City's owners are providing rocket fuel.'

This was a comparison that would be made repeatedly, that Manchester City's owner since September 2008, Sheik Mansour bin Zayed Al Nahyan, vice-president of the United Arab Emirates, multibillionaire and member of the ruling family of Abu Dhabi, was lavishing a fortune on United's neighbour. Unlike the Glazers, Mansour never needed to borrow, there was no question about his direct access to fabulous wealth.

The contrast was stark, and in January 2010, with the loss to Leeds and the Glazers trying to sort out their borrowings again, it was savagely exposed. United pressed ahead with the bond issue. Woodward was off on a whirlwind tour of prospective investors arranged for him by J.P. Morgan, taking in Hong Kong, Singapore, Paris, Edinburgh, London, Amsterdam, Frankfurt, New York, Boston and Los Angeles.

Key to his pitch was the bond prospectus, a thirty-two-page dissection of the club's finances and its prospects, detailing the profits but also likely risks that any buyer of the bond would face. For the Glazers, used to shrouding the money side of the club in a veil of strict security, never giving interviews or providing explanations themselves for anything, this was a rare and dangerous departure. It had to be done, however. Nayani warned them as much: 'Joel Glazer's reaction was as sanguine as ever, reminding me how the outcry and protests following previous leaked business plans had eventually subsided.'

The difference on this occasion was that for years the fans had been starved of real detail. There had been speculation aplenty but now they were being supplied facts, stated in a legally watertight document.

Of course, the prospectus was not meant to be public, but there were enough opponents of the Glazers around the world, recipients of the PDF, to ensure that it would leak.

The two contrasting sides of United under the Glazers were vividly highlighted: Woodward was receiving an enthusiastic response from the financial community, but on the other side of the world, back in Manchester, the United community was in uproar. Their anger was fuelled by the UK media.

Made public for the first time was a veritable take-your-pick of aspects of the Glazers' ownership to stoke the fire:

- £70 million of club cash used to pay down the PIKs
- the club saying it 'cannot assure you that our business will generate sufficient cash flow from operations or that future borrowings will be available to us in amount sufficient to enable us to pay our indebtedness, including the Notes, or to fund our other liquidity needs'
- £38.6 million of club cash lost on an interest rate swap that went wrong
- proudly boasting 'we have been able to consistently increase matchday ticket prices for both general admission and seasonal hospitality seats at levels above the rate of inflation, particularly following the recent expansion of Old Trafford'
- a £10 million loan made to the Glazer siblings
- £10 million paid to the Glazers in 'management and administration' fees.

It made for shocking reading for those who still held on to the belief that the people who ran Manchester United were interested at all in the wider benefit of the club or the game. United's PR machine was unable to say very much, their lips sealed by the heavy legal disclosure rules governing bond issues.

There was a flurry of newspaper stories, all on the same theme, that United was in deep financial trouble and that this was an 'emergency' bond issue. Ironically, the opposite was the case: thanks to Woodward's Black Box of tricks, United's operational revenues had never been stronger; they were raising the debt precisely because they were in excellent shape.

'They boast of having 469 million [the visitors to the club's social media pages extrapolated] followers around the world but then warn that they may have to sell their own stadium,' wrote the *Daily Mail*. 'They are the most valuable football club in the world – worth £1.2 billion according to *Forbes* – but have no money of their own to buy players. This is Manchester United 2010; Manchester United the Glazer way. Fears of financial meltdown have stalked the dreams of supporters since the Glazer family took their club into private ownership in 2005. Now – as they tour the world trying to raise £500 million to ease the burden of debts worth £699 million – United's owners have put down in black and white just what their four-and-a-half turbulent years have done to England's most famous football club.'

Meanwhile the financial roadshow was signing up would-be investors. In London, Woodward was joined by Gill, the pair of them flanked by replica Champions League and Premiership trophies. The business pages reported differently from the sports pages. From Henry Winter's *Daily Telegraph*: ' "This is a well-run company whose owners have demonstrated it can get bigger and more successful," said one banker with knowledge of the sports market. "People will be attracted by the emotional link to United as well, but this is not a flaky investment. There is more risk in football than many other industries, but United are better protected than any other club." '

At United's first match since the bond issue, at home against Burnley on 16 January 2010, predictably the protests were severe. There were anti-Glazer chants, and the unfurling of a giant 'Love United Hate Glazer' banner. The same *Daily Telegraph* reported: 'No matter how strenuously Manchester United attempt to keep a lid on comment about the club's financial situation they cannot control the 75,000 voices of those supporters who continue to pay to watch Ferguson's team and the mutinous air within the stadium during the closing stages of this game, when a series of vitriolic chants against the Glazer family, the club's owners, rang around the ground, would have had the bond salesmen squirming in their seats. After all, there was little mention of revolting fans in the prospectus.'

The mood in Manchester darkened further after a clerical error meant United's latest company accounts were published ahead of schedule. They showed that the overall debt had increased from £699 million to £717 million. More stories, more protests.

None of it appeared to bother the international investors. Nor did a speech by President Barack Obama attacking the greed of banks and calling for tighter restrictions on their 'casino' activities, which pushed the equity and debt markets downwards.

All that excited potential buyers of the United bonds was the club's future growth forecasts. Woodward's Black Box was more than delivering.

Regardless of the negative press, the anti-Glazer demonstrations, revelations about payments to the Glazers, United's debt mountain and utterings from Obama, the bond was more than twice oversubscribed, with most of the investors coming from the US. Even the fickle nature of football itself did not matter. Forget the likelihood of defeats on the pitch and the ever-present threat of relegation (it had happened several times before, could happen again), as far as United's finances under the Glazers were concerned, the only way was up. Mesmerized by the smooth sales pitch from Woodward, the actual game, what it was all about, was reduced to little more than an afterthought. This was about branding, monetizing, brand stretch, cost-benefit, EBITDA (Earnings before Interest, Taxes, Depreciation and Amortization), growing a franchise, return on investment, globalization.

On 23 January 2010, United played Hull City at Old Trafford. Wayne Rooney scored four goals in a display of brilliant skill and raw power. That was one abiding memory; the other was of much of the Stretford End decked out in the green and gold of Newton Heath. For a full ninety minutes they harked back to the origins of United, twirling green and gold scarves, and chanting, 'We love United, we hate the Glazers'.

Such was the outpouring of feeling that Ferguson intervened. He tried to pour water on the flames but failed; noticeably he did not leap directly to the Glazers' defence.

In his programme notes, the manager wrote: 'The family of Manchester United is under pressure as a result of all the issues and controversies surrounding the ownership and financial situation of our club. Everyone is entitled to their opinion, and to express disapproval if they don't like what they see around them. I'm not slow to express disapproval myself if there is something I don't agree with – even in the boardroom with the directors. But once I walk out of the meeting, I get on with my job as manager of the team. Some of our fans are clearly unhappy with the financial position, but we mustn't allow the situation to become divisive. The danger, as I see it, is that we could be presented as being split, which could be harmful and inaccurate because I believe the vast majority of United fans are behind us. This is not about stifling criticism; it's simply a plea to stand together rather than take action that will damage ourselves more than anyone else. Manchester United is bigger than me, the players, the directors, officials and the fans and, particularly at this critical stage of our season, we need to pull in the same direction.'

Fergie's plea was ignored. Duncan Drasdo, of the Manchester United Supporters Trust, responded: 'He talks about the Manchester United family and he's right; all strands of the family must come together to accelerate the change of ownership because we certainly don't see the Glazers as part of the United family. I thought Fergie's words smacked of a conciliatory gesture to the supporters and that he understood our concerns. He has not defended the Glazers in his notes!'

What was riling the fans was the nagging thought that with the Glazers in charge, United had become a 'selling club'. At Fulham, we're used to seeing our best players snapped up by bigger, richer clubs – Louis Saha, Ryan Sessegnon, Harvey Elliott, Fábio Carvalho, to name just four recent Fulham sales. The roll call of those we adored, who we revered and sang of as 'one of our own', only to see them go, is long. While we're resigned to it, every time one departs, we hurt.

Supporters at the glamour clubs don't know what that's like. If their manager wants a player, they go out and buy them – frequently from a club like Fulham.

The previous summer, soon after concluding a world-record shirt sponsorship with Aon for a reported £80 million, United had sold Cristiano Ronaldo to Real Madrid, also for £80 million. The Portuguese superstar had won everything there was to win at United. He'd been persuaded to stay on once before but he could not be held back any longer. He was popular at United, with the backroom staff as well as his teammates and fans, but there was no keeping him.

Ronaldo could also be fitful in terms of performance levels and, on a positive note, the belief among the fans was that the proceeds from the sale of him and Carlos Tévez, another transferred star, would enable Ferguson to buy two or three more consistent, world-class replacements.

But that hadn't happened. Ferguson's recent buys had been the far-from-inspiring, injury-prone Michael Owen, Antonio Valencia and Gabriel Obertan. The Ronaldo cash remained largely unspent. The fans speculated that the money was required elsewhere, possibly nabbed by the Glazers to help pay off their borrowings.

So unrelenting were the claims that, for once, United broke cover, issuing a statement in January 2010: 'Manchester United is the most profitable football club in the world. Last year, on a record turnover of £278 million, the club made a record cash profit of £91 million. Interest payments were £41 million and wages accounted for less than half the turnover. The recent bond issue has been very successful and provides the club with certainty in its interest payments, as well as great flexibility with the removal of bank covenants. The cash from the sale of Cristiano Ronaldo is available for Sir Alex to spend and it will be spent on players who are available for purchase and who the manager thinks can improve the squad, not to prove to pundits that it exists.'

It had zero effect. The City of London financier Keith Harris, interviewed by the BBC, made the arresting claim that 'Seventy-five pence of every pound that [Manchester United] fans are spending is now going to the Glazers either for themselves or to pay debts.' It wasn't strictly true, but as mud went, it stuck pretty well. Ordinary United fans were donning green and gold in ever greater numbers, reciting anti-Glazer slogans, waving abusive placards and banners; worse, some wealthier, well-connected followers had been discreetly meeting and discussing whether they could do anything to unseat the owners.

These were people who – schooled in stellar careers in finance and business – were used to coming up with solutions, who liked to find a way if there was a way to be found.

Harris, in his BBC interview in January 2010, had hinted at their existence when he mentioned that a group of investors, the 'Red Knights', were contemplating buying out the Glazers. 'It's too early to say how much money would have to be raised. I would hope that there would be sufficient money in addition to that to show the Glazers they could take a profit and put the ownership into more caring hands.'

A few weeks later, on 28 February 2010, the Carling Cup Final at Wembley between Aston Villa and United was notable for the tens of thousands of Reds donning green and gold – so much so that you looked for the team wearing green and gold in vain. *The Wall Street Journal* commented: 'First sports fans wanted their teams to win. Then they wanted fancy new stadiums with sleek amenities and gourmet food. Now they want ownership to have a healthier balance sheet. The family of American businessman Malcolm Glazer, owner of the English Premier League's fabled Manchester United club, is locked in a strange battle of wills with part of the soccer club's rabid fan base.'

My phone went. The voice on the end was that of Jim O'Neill, the chief economist at Goldman Sachs. He wanted to meet, later that day if possible; there was something he wanted to run by me.

We met at The Kensington Wine Rooms at the top of Kensington Church Street. Over glasses of a fine white Burgundy, he cut to the chase. 'It's early days and definitely not yet for publication. A group of us is thinking of buying United. The idea is that we'll each put in £10 million-plus. We'll buy the club and have some left over to buy players. We're calling ourselves the Red Knights. What do you think?'

All I could think of was my own experience of fundraising for a charity and for a large, new theatre. It wasn't the same but it's what entered my head. Wealthy folk would say they'd come in, that they would put money in or sponsor this or that, and then, next, there would be their lawyers on the phone, wanting to see the terms. 'You're entering a minefield,' I said. 'They will fight among themselves. Their lawyers will want to know if they're getting seats on the board, how it's going to work. Good luck with that.'

Then I asked if there were enough rich Reds out there. The last published figure, an estimate for United's worth, was £1.2 billion. Could he raise that amount? 'Easy,' he replied. 'Have you any idea how many wealthy United supporters there are?'

But they would be doing it for love, I guessed, not to make a profit, not immediately anyway. He nodded. He was still confident there was enough of them.

What, he asked, did I suppose the press would say? This was what he really wanted to know. There, I was confident: they'd love it; they'd never liked the Glazers.

Where was his friend Fergie in all this? Here, O'Neill was not so forthcoming. He and Ferguson were pals, but he said it was difficult for Ferguson – the manager was, after all, employed by the Glazers; he was on their payroll.

The Red Knights could work, I agreed. We clinked glasses. He would call me and let me know how he was getting on. Subsequently, Mark Kleinman of *Sky News* received a tip-off that the Red Knights had been meeting in London to discuss a £1 billion bid for Manchester United.

I'd known Jim O'Neill since 2001, ever since he came up with the acronym BRIC to describe the rising economies of Brazil, Russia, India, China.

He had been born Terence James O'Neill in 1957, and grew up in Gatley in Manchester. 'One side of the road was Cheshire,' he said, mimicking a posh Cheshire accent. 'The other side was Manchester,' he added, reverting to his usual broad Mancunian.

He's blessed with a dry, sharp, self-deprecating wit and a direct, often irreverent manner. He's no respecter of fools or pomposity. A typical Manc, all told. His was a working-class background – his father was a postman from Moss Side. He had three sisters. 'Dad left school at fourteen and he was determined we'd all get a good education.'

From primary school in nearby Wythenshawe, O'Neill was offered a place at William Hulme's, the nearest fee-paying school. He turned it down – 'because they didn't play football' – in favour of Burnage, the comprehensive attended by Noel and Liam Gallagher (both City supporters; best not to mention them in the United die-hard O'Neill's presence).

'I didn't take education that seriously,' he said with a rueful grin. Football was his passion. It still is – he watches United home and away whenever he can. He was a director of the club for a brief period, leaving when the Glazers arrived, and has season tickets, sitting with the same friends from his youth (if he can't go, he leaves his tickets behind the bar of a pub near Old Trafford for a mate to use).

He chose Sheffield University because he was keen on football. 'I got drunk and played football for the university.' And he studied economics.

He moved to Goldman from Swiss Bank Corporation in 1995. 'Goldman got wind I was unhappy and made me the offer of a partnership.' As is the case today, Goldman rarely hired people directly as partners. 'It was a huge honour. I was nervous about joining.'

He was not detained just by BRICs. O'Neill established a formidable reputation for correctly predicting currency movements relative to the US dollar. He also displayed an aptitude for devising new models to approach different problems. Gavyn Davies, his predecessor, described him as 'the top foreign-exchange economist anywhere in the world in the past decade'. *Business Week*, the US business magazine, hailed O'Neill as 'Goldman's rock star'.

O'Neill was fortunate enough to be a partner when Goldman floated in 1999. The shares he received then, plus his pay packet down the years, made him extremely wealthy. In 2015 he was made a Treasury minister in David Cameron's government and a life peer, Baron O'Neill of Gatley. These days, he's an investor, philanthropist, pushing the Northern Powerhouse project aimed at revitalizing the economy of the North of England, crazy about Manchester United.

O'Neill's forthright style – once a Manc, always a Manc – had previously got him into hot water. During the Woodward roadshow selling the bond, O'Neill was at a conference in China and told a newswire what he thought. 'There's too much leverage going on with Manchester United, it's not a good thing. I'm not a buyer of the bond.' Hardly earth-shattering, given his well-known animus towards the Glazers and his love of the club. But then O'Neill's employer, Goldman Sachs, was part of the syndicate of banks that was advising on the bond sale.

The original Red Knights were O'Neill, Paul Marshall, co-founder of the Marshall Wace hedge fund, and Guy Dawson, Nomura banker and founder of Tricorn partners, the corporate advisory firm. Mark Rawlinson of Freshfields was back, supplying legal advice, as was Finsbury on PR.

After the *Sky News* story, there was saturation media coverage, with the result, says Rawlinson, that 'people were phoning up, saying "I want to be a Red Knight, I want to stump up £10 million."'

In no time at all, he and O'Neill were confident, they could get eighty names or pledges worth £800 million. 'Money wasn't the problem, we could get £800 million in equity and we could get the same again in debt,' says Rawlinson.

Debt? This was one problem with the Red Knights, that they were City whizzes, not so different from the reviled Glazers themselves, who were prepared to use similar, clever financing techniques as the Glazers. What they were offering that was different was that they were not the Glazers and that they adored the club, they were true fans. They would not be absentee landlords.

Stefan Szymanski, a leading expert in the economics of sport, wrote: 'There's no doubt that the frontmen for the Red Knights are genuine United loyalists, but are they only the squires? Given that United are known as the Red Devils, it seems appropriate that the Glazers are becoming the most demonized owners in football history. But it is unlikely that getting rid of them will divorce the profit motive from owning Manchester United. What seems surprising about much of the opposition to the Glazers is the presumption that they care less than the fans about the club's success. How could they ever make a profit without it? Perhaps more than any other potential owners, the Glazers depend on the team winning. If the Red Knights triumphed it would require a colossal investment. A shrewd supporter should ask this: either the Red Knights are simply altruists or if not, how on earth will they get a return on their investment?'

There was contrasting treatment between the business and sports pages – the former eulogizing the financial credentials of the Red Knights, the latter being critical. Martin Samuel, doyen of sports writers, wrote in the *Daily Mail*: 'O'Neill is the head of the Red Knights, a group of City experts – no, stop giggling at the back – and Manchester United fans who are discussing the overthrow of the Glazers at Old Trafford. The irony is that Sir Alex Ferguson seems content with the current owners. So, on one side, the man who came up with BRIC; on the other, the man who came up with two European Cups, eleven league titles, five FA Cups, four League Cups, one European Cup Winners' Cup, one World Club Championship, one

Intercontinental Cup and a European Super Cup. There is only one Red Knight that needs to be kept happy in Manchester.'

Sharply pointed, but not necessarily fair. Ferguson and O'Neill were close, and the United manager was constrained in what he could say.

Keith Harris, who was not a leading Red Knight but was closely following events, came up with a proposal of his own: the City financier called for a boycott of season tickets. At this, Gill and Ferguson had something to say.

Here was David Gill: 'Keith Harris will go anywhere with some publicity around, that's his modus operandi, but his track record in football isn't anything to write home about. But these are credible people and they do what they think is in the best interests of the club . . . Their idea of having twenty, thirty or forty very wealthy people owning and running Manchester United, I just don't know it would work in practice. The better-run clubs have clear single decision-making that is quick and efficient . . . What the Glazers have done is let me and my team run the business, they've let Sir Alex Ferguson run the football side.'

Ferguson, when informed about the proposed boycott, said sarcastically: 'Now that is a great idea. And that's come from an intelligent guy, has it? There's no chance of that. I don't mind people protesting. I went on an apprentices' march myself when I was younger, so protesting is not a problem for me.' What Ferguson did not like, he said, was if protesting affected the team's performance. 'I've no issue with the Red Knights. I'm quite friendly with a couple of them and don't deny them their right to protest. If they want to try to buy the club, it's entirely up to them.'

The Sun was ruder. 'Who will actually run the club if they gain control? Red Knights would boldly put themselves up for that talk on the basis that the whole thing was their idea. Let's get this straight. Nine fans want to buy the club with other people's money.'

Despite the reservations, the Red Knights seized the popular imagination. They were fans, locally born and bred in many cases, super-successful, and there was an undoubted aura attached to the name of a Manc from Goldman Sachs, even though the powerhouse bank was not involved.

The Red Knights knew how to play the system, to manipulate the media. Up popped a story in the *Observer*, saying that 'Senior City financiers allied to the wealthy consortium planning a takeover of Manchester United claim Sir Alex Ferguson is supporting the controversial bid. Several key sources have told the *Observer* that they believe that the Old Trafford manager would be prepared to invest his own money in the club if the bid by the group known as the "Red Knights" were to succeed.'

One source told the paper it was a 'killer blow' against the Glazers; another said, 'We all know we have his support, that he likes the people involved but we can't embarrass him.'

In all likelihood, in private, Ferguson had indicated his support – the Red Knights, O'Neill in particular, were his friends – but the *Observer* story was a step too far, in public he had no choice other than to deny it.

The Red Knights turned up the pressure. They announced that Nomura, the Japanese investment bank, and employer of Dawson, would be drawing up a formal bid document. Details soon leaked: fifty investors would be putting in £10 million each; another £250 million would be raised by issuing securities to United supporters in the UK; the £500 million bond would be retained. The club would have a notional value of £1.25 billion.

There were signs of tension, though. One newspaper report spoke of 'egos and testosterone' among the individual backers. O'Neill was all for them doing it entirely out of love and support for United;

some, though, were said to have extra motivation, including seeking seats on the board and dividends.

'The money was not the problem,' says Rawlinson. 'People would always lend us the money. The problem was that the Glazers were not willing to sell.'

Were the Glazers actually prepared to sell? The answer was a resounding 'no'.

As Joel said to Nayani when the latter first phoned to tell him about the Red Knights, 'The message is simple. Manchester United is absolutely not for sale. We are in it for the long-term, we love owning the club.'

Says Rawlinson: 'The Glazers refused to engage with us. We had no way of getting them to engage. We did not know what United was worth because the Glazers would not tell us. Normally you would say, "We can go to X but if you want us to go to Y then you have to share information with us." They would not do that; they were not interested.'

He adds: 'Their silence was saying to us, "We've only owned the club for four or five years, we like it, the TV income is taking off, so fuck off."'

The assumption was that the Glazers hated the protests and the personal attacks, loathed being in the public eye, and that – faced with a serious bid from a bunch of supporters, one that ticked the boxes PR-wise – they would sell. It was never checked out though. It was a reasonable stance to take, but for it to work, the Glazers had to behave as normal investors might. A normal investor would say 'enough, to hell with it, I'm out of here, show me the money'. But in that sense, the Glazers were not normal – they were prepared to put up with the opprobrium, the personal attacks, as the *price* for owning Manchester United.

What an asset they owned. It was decided that after months of horrendous press, the Glazers should go on the offensive and stress to journalists that the club was in great shape. As usual they would not speak to the media themselves, so Woodward was dispatched to hold fourteen forty-five-minute sessions with influential reporters and commentators on the business of sport.

He was instructed, in answer to the question about the Red Knights, to keep it short and sweet: 'The club is not for sale. No comment on the Red Knights.'

When it came to the facts and figures, he was the opposite. He poured out boast after boast: the club had 113,000 members who got first refusal on matchday tickets, so if there was a boycott of season tickets more than enough of them would step forward and snap up the seats; more than a million United credit cards had been sold in South Korea alone and the club was paid a royalty for each one; Saudi Telecom expected to sign 50,000 Manchester United supporters in the first year of their exclusive partnership with the club, in reality they got 400,000 – in just the first week; and on it went.

The message was clear: there was no way the Glazers were selling. Manchester United was not for sale. The Red Knights had no choice than to try to retreat with honour. In June 2010, they said they were ending their bid but 'we will only attempt to purchase the club at a sensible price.'

At Old Trafford, it was business as usual. United versus Stoke saw a new round of protests, more wearing of the green and gold, fans clashing with police in front of the East Stand, a smoke bomb being set off in the Megastore, stink bombs let off near the directors' entrance and a plane flying over Old Trafford trailing a 'Glazers Out' banner and a number to text in support.

But compared with what they were making from owning United, and what they stood to make in the future, the Glazers were prepared to withstand whatever was hurled in their direction.

ELEVEN

New York, New York

While the Glazers seemed impervious to the campaign waged against them, they were also seemingly unbothered by another consequence of their ownership of Manchester United – the debts of £700 million they'd accrued in order to buy the club.

For that they had to thank Malcolm Glazer, who realized early on in his career that by borrowing from others, you could do bigger deals, repay them, and be left with whatever it was you'd bought. Better still, you could put the security for the debt on the business or asset you were buying so the risk wasn't even yours.

For someone like me, who grew up in a household where my parents could not abide debt of any sort, who worried if they borrowed even a tiny amount, Glazer's approach was anathema. As a generation brought up in the war years and on tales of the Great Depression, my folks would have regarded it as dangerous and irresponsible; 'not right', I can hear my mother saying.

Malcolm Glazer had also known straitened circumstances and he loathed spending money himself, but if the cash was someone else's, that was OK by him. If only we'd had his audacity, we too – you too – could have owned Manchester United.

In October 2010, the two faces of United under the Glazers came again to the fore. Thanks to Woodward's Black Box and the driving of deals, the club's commercial revenue climbed. In 2005, it was £48.7 million. In 2010, it was £81.4 million. That year, annual operating profits exceeded £100 million for the first time. But the club disclosed a loss of £80 million, largely thanks to charges from the bond refinancing of £67 million and the failed interest-rate swap. *The Daily Telegraph* headline was 'Operating profits at Old Trafford top £100 million', whereas *The Times* chose: 'Anti-Glazer protests set to be revived by £67 million loss for United'.

Chief executive David Gill briefed away, saying the club had amassed a cash mountain of £165 million and had not spent the money from Ronaldo's sale and was under no pressure to sell anyone else. Writing in *The Daily Telegraph*, Paul Kelso commented: 'The accounts published yesterday demonstrate once again that, despite the objections of the supporters ranged against them, the massively leveraged business model they imposed on the club is doing what they intended. A debt burden of £700 million may make some of us queasy but not apparently the Glazers.'

Joel Glazer was, though, perfectly capable of intervening personally when it mattered, when the club's commercial reputation and standing were threatened, something that came to a head with Wayne Rooney, soon after those results were posted.

The club's biggest star wanted out. His people were telling the newspapers that contract talks had broken down, that the twenty-four-year-old England international was rowing with Ferguson. Rather than be seen to be demanding and only interested in lucre, his desire to leave was spun against the Glazers. His angling to go reflected concern about the club's lack of ambition. Henry Winter in *The Daily Telegraph* did not hold back: 'The Glazers will dispute the allegation they are "leeching" off United but the recent annual accounts, with interest repayments gorging on profits, makes grim reading for United fans . . . To lose one star like Cristiano Ronaldo could be considered a misfortune. To lose another, in Rooney, looks more than carelessness; it looks like the dreaded hand of debt holding United and Ferguson back. The shame of the Glazers' regime is now fully exposed.'

Rooney stuck the boot in, saying, 'I met with David Gill last week and he did not give me any of the assurances I was seeking about the future squad . . . about the continued ability of the club to attract the top players in the world.'

Joel had always valued Rooney as a player, but this was also damaging in another direction: talk of no money, of no ambition, could jeopardize future sponsorships and profitability. Joel picked up the phone and reassured Rooney about his plans for the club and offered him £200,000 a week. Rooney stayed.

More often, though, the Glazers would remain behind their wall of secrecy, inviting questions and providing no answers.

Towards the end of 2010, the £220 million of PIK notes was dogging their smooth ascent. As if to highlight the cavalier use of the PIKs, the notes were now accruing interest at a whopping 16.25 per cent a year. This had increased, because under the tough terms forced on the Glazers by the hedge funds, the club's overall debt now exceeded its earnings by more than five times, so up went the interest. The recently completed bond issue, by contrast, had cost the Glazers only 9 per cent.

Then, they announced the PIKs had gone. As if by magic, the notes had been redeemed. Just like that. The club stated that none of the Ronaldo cash had been used. As to how, exactly, they'd been paid back, the stock, robotic Glazer answer of 'no comment' applied. This invited speculation that the Glazers had sold off a stake in the club to raise the funds to pay them off, or that they'd sold investments in the US or they'd taken out another loan at a lower rate. No light was shed. The very private owners preferred to keep everyone in the dark.

'They found a way of repaying them,' said someone who studied the Glazer finances – as far he was able. 'I don't think it was in the UK. I suspect they borrowed more money against assets they owned outside the club. Who knows? They've never said.'

Removal of the PIKs paved the way for the Glazers to realize some cash, for the club to float once more on the stock market. Even though the family had said they had no intention of selling, the Red Knights' interest in buying United had caused some of the siblings to consider what United was worth.

Of Malcolm's six children, Joel, Avram and Bryan were most interested in running and growing United. Kevin, Edward and Darcie, less so. The latter trio are thought to have been keen to cash in their assets. In 2011, the Glazers explored obtaining a listing on a stock market in Asia, where United had its biggest, most passionate following – either in Singapore or Hong Kong. They were looking to raise £400–600 million.

At first, they picked out Hong Kong. Their appetite was whetted by successful floats of upmarket western brands, such as luggage firm Samsonite. Luxury fashion house Prada was another yardstick. Then they decided to switch to Singapore, which was prepared to 'fast-track' a flotation. In September 2011, they secured approval from the Singapore Stock Exchange to list United's shares. They said they were looking to raise up to £635 million to pay off some of the club's debts by selling about 25 per cent of the parent company's shares. That's what they said, although a large slug of the cash was bound for the Glazers themselves.

Their timing was awry. The bull market had passed and conditions were turning volatile, not a good moment to be bringing a company to market. In spring 2012, Graff Diamonds, the British gems retailer, had to abandon its $1 billion share sale in Hong Kong. So even if the Glazers were to succeed in getting the flotation away, they might not get the price they wanted.

Another complication was that, typically, the Glazers wanted to sell the shares but guarantee they kept control. Presumably, the other three brothers were not prepared to let go. The ruse they and their advisors came up with was to split the shares into voting and non-voting shares, which would allow the family, owners of the voting shares, to retain full control.

Come June 2012, and they'd moved the crosshairs again, to New York. Bloomberg claimed the switch was aimed at securing a higher valuation. But there was another reason: Malcolm and his family wanted to pursue the two classes of shares idea, to retain control, and two classes of shares were more common in New York flotations and more acceptable to US investors than elsewhere.

The United shares would be split into A and B classes; the A shares would be offered for sale to investors on the New York Stock Exchange, while the Glazer family retained ownership of the B shares, which carried ten times the voting rights of the A shares.

In July 2012, in a 121-page filing with the Securities and Exchange Commission, United said it was listing on the New York Stock Exchange. The club said it was selling 16.7 million shares at between $16 and $20 each.

But it also revealed that revenue had fallen in the last year. United had been knocked out of the Champions League at the group stage, leading to a 11–13 per cent drop in broadcasting revenues – down to £102–4 million. Total income for the year to June was between £315 million and £320 million, down as much as 5 per cent from the previous year.

The Glazers, however, cited a new valuation from *Forbes*: $2.23 billion, up more than $1 billion in little more than two years.

Buried in the 121 pages was the disclosure that the Glazers had reorganized the ownership structure of United, via the Cayman Islands. Manchester United Limited, as a Cayman Islands company, would, the document says, remain owned by the 'linear descendants'– the five sons and one daughter – of Malcolm Glazer. Not only would buyers of the non-voting shares have no say, but there was never any intention even to pay them a regular dividend. Their only chance of a profitable return would be to realize a future gain, should the company registered in the Cayman Islands sell the shares.

It's harder to think of anywhere so far removed from Old Trafford and the nearby Manchester Ship Canal than the clear blue water of the Cayman Islands. Discovered by Christopher Columbus in 1503, when his ship was blown off course, by 1530 the islands had been named the 'Caimanas' – derived from the native word for the crocodiles that used to dwell there. The earliest settlers arrived in the mid-seventeenth century; they were deserters from the British Army in Jamaica, and inhabitants still speak English with a Caymanian flair. Even though rope-making (using the local silver thatch palm) and catboat racing are the main island activities boasted about in the tourist literature, in reality the islands are famed principally for international financial services, enabling people from across the globe to hide their wealth.

Those who invest here might do so because they shouldn't have the money, it doesn't belong to them, they got it illegally; or they might not want others – prying relatives, employers, business associates or tax inspectors – to know they have it. Cayman is happy to be that safe haven. The importance of the trade is obvious in George

Town, the capital. The flash glass buildings set back from the shops selling flip-flops, hats and sun creams along the waterfront aren't hotels, but offices, workplaces for accountants, lawyers and 'wealth' advisors.

There are 100,000 companies in Cayman as a whole, but there is no sign of the companies' physical presence. That's because they only exist in Cayman on paper. They're shell companies. They pop up right across the world, as the owners of apartments in New York and London, names behind villas and yachts and, yes, shares in companies that own football clubs.

When Hurricane Ivan hurtled towards the Cayman Islands in 2004, a fleet of light aircraft took off from Cayman for Miami. They were carrying computer hard disks, storing details of a large slice of the world's money. When Ivan had blown its way through, the planes flew them all straight back again.

Cayman levies no income tax on individuals and no corporate tax of any kind. Companies registered there do not need to file a tax return, so it's a secret how much they make.

The former UK business secretary, Sir Vince Cable, called such locations 'sunny places for shady people.' *Sunny places for shady people*. Under the Glazers, Manchester United called it home.

The document shared with the Securities and Exchange Commission also revealed that United had signed a new deal to have its shirts sponsored by US car maker Chevrolet. The automobile firm took over from Aon, and the sponsorship was for seven years, starting in 2014–15, for an undisclosed amount.

If that looked good – this was the first time ever a US automaker had ventured into European sport – and the timing was impeccable, the actual numbers that reached the market were jaw-droppingly spectacular: $559 million or £64 million a year for seven years. That was an incredible sum, breaking all sorts of records. Even within

General Motors, owner of Chevrolet, it made no sense and rather, it set off alarm bells. Suspicions were raised as to what had really taken place, that the Chevrolet sponsorship was merely a carrot for US investors, used to excite their interest and get the flotation away.

Within forty-eight hours of the sum being revealed, Joel Ewanick, GM's marketing chief who led the negotiations, such as they were, left the company. GM sources said he failed to disclose the deal's full cost to the car-maker. Ewanick 'failed to meet the expectations the company has of an employee', said GM.

Chevy was looking to push its marketing and sales internationally and was a well-known US domestic brand but it had no overseas presence. In the UK, its profile was virtually non-existent. One consequence of the contract was that United players and staff were obliged to turn up at the Carrington training ground and be photographed behind the wheel of a Chevrolet. Compared to the players' usual, and better-known, high-performance Ferraris, Lamborghinis, Porsches and Aston Martins, the sight of the stars driving mundane Chevrolets appeared incongruous.

Woodward and his team had sold to Chevrolet the prospect of United's global reach, the hundreds of millions of viewers on TV, 76 million followers on Facebook and 31.6 million on Twitter.

'It really opened the doors at a time for American brands to see the value of international soccer, which is such a global phenomenon,' said Randy Bernstein, CEO of Playfly Premier Partnerships, a leading sports consulting firm specializing in sponsorships.

Chevrolet was now the primary shirt sponsor for the team, with its iconic golden bowtie emblem on the front of the team jerseys. Chevy also created the 'Chevrolet China Cup' for United's pre-season tour. As always, Asia was the great driver for the Americans, for the Glazers and for Chevrolet – they were told repeatedly that the continent was home to almost half of soccer's global fan base and would-be owners of Chevrolet cars and trucks. The 121-pager boasted that 'over 5 million items of Manchester United branded licensed products were sold in the last year'. The club had opened an office in Asia to try to attract new sponsors there and was in the process of opening another one in North America. United had launched retail stores in Singapore, Macao, India and Thailand to try to capitalize on its popularity in Asia, and intended to open more.

Europe was also the other main draw. 'I believe that the borders for marketing and advertising have come down precipitously over the last number of years,' Bernstein said. 'American companies are starting to advertise globally, [and] global companies headquartered outside the US are starting to advertise here.'

Ewanick stuck to the script even after losing his job, saying that the partnership would bring Chevrolet increased brand exposure, purchase consideration and awareness around the world worth 'over four times' the sponsorship's cost.

Said Ewanick: 'The way this was going to work overtime, I would say that for the amount of money we were talking about, it was the biggest no-brainer I've seen.'

It clearly worked to an extent, as United and Chevy agreed a six-month extension before the deal ended in December 2021. 'Too much money, not enough focus,' Bernstein said of the sponsorship. 'But a decade later, you look at it as not that far-fetched as people at the time felt.'

Was the Chevy deal inflated to make the share sale a success? Arguably, the IPO (initial public offering) would have been successful without Chevrolet. In that sense, there was no pressing urgency to do the Chevy deal in order to get the shares away. But there's also no doubt it certainly helped.

And if it was not so expensive for Chevrolet, why did Ewanick depart so abruptly?

In March 2021 Chevrolet was replaced by global tech company Team Viewer. The German software firm secured a five-year shirt sponsorship deal worth £235 million or £47 million a year – an annual drop of £17 million on the partnership with Chevrolet. 'There's no doubt there was close linkage between the New York Stock Exchange flotation and the sealing of the deal with Chevrolet,' said a leading protestor in the City. 'It's my belief they could not have done the share sale without the Chevrolet contract. The timing was too good and the amount – there was something not right about it.'

The 'strategy' for United was set out, specifying how the Glazer family intended to 'increase our revenue and profitability, by expanding our high-growth businesses that leverage our brand, global community and marketing infrastructure'.

The Glazers intended to develop areas including 'global and regional sponsors, retail, merchandising and product licensing, exploiting new media and mobile opportunities, enhancing the reach and distribution of our broadcasting rights [via United's MUTV channel] and diversifying revenue and improving margins'.

The document proclaimed: 'We believe that we are one of the world's most recognizable global brands with a community of 659 million followers' (up from 333 million in only a few years); and it predicted that football's popularity and profitability around the world would continue to grow.

It set out risk factors that investors should consider before buying the shares. These included warnings about maintaining football's popularity and crowds at Old Trafford holding up despite the recession; and that United's debts, wholly imposed by the Glazers' original takeover, 'could adversely affect our financial health and competitive position'.

For the first time, the document publicly spelt out that the debt, still at £423 million, despite the £500 million United had paid out since 2005, could affect the club's ability to compete for players and soak up cash. This was the impact of the Glazer debts which their representatives had always denied.

The Glazers were to receive half the sale proceeds. Duncan Drasdo, chief executive of the Manchester United Supporters Trust, called it 'another slap in the face'.

Some investors were equally unimpressed. 'They are getting a shoddy deal,' said Michael Jarman, chief equity strategist at H2O Markets, an ex-professional footballer and a United fan himself. 'Investors are not idiots and there is simply no value in the company. The Glazers want to have their cake and eat it – the share structure shows they want to retain complete and utter control.'

He said there were plenty of other more attractive investments, where shareholders get a dividend and the chance of capital growth.

Jarman said that 'debt free, Manchester United is a good business', but it was clearly not debt free. As a result, he argued the club was massively overvalued.

Then there was a setback. The planned IPO in New York had to be temporarily postponed because of volatile US markets.

Once conditions had calmed, United was back, announcing it would sell the shares at $14 each, below the hoped-for $16–$20 range.

On 10 August 2012, the New York Stock Exchange's opening bell was rung by Joel and Avie Glazer, while Woodward, Gill and other club executives looked on and applauded. Traders wore United shirts and the NYSE's floor was covered in Astroturf.

Stefan Szymanski, the expert in sports economics from the University of Michigan, said that – even with the lower share price – Manchester United was still 'the most valuable sports franchise in the world, and the American investors are looking at this as a franchise.

'Given the way they have tried to sell this off, with no voting rights, no dividends, and limited disclosure [of financial information], it is a testament to the strength of Manchester United as a football club and its popularity internationally, that they have managed to do this well,' he said.

The shares began trading under the ticker name MANU – Tony O'Neill would not have been impressed. Ten per cent of the club was sold in the IPO, raising $233 million (£150 million), a third less than hoped. The shares started well, rising slightly to $14.05 per share, before slipping back. They closed the day at the offer price of $14 each, valuing the club at $2.3 billion.

The club reduced the share price because more investors were comfortable with that figure. Most top-drawer institutional investors were keen on $14 and that appealed to the Glazer longer-term view, to build a more heavyweight shareholder base.

One surprise investor was billionaire George Soros, whose investment company bought 3.1 million class A shares or 1.9 per cent of the club, valued at $40.7 million.

In May 2013, Sir Alex Ferguson's retirement was carried as front-page news by thirty-eight newspapers around the world, including *The New York Times*. In the UK, some papers produced 10–12-page special supplements to commemorate the occasion.

Ferguson had come close to going previously, back in late 2001, but had changed his mind. Then he was flush with the success of Rock of Gibraltar. He said he would be going at the end of that season. 'When I leave Manchester United, I'm finished with football for ever. Full stop. So, yes, I will walk away. I've been doing this for twenty-eight years and that is a long time. The important thing in life is to count your blessings and not to think that you can go on for ever.'

Then, on Christmas Day 2001, his wife Cathy and their sons talked him out of it. 'We've just had a meeting,' said Cathy, coming into the room as Ferguson was on the sofa, nodding off watching television. 'We've decided. You're not retiring. One, your health is good. Two, I'm not having you in the house. And three, you're too young anyway.' He would stay as manager for another eleven years.

This time, though, it was for real. He was off. He would remain an ambassador to the club and a director, but otherwise he was gone. Ferguson agreed a new contract that would see him paid a reported £2 million a year by the Glazers. For that he would attend matches and club events and press the flesh. He would also, it went without saying, remain silent and do nothing to jeopardize his relationship with them.

He would not be on hand to guide his successor. 'Alex felt he was due the retirement he deserved and he didn't want to be like Sir Matt, who hung around and interfered. Alex did not show up at Carrington for a long time afterwards,' said someone close to the club.

His departure was heavily choreographed. It had been coming for a while – he was now seventy-one years old and it was not unexpected. The players presented him with a 1941 Rolex from the year he was born, with the time set at 3.03 p.m., the time he had been delivered as a baby in Glasgow. He also received a book of photographs covering his reign at United, with his grandchildren and family across the centre-spread.

He'd decided to formally quit around Christmas 2012. Cathy had lost her sister, Bridget, and was struggling with the bereavement. 'Joel understood. We agreed to meet in New York, where he tried to talk me out of retiring. I told him I appreciated the effort he was making and thanked him for his support. He expressed his gratitude for all my work.'

In New York they talked about his successor. 'With no prospect of a change in my thinking, the discussion turned to who might replace me. There was a unanimous agreement – David Moyes was the man.'

This was Ferguson, writing in his book *My Autobiography*. Given the Glazers' lack of football nous and Ferguson's slice of it, quite what he meant by 'unanimous' was difficult to say. Probably, Ferguson proposed Moyes and they agreed, which would make it unanimous.

On 3 May 2013, Moyes was shopping in Manchester with his wife, Pamela, visiting a jeweller to get the strap adjusted on the watch she had bought for his fiftieth birthday, when Moyes's phone went. It was Ferguson. 'Can you come over to the house?' said the United manager.

Half an hour later, Moyes was at Ferguson's home in Wilmslow. Ferguson made him a cup of tea then got straight to the point: 'David, I'm retiring, you're going to be the new manager of Manchester United.'

It was done. There and then. Moyes, who was managing Everton, would be crazy to turn down the opportunity to run the biggest club in the world, one with the greatest history, the largest following and a team full of stars.

They did talk about the job that would need doing. United had just clinched the Premiership title for the thirteenth time in twenty seasons. Some of the team were ageing, there was the need for a refresh, the academy was not producing the stream of first-team players like it should (they had let it fall behind academies elsewhere, notably those at Manchester City and Chelsea), but otherwise all was good. 'Within the hour', wrote Jonathan Northcroft in *The Times*, 'Moyes was leaving Wilmslow, the biggest job in football his.'

Moyes then met Woodward and the Glazers to finalize terms. A six-year contract was his, deliberately chosen as the same length of time it took Ferguson to win the English title after arriving from Aberdeen in Scotland in 1986.

Writes Ferguson: 'The Glazers liked David. Right away they were impressed by him. The first point they will have noticed is that he is a straight talker. It's a virtue to be straightforward about yourself.' He felt certain that 'David would have no trouble embracing our traditions. He was a fine judge of talent and laid on some marvellous football at Everton when he was allowed to sign a higher class of player.'

Whilst there was no great record of achievement behind him, Moyes was generally thought to have done a good job in straitened circumstances at Everton. This was his shot at the big time.

He was entirely in Ferguson's image. They were fellow Scots, but more than that: their families actually knew each other. Said Ferguson: 'I knew his family background. His father was a coach at Drumchapel, where I played as a lad. David Moyes senior. They have a good family feel about them.'

Added Ferguson, suggesting the family relationship was not an influence while managing to imply that it was: 'I'm not saying that's a reason to hire someone but you like to see good foundations in someone appointed to such high office.'

Avie Glazer broke with tradition and did say something, hinting there was no one else, that no other manager had been looked at. It was all down to Ferguson's choice. 'The search for a new manager has been very short. Alex was very clear with his recommendation.'

On 8 May 2013, the official statement that Ferguson was leaving sent the shares in New York down 5 per cent. United was now a quoted company yet it was behaving like a private one. Most publicly listed companies would not have appointed someone to such an important role in such a cavalier fashion – for such a senior, vital post, one they knew was falling vacant, they would have done their homework, their due diligence. Executive search and psychometric experts would be drafted in to assist in the quest. Most football clubs are not listed, so replacing the manager is not conducted so rigorously. But United was quoted, investors had put their cash into the stock, so arguably it should have been – except United wasn't really quoted either; total control resided elsewhere.

There had been another bombshell for the club. David Gill was also departing. He'd told Ferguson back in February that he would be standing down as chief executive at the end of the season. 'Bloody hell, David,' said Ferguson.

So, effectively the company COO, Ferguson, and the CEO, Gill, both went together. No attempt appears to have been made to stagger their departures. On both sides of United, playing and non-playing, new brooms would be deployed simultaneously. In Gill's case, the club went public straight away, in February 2013, saying he would be leaving his post in the summer and that Woodward would be taking over as executive vice-chairman. Again, though, there was no search; the Glazers decided and that was it; the investors, those who owned the non-voting shares, did not have a voice.

Gill, like Ferguson, was kept on the payroll, and like Ferguson will not speak without the Glazers' permission.

Kieran Maguire, teacher on the Football Industries MBA course at Liverpool University Management School and author of *The Price of Football*, is scathing. 'From a management point of view a good business prepares for change and prepares for senior management change. They have succession plans. Alex Ferguson, who was effectively the coach and director of football, left at the same time as David Gill. Ferguson was replaced with David Moyes, and Gill, who was a football person, was replaced by a rugby person [Woodward is keen on rugby] in Ed Woodward. Gill was Marmite to the fans, but as chief executive he was excellent. David Gill also knew football. You can't level the same plaudit at Ed Woodward.'

Gill, said Maguire, was across both sides, football and non-football. 'Football is a funny industry, often it's about backing yours and other people's judgement. But to do that you have to be confident; you have to know football. David Gill backed Sir Alex while running the club, he was a good go-between, between the board and the team.'

With Woodward in charge, says Maguire, it was different. 'There was no footballing strategist at the club. Woodward was excellent in many respects; he was very good at product monetization and brand extension, all those things. He was great at finding a snack partner in Malaysia – but that doesn't mean he made a good CEO of Manchester United.'

Mitten says he discerned a change. Gill and Ferguson were close, they operated as one. Now there was a distance between the club and manager. 'It was as if Ed Woodward and Richard Arnold [Woodward's successor on commercial and now the chief executive] said "we're our own men, it's not about the David Gill, Alex Ferguson axis any more. We'll make our decisions in our way."'

Above them was Joel Glazer who, with the two football heavyweights now gone, became more involved in decision-making. He and Woodward spoke several times a day by phone.

Apart from the manager, there was no football brain at the most senior level of the club. Unlike its rivals, United did not employ a director of football to look after the football side.

From the beginning, the signs were inauspicious. Despite the rush to appoint him, Moyes could not take up the job for a full two months until his Everton contract ran out. The parsimonious Glazers could have bought him out but did not want to have to pay Everton his final two months' wages. They took the view they could wait.

Those two months coincided with a period when they could have been wooing the available Gareth Bale to join them, but instead the Tottenham star was seduced by Real Madrid, and Cesc Fàbregas was also leaving Barcelona. Bale, Fàbregas and their agents could not wait for Moyes to be installed – time was of the essence – and both opportunities were lost.

That first post-Ferguson and Gill transfer window in 2013 set the tone. Under Moyes and Woodward, United signed Belgian midfielder Marouane Fellaini from Everton but missed their other 'buy' targets. This prompted coruscating criticism. *The Daily Telegraph* commented, 'In a summer when, in the words of Sir Alex Ferguson, Manchester United were ready to "push the boat out" to attract the biggest stars to Old Trafford, the reality was that the new man at the helm could not even steer the ship out of Salford Quays.' United, continued the paper, 'made all the right noises about luring Cristiano Ronaldo back to the club from Real Madrid, pursued Barcelona midfielder Cesc Fàbregas and toyed with the idea of moving for Robert Lewandowski.

'But the transfer window closed with United suffering the humiliation of missing out on most of their leading targets following a disastrous first attempt at transfer business by chief executive Ed Woodward.'

Forget that six-year contract and the Glazers waiting as long as their predecessors had done for success after Ferguson was appointed. Moyes lasted only ten months as United manager. He started in June 2013 and was sacked in April 2014, with United in seventh place and, crucially, unable to qualify for money-spinning European competition.

It was harsh on Moyes, who thought he was there for the long-term. 'If I knew I was only to be there only ten months I would have done things a lot differently,' he said.

No sooner had he started than he realized that the job, as mapped out by Ferguson in his Wilmslow home that Saturday afternoon, was in reality a lot bigger. 'There was a massive rebuilding exercise to be done.'

Even though they might have expected a planned succession, as other quoted companies would have used, investors could not say they were not warned. The NYSE prospectus did state: 'Any successor to our current manager may not be as successful as our current manager.'

Moving on from Moyes, the Glazers, now advised by Woodward, lurched to the other extreme, hiring the highly decorated veteran manager Louis van Gaal.

Van Gaal behaved like 'some sort of Dutch aristocrat' said someone familiar with his period at the club. 'It was weird. He had a rigid way of playing which was depressing to watch and presumably depressing to play, and he was this crazily strict disciplinarian, so an experienced pro would be fined for being one-and-a-half minutes late to training. This wasn't someone swinging the lead but a conscientious pro who probably got held up in traffic. He still got fined.'

Soon, the ex-Ajax, Barcelona, Netherlands and Bayern Munich boss was openly questioning whether United were 'too big a club' for their own good.

It was damning criticism, that commercial demands could hamper the team's success. 'Maybe it is too big a club. Not only in a sporting sense but also commercially. We have to do a lot of things that normally I don't allow. I have to adapt to this big club but I think also this big club has to adapt to Louis van Gaal. I hope we can have some balance to that.'

What prompted van Gaal's outburst about the club was a pre-season tour of the US, which is where the sponsors and the money were. 'We have to prepare the season and when you have commercial activities and dreadful distances, having to fly a lot and the jet lag, it is not positive for a good preparation.'

From the US, Woodward publicly defended the tour. Woodward, the CEO and commercial man, was dismissive of the worries expressed by the hugely accomplished United football manager: 'This is a very good country [for us] from a potential sponsorship perspective, a potential media perspective.'

Then he showed where the club's focus now lay, which was no longer in its heartland, but thousands of miles away from Old Trafford, Carrington and The Cliff. 'We've got more fans here than we have in the UK.'

TWELVE

Not so Super

O n the pitch, post-Ferguson, United did not reach the heights that had almost become the norm under its former manager.

Ferguson had set the bar high; his had been a golden period of achievement and it was always likely that no successor, however good, could ever equal it. This is not unique to United – most successful managers are followed by those who fail or don't succeed as well. One exception was Liverpool, where Bill Shankly was followed by Bob Paisley and later, Kenny Dalglish, but only then showed promise in fits and starts until Jürgen Klopp arrived.

The United fans, though, had got used to winning, to being champions domestically and in Europe, or at worst to be challenging for the major prizes. Their level of expectation, their sense of entitlement, were similarly raised. So too was their idea of how United should play, with élan and verve. When the team struggled to deliver on both fronts – winning and winning with style – the fans' frustration with the Glazers only increased.

Nevertheless, while they were raging and complaining at Old Trafford and in the fan forums and fanzines, aided and abetted by a posse of former players turned pundits whose presence only served as reminders of the glory days, and who liked to compare their past with the present, the Manchester United commercial juggernaut rolled on.

Woodward's marketing operation had outgrown 50 Pall Mall and moved to Stratton House at 5 Stratton Street, near Piccadilly and the Ritz Hotel, and next door to Langan's Brasserie. United was based on the discreet, upper floors of the grand building shared with two leading hedge funds, Egerton Capital and Calibrate Partners.

More deals continued to be struck, such as the one with Aperol Spritz to be its 'official spirits partner'.

Bob Kunze-Concewitz, chief executive of Gruppo Campari, Aperol's owner, said: 'We see it as a perfect combination. We share the same values. It is about success. It is about winning. It is about celebration.'

United's world was more split than ever, between the forever expanding commercial side and the power of the United brand, and the increasingly downbeat, lacklustre playing side. It was a curious juxtaposition: United ploughing on, winning as a money-making venture but failing on the pitch. They were out of step and lacking a joint focus.

Typically, Gruppo Campari was starstruck, saying it was delighted to be tapping in to the United marketing network, but in truth there was little success or cause for celebration among the supporters, many of whom devoted a sizeable chunk of their wages to following their favourite club, even when it was not winning, something that did not seem to matter to the owners.

Woodward was constantly singled out for abuse by the angry fans as executive vice-chairman, but he lasted in the job nine years – proof, as if it were needed, that the Glazers were not moved one iota by the protests. The supporters called for his head repeatedly but were ignored, and why not, since from the Glazers' perspective he was delivering on the all-important revenue front. The various groups of remonstrating supporters and critical commentators might as well have been shouting at the moon, such was the impact they had on the Glazers and their management of the club.

One recurring issue was transfers and the quality of United's buys. Woodward would insist that United was one of the most powerful clubs in the world and that there was no limit to the transfer budget, but then United appeared to go through fallow periods, when the club was not buying while others were, which only raised the fans' blood pressure further. Then, when United did enter the market, it was often too late, an available player had gone elsewhere. All the dealings had to be finally approved by Joel in his office in Maryland, and it was not always forthcoming or was delayed. Even though he'd given instant approval for the purchase of Wayne Rooney when he was asked as a minority shareholder in August 2004, in charge Joel did not like to take decisions quickly – a trait that did not help in the race to land big-name buys.

It did not help either that Woodward, while having a sharp commercial brain, did not have the same footballing contacts and standing within the game as his veteran predecessor, David Gill.

For a long time, targets had been identified by Ferguson, using little more than his own instinct or acting on a tip-off from one of his trusted scouts. Then the player was actively and often successfully pursued by Gill.

Not that the duo was infallible. Ferguson, with Gill, made mistakes, but they tended to be regarded as untouchable by the supporters and forgiven. That generosity was never afforded to Woodward, who was regarded as the 'Glazers' man' and therefore always to be loathed.

Ferguson, for instance, had in 2009 turned down the chance to buy Karim Benzema for £30 million, saying it was too much. Benzema had gone to Real Madrid and his track record there – he was subsequently both UEFA Player of the Year and winner of the Ballon d'Or – suggests that £30 million was a bargain.

In January 2010, after the Ronaldo money had still not been spent, after he'd rejected Benzema and others, Ferguson defended the lack of buys, saying it had nothing to do with the Glazers, they had not put the brake on purchases, but it was because he believed there was 'no value in the market'. Said the Scot: 'We have got the money. There is no question about that. I just don't see that player who can make a difference for us in terms of value or ability.' It was a ludicrous claim, almost certainly masking the Glazers' unwillingness to spend at that juncture but, because he was Fergie, he was allowed to get away with it – if Woodward had made the same claim, all hell would have broken loose.

Other clubs had pushed ahead and developed more sophisticated player research techniques, building more extensive scouting networks and using data analytics. They'd also fostered, as in the case of Manchester City and Benfica, close ties with foreign clubs, who would feed them rising stars. At the same time, as Moyes was shocked to discover, the much-vaunted United academy system had been allowed to decline. It was not producing the same quality young players as previously.

The rot had set in during Ferguson's reign, but his genius and force of personality had largely disguised it. But with him gone, and Gill too, United's fragility was cruelly exposed. 'Woodward got involved in transfer decisions and he had his pants pulled down,' says journalist and fanzine editor Andy Mitten.

United did spend money, no question. Often post-Ferguson it was on established stars who then, for a variety of reasons, did not perform. Smarter analysis and greater experience might have spotted a possible flaw in their make-up. Meanwhile, other clubs were also buying players, but to the chagrin of the United supporters theirs seemed to be more sure-footed, making a neater 'fit'.

Not that the United faithful would be necessarily negative at first. This whole period was characterized by United bringing in marquee names such as Alexis Sánchez, Romalu Lukaku, Ángel Di María, the fans applauding and then the transfer not working out. It didn't make a difference, they still hated the Glazers, still called for them and Woodward to go. 'The supporters are allowed to change their tune, Ed Woodward can't,' says Mitten. 'The reality was that player recruitment was not as sharp as it used to be or could be, and that's what ultimately mattered.'

Luck played a part, and with the managers, too. United wanted Klopp when he became available as manager, but they were already committed to van Gaal. They loved Pep Guardiola, but he'd already given his word to Manchester City. The one time the Glazers did respond to the fans and media, and moved Ole Gunnar Solskjaer from caretaker to permanent manager, they got it wrong.

Woodward played the cards he was dealt. When José Mourinho became manager, he told Woodward he would like to add the central defender Harry Maguire from Leicester. But he did not want to go above £50 million, that was José's absolute maximum – beyond that Mourinho said would be silly. Woodward went along with his manager and they let Maguire be.

Not long after, now with Solskjaer in command, United returned to Maguire. The Midlands club was under no pressure to sell – one of the consequences of rising TV receipts was that less well-off Premiership clubs did not need to rush to sell as they had previously. United eventually landed Maguire for a world record £80 million for a defender in August 2019 – some £30 million above what Mourinho would have paid.

From having had one manager for so long, post-Ferguson they raced through them in quick-fire succession: Moyes, van Gaal, Mourinho, Solskjaer, Erik ten Hag. Trophies were hard to come by, a scarcity made worse by the dominance of City under Pep Guardiola and a resurgent Liverpool with Jürgen Klopp. It was United's misfortune that it just so happened that two of the best managers in the world ever were installed at City and Liverpool at the same time and it was very difficult to knock them off. Manchester City and Liverpool pushed the bar high, to the extent they were on top of Everest and everybody else was at base camp.

You make your own luck, though, and it was undoubtedly United's failure in not getting the right manager. They did not secure Guardiola and Klopp, for whatever reason, while others did. United drew on process, on recruitment advisors and data – but, crucially, not market nous – and missed them.

The fans might have been distraught, but were the Glazers? Because this is what Woodward said in May 2018: 'Playing performance doesn't really have a meaningful impact on what we can do on the commercial side of the business.'

He said it in a call to investment analysts to explain United's quarterly earnings. In a sense he was speaking to his audience; that's what they wished to hear, that the team's failure to win was not impairing United's money-making ability. Like the comment about the US having more fans than the UK, Woodward's remark struck the wrong note outside the City and Wall Street.

It also wasn't strictly true, as the NYSE flotation prospectus had shown, TV income was boosted by a good run in the Champions League. Still, Woodward was able to strike deals with more 'official partners'. Currently, the club's website lists twenty-five 'global' partners. They include Apollo tyres, Cadbury chocolate, Maui Jim (a Chinese manufacturer of lenses), Chivas whisky, and Mlily, 'the Official Global Mattress and Pillow Partner of Manchester United'.

'It's about margins,' said Pomi Khan, CEO of Mlily UK, which agreed the partnership in 2016 and extended it to ten years in 2018. 'For a team like Manchester United, playing in the greatest, most competitive league in the world, every added advantage counts for its players. One of those advantages is by ensuring their players get the healthy, regenerative sleep they need to recover quicker and perform at their best.'

Then there are the official 'regional' and 'financial' partners. Among them, currently, are the Hong Kong Jockey Club and CB Bank, 'Official Financial Services Partner of Manchester United for Myanmar'.

The money pouring into the club was not lavished on refurbishing Old Trafford, Carrington or The Cliff. In 2005, when the Glazers took over, Old Trafford's capacity went up to 76,000. Second was Newcastle with 52,000. Since then, others have moved, or expanded their grounds, so Spurs now play in front of 62,850, Arsenal's capacity is 61,000, West Ham's is 62,000 and Manchester City's is to rise to more than 60,000, as will Liverpool's. United, by contrast, has stood still.

It grates with the fans, not least because Old Trafford's décor and appearance has been allowed to slip as well. It's still the largest Premiership stadium, but the facilities – compared with the major new and redeveloped domestic and European venues – are poor, and that hurts. United is the biggest club in the world and its supporters expect the best. Like playing world-class football with world-class players and winning, they see it as a right, as where they belong.

At Fulham, I sit in the Johnny Haynes Stand, built in 1905 and Grade II-listed by English Heritage, complete with the original narrow turnstiles, wooden seats and wooden floor, and barely any legroom. I'm happy ensconced in my living museum, but then Fulham is not United.

What is galling for United fans too is that not all of Old Trafford has been ignored. The executive boxes have been upgraded, as have the dressing rooms. The fans see the pecking order: corporate fat cats first, players second, genuine supporters third.

That's a view reinforced by the fact that Old Trafford is permanently sold out. As United's fan base has grown, so has the demand for tickets. The Glazers could have increased the capacity and still have sold all the seats, but they never did. Only recently has there been talk of expansion.

That indicated to the fans the Glazers did not want to invest in the club's spiritual home. It also indicated the Glazers were content raking in the proceeds from the commercial deals while not paying attention to United's beating heart: the playing of football and the sheer joy in watching it. Nothing beats physically being there, with the players, officials, fans, and seeing a game unfold, and experiencing the shared delight and agony – something the owners rarely did themselves.

'The Glazers' failure to put money into a project that at most would have cost hundreds of millions is symptomatic of their attitude towards investing in Manchester United,' rails Mitten.

Carrington also suffered, as did The Cliff. 'Carrington was state-of-the-art when it opened in 2000, but that was decades ago,' says Mitten.

It didn't go unnoticed either that when the Glazers did make improvements, nothing tended to occur quickly. They were made slowly, taking an age, suggesting they were being done begrudgingly.

Their approach meant that the Glazers were responsible for the advent of a word that made it into the online Urban Dictionary: 'Glazernomics'. It's defined as: 'The branch of knowledge concerned with the production, consumption or transfer of wealth to oneself, at the detriment of all others.'

When Mohamed Al-Fayed owned Fulham, the billionaire Egyptian would appear on the pitch before every home game, waving a scarf in the team's colours and rapping, 'We're not Real Madrid, We're not Barcelona, We are Fulham FC, And Al-Fayed's the owner' to the tune of 'Volare'. There was something amusing about the spectacle of the Harrods tycoon fooling around. But we fans did not find the words especially funny: while we liked Fayed and we were grateful for his largesse, we yearned for our football club to be like Real Madrid or Barcelona.

Or Manchester United. It's the dream of countless fans everywhere that their club might sit astride their league system and Europe. We can do it two ways: play amazing football with our existing players and squad; or hope that a sugar daddy will buy us and add superstars and a fantastic manager and take us on an incredible journey. Either route is the stuff of fantasy, it's what sustains us.

As the football cliché says: 'It's the hope that kills you.'

Occasionally, there are miracles, like the night Fulham beat the Goliath of Juventus, Italy's most successful club, 4–1 at the Cottage. In the Europa League, Fulham were trailing 3–1 from the first leg in Turin. We did it, or rather Bobby Zamora, Clint Dempsey and the rest of Roy Hodgson's marvels did it. With the aggregate score level at 4–4, Dempsey produced a perfect parabola of a chip for the winner. Mayhem erupted.

On the bus on the way home, an old boy sat, his Fulham scarf wrapped around his neck and clutching a match programme, in tears. 'I never thought I'd ever see anything like that in my lifetime,' he said.

Dreams can come true, or so we like to believe. It's also why we go: to be there when they do.

The problem for the Glazers and for other owners of the biggest clubs is they would rather we didn't have that belief, that there should never be any prospect, even via a dream, of clubs lower down joining them, not for any length of time. Because, by definition, if a small club jumps up, a big one must fall. And they want to cement their place at the top, not allow it to be challenged and taken by others. That way they guarantee more lucrative commercial spin-offs and boosted TV rights, as sponsors and broadcasters are prepared to pay more for the clubs that command the largest followings and audiences. For this, the Glazers were prepared to attack the infrastructure and, with that, the culture of the beautiful game.

The first sign that they desired to shake up the structure of the sport to their financial advantage was 'Project Big Picture' in 2020 (by now people should have been very wary of anything prefixed with 'Project' where the Glazers were concerned).

It was a plan put together by them jointly with John Henry, the American owner of Liverpool. The present system is geared towards benefiting the biggest clubs in the Premier League, traditionally the 'Big Six' of United, City, Liverpool, Arsenal, Spurs and Chelsea. The lion's share of the money going into the game goes to these glamour sides. After that, it filters down, so that clubs in the English Football League, the second tier, receive a lot less and, in the lower reaches of the EFL, a tiny fraction compared with those at the top.

United and Liverpool – arch-rivals on the pitch but pals, it seems, when it comes to their rich US owners trying to extract more cash from the sport – proposed what appeared on the face of it to be a fairer distribution, giving £250 million to the EFL clubs as well as 25 per cent of the money from the Premier League broadcasting rights sale.

The Premier League would be cut from twenty to eighteen clubs, supposedly to relieve fixture congestion and the Carabao Cup, the old 'League Cup' would be ditched. Enhanced voting on some issues would be granted to nine clubs in the Premiership with the longest consecutive number of seasons in that division, but just six votes were needed to pass changes in the regulations. The Football Association, which has a 'golden share' when it comes to voting on major changes in the Premier League such as voting rights and relegation, would receive an ex-gratia payment of £100 million. All very good, except – as Kieran Maguire says – 'the (red) devil is in the details.'

On inspection, the £250 million to the EFL clubs was not a donation but a loan, to be repaid from future share of broadcast revenues. Some 25 per cent of the collective broadcast revenues would be of the revenues from a much smaller package of games, since the Premiership clubs were going to be allowed to sell their own rights for up to eight games a season internationally, and the proceeds would all be kept by the club. This was something that United, which would get the biggest TV audience, dearly wanted, so it could negotiate its own rights and secure more than by being part of any collective offering. 'By taking some of the matches in house and keeping all the revenues, the gap between the Big Six clubs and the remainder would increase substantially,' says Maguire. 'The Big Six clubs already average £350 million higher revenues than the remaining clubs but this isn't enough for the owners of Liverpool and Manchester United.'

Reducing the size of the Premier League and scrapping the Carabao would remove fixtures against unglamorous clubs that Liverpool and United cannot sell premium-priced hospitality against, and it would free up the fixture list for more highly profitable European matches should that league widen . . . and it could also mean a later start to the season which would allow for more lucrative, sponsor-wooing pre-season tours.

Changing the voting rights would allow just six clubs to determine the future of English football (guess which six they would be).

The enhanced voting rights was just a carrot to get the other nine clubs to view this proposal favourably.

It didn't work. Project Big Picture was rejected by at least fourteen clubs at a Premier League meeting. Those voting against saw through a scheme that was aimed at bringing individual TV negotiating rights to United and Liverpool and the other members of the Big Six, which would allow them to scrap some matches they did not want and open up the fixture list for more European games, and gain control of the Premier League.

Concepts such as collectivity and democracy, expressed in the principle of one club, one vote, were anathema to them. Equally, they were not moved by the thought that to fans of lesser clubs a match against one of the Big Six and United especially – it's the one that fans up and down the country first go to when the season's fixture list is announced – or playing them in the Carabao on a midweek night, means everything.

As Maguire says: 'The present 58 per cent of total revenues shared by 30 per cent of clubs is not enough in the eyes of their owners, and to quote Gordon Gekko in *Wall Street*: "Greed is good. Greed is right. Greed works."'

Undeterred by the failure and negative reaction to Project Big Picture, the Glazers, as was their fashion, came back, this time with a proposal for a European Super League. In April 2021, it was announced that twelve major European clubs would be founding members of what was intended to be a twenty-team league, the European Super League. The proposed competition would comprise twenty clubs that would take part in matches against each other. Fifteen would be 'permanent members', holding their places for the length of their commitment, initially twenty-three years, while five places would remain open to teams who performed best in their country's most recent domestic league season.

They would all be split into two groups of ten clubs, playing home-and-away games in a round-robin format. Then the top teams would qualify for the later stages, run as a knockout.

The Super League clubs would have access to 'solidarity payments', which would be in excess of €10 billion and the founders would receive €3.5 billion to support 'infrastructure investment' plans and to offset the impact of COVID-19. The founders would share 32.5 per cent of commercial revenues, 32.5 per cent would be shared among all twenty Super League teams; and 20 per cent would be distributed on the basis of performance. The remaining 15 per cent would be distributed according to the size of the clubs' TV audiences.

As for the rest, the poor relations outside the Super League, they would receive a 'solidarity payment' of €400 million. 'This Super League is not a competition for the rich, it's a competition of solidarity to save football, by the great and the modest,' claimed Florentino Pérez, president of Real Madrid and, along with the Glazers and the Agnelli family (owners of Juventus), a key architect of the enterprise. 'The great and the modest' – incredible.

The move was instantly and widely condemned by fans, managers, other clubs, media, politicians, even British royalty. Prince William, who is the FA president and an Aston Villa supporter, tweeted: 'Now, more than ever, we must protect the entire football community – from the top level to the grassroots – and the values of competition and fairness at its core. I share the concerns of fans about the proposed Super League and the damage it risks causing to the game we love.'

What especially rankled was that the new Super League would not have relegation, same as in the US major sports leagues. The American owners of the European football clubs were revealing what they really wanted at last.

In England, there are six teams, possibly seven with Newcastle now having Saudi backing, with the wherewithal to regularly expect Champions League football. They want it for the extra income and profile it brings. The difficulty is that under the present rules only four clubs from the Premiership qualify for the Champions League. And six into four does not go.

'They need to improve their revenues beyond the Premier League,' says Maguire. 'That means being in the European Champions League regularly and that means not losing Premiership matches.'

History shows that can't be guaranteed, that even the mightiest clubs can be relegated, let alone qualify for the Champions League. That's dismaying to the Americans who want the promise of constant success, and the cash that generates.

'The Super League is a fantastic idea, if the only reason you own a major football club is to make money,' says Maguire.

Everton, Nottingham Forest, Leeds, Prince William's own Aston Villa, they were all winners in the past, all big clubs that went on to know hard times. There are many others. 'With the Super League, six into six does go, so problem solved.' They would no longer have to win to be in Europe's – the world's – top competition. Says Maguire: 'It would lower player quality; lower the level they need to spend to win the Premier League – but it would increase their club's value.'

The Glazers, Agnellis and their exclusive troupe wanted to remove the uncertainty; they wished to be certain of remaining at the very summit of the sport and counting the millions that brings.

There was an arrogance to their approach. The Super League's public relations was dreadful. They offered no real explanation for the scheme; they seemed to assume that because of who they were, the plan would be accepted.

There was no 'softening up', the news was sprung without warning. Even the TV companies that pay and partner them did not know. The founders failed, miserably, to get the advance backing of influential figures – possibly for fear of leaks – but it meant they were left gasping when someone like Klopp spoke out in opposition. Star players, too, joined in the opprobrium.

Neither did they appear to have thought about how the sport's snubbed governing bodies might react; that they could and would bar players at the Super League clubs from playing for their national teams.

What they were clearly not expecting either was the furious reaction from royalty, from governments, especially in the UK, from Prime Minister Boris Johnson. Woodward saw Johnson in Downing Street shortly before the Super League was announced. He'd gone to Number Ten, on 14 April 2021, to meet Dan Rosenfield, the Downing Street chief of staff. It was later reported that Woodward had gone to butter up Rosenfield and Johnson, to sell them the notion of the Super League and seek their support.

Woodward did go and he saw Rosenfield who he knew, but by chance he was taken to say hello to Johnson who was sitting in his office. After Woodward was introduced, Johnson made reference to football needing to get the crowds to return (after the pandemic) and how good it was that a club of Newcastle's size were on the way back. There was no mention of the Super League, but Johnson had appeared friendly enough.

Four days later, on 18 April, came the Super League announcement and the lighting of the blue touchpaper. Out, all guns blazing, came Johnson. The founders were betraying ordinary people, he said. He declared that he would drop a typically unspecified 'legislative bomb' on the proposal.

The Super League were thrown into disarray by Johnson's reaction. He has no abiding interest in football, but they'd reckoned without his opportunism. The level of rage against the Super League went right across the political spectrum, right across society, North and South. Not one to pass up the chance to climb aboard a bandwagon, to be seen to be caring about a sport enjoyed by millions, Johnson duly joined in.

Some in the club were against the Super League. Others were in favour. What the management thought didn't really matter: Joel Glazer was keen and he went for it.

Shortly after its unveiling, the Super League saw the withdrawal of the six English participants, including United. It was dead in the water, for now. In the future, the Super League pitch may well be taught at business schools as a case study in how not to launch something, it was that awful. Yet the schism that drove the clubs to contemplate forming their own 'super league' remains. If someone comes along with wads of cash and buys a club and sets about acquiring superstars, its fans are thrilled. They don't stop for a second to question how those wealthy people and companies became rich, what actually motivates them. Liverpool supporters welcomed a US tycoon like John W. Henry swooping in to purchase their club, without thinking why. Henry is not doing it out of the goodness of his heart, he does not operate a charity, this definitely is not *pro bono*. He has a profit imperative, as have the Glazers and the proprietors of several of the breakaway clubs. For them, the club is one more addition to their worldwide investment portfolio.

Fans and owners share a common bond: they want their team to do well. But for many businesses and corporates behind the biggest, most commercially successful and internationally marketable clubs, that is just a step towards making even more money. So, when that objective is exposed by the blueprint for the Super League, something called 'the football community' reacted in horror.

The 'football community' and government and politicians and some sections of the media have seemingly got their way, but – with the owners not getting theirs – no one should be shocked and disappointed if some of them walk away to put their capital somewhere else, and funding leaves their clubs and the game. Or perhaps they might try again. An expanded Champions League will not suffice. What the owners are seeking are guarantees – of always having a place in Europe's premier competition, of being able to bag hugely lucrative deals and other spin-offs. A league that delivers those prizes will be back.

Two weeks after the Super League went public in April, a planned peaceful protest against the Glazers outside Old Trafford turned ugly. On Sunday 2 May 2021, United were due to play Liverpool behind closed doors because of Covid restrictions. Up to 2,000 fans assembled outside the ground on the stadium forecourt at 1 p.m., with the match due to kick off at 4.30 p.m. It was calm at first, then a group of about 200 fans broke into the ground, and began throwing flares, firecrackers and bottles. Club staff locked themselves into their rooms for safety.

Some of the fans breached security barriers and made for the players' tunnel, the 'Munich Tunnel'. They tried to force open the gates and they attacked police and camera crews. They were ejected and got in a second time, via a disabled entrance. More fighting ensued. Meanwhile, the violence had spread to the forecourt. As the police tried to clear the area, more flares, bottles and cans were hurled. In all, thirty-five assaults against police were recorded. One officer said missiles were being thrown at them 'like confetti'.

Another group had gathered outside the Lowry Hotel where the United players were staying. They surrounded the team coach and chanted: 'We decide when you will play.' More flares were lit and they held up banners saying: 'Glazers out Woodward out'.

Eventually, the police called a halt and abandoned the game, to be rescheduled for a later date. It was the first time a Premiership match had been postponed because of fan behaviour.

Multiple arrests were made and a series of trials held in

Manchester. The first was for Jake Cottee, from Kent, for violent disorder and criminal damage. The court heard how he'd pushed over a Sky camera on a tripod, causing £63,000 worth of damage, and thrown missiles outside the ground.

Defending Cottee, his barrister Jonathan Dickinson said the devoted United fan, who has followed the team across Europe, had otherwise led a hard-working and 'blameless' life. Cottee had an 'extremely well-paid job' working as a service technician in the offshore wind industry. He described Cottee's actions as an 'out of character afternoon of madness', committed while his 'adrenaline was running high'.

Cottee, 'like many of Manchester United's supporters at that time was particularly unhappy at the involvement of the club's owners in the European Super League.'

Dickinson said Cottee was 'genuinely shocked' at his own behaviour, and that he never intended to harm anyone. He was sentenced to twenty months in prison, suspended for two years, and ordered to carry out 200 hours of unpaid work. He was also required to pay £12,000 towards the damaged camera.

One of those who went on the pitch, who gave his name as Ryan, said: 'The protest went better than expected. The whole idea was to cause disruption and I believe that's what's been achieved. The atmosphere was unreal. I myself have spent my life idolizing this club and to watch how the Glazers have used the club has angered and disappointed me. The scenes on the pitch were unreal, we achieved what we needed to and took it further by making it onto the pitch. Do I agree with causing damage? Absolutely not, but what do Manchester United really expect? They have been told for years.'

Another, Jamie, from the *United We Stand* fanzine, said: 'This is all to do with the Glazers. It has been a long time in the making because we protested in 2005 [when they bought the club], and again in 2010.

I can understand people saying: "It's just because you're not winning things any more." But that's not the point – this is about a football club and a community that surrounds it.'

Said Jamie: 'The general outrage about the Super League has provided momentum: it's now or never. I have seen plenty of Liverpool fans on social media who have backed what we've done. There had been talks in the last couple of weeks about them joining us on Sunday but it would have been too hard to facilitate. It would have made a hell of a statement.'

Manchester United Supporters Trust said: 'The owners have taken £1 billion out of the club and we have witnessed decay and decline both on the field and off it. The invasion of the stadium isn't something we expected, and it is rumoured a gate was opened for fans, but even if that is not the case, we believe the vast majority of Manchester United staff are sympathetic with the views of the fans.'

Gary Neville, who was covering the match for Sky, raged: 'This is the consequence of the owners of Manchester United's actions two weeks ago [the Super League]. There's a general distrust and dislike of the owners, but people weren't protesting before this happened. Generally, the Glazer family, along with a number of other owners of football clubs in this country, were conniving and scheming behind everyone's back to walk away with the crown jewels. Today we've seen people protest at that.'

What was telling, in the face of that, was the almost ambivalent response from on high. 'A dangerous situation that should have no place in football,' was how the Premier League reacted.

United said: 'Our fans are passionate about Manchester United, and we completely acknowledge the right to free expression and peaceful protest. However, we regret the disruption to the team and actions which put other fans, staff, and the police in danger. We thank the police for their support and will assist them in any subsequent investigations.'

What there wasn't then was any acknowledgement that the fans' anger was justified.

As ever, the feeling that the fans belonged at the bottom of the heap, that they did not merit a voice, that they were not worth listening to, persisted.

THIRTEEN

Mea culpa, not

The Glazers were taken aback by the response to the Super League, to their close involvement in the ill-conceived, widely condemned scheme.

What was a long-running sore between them and a section of Manchester United supporters was in danger of becoming something much worse – uniting all of football against the family.

With this at the forefront of his mind, Joel broke with what had become the owners' traditional silence and began engaging with the fans and trying to explain. It was quite a watershed moment. The trouble was, he continued to display that same lack of empathy which had been so prominent ever since the Glazers had first owned the club, and showed the familiar, obstinate refusal to really change tack.

He wrote open letters, promising better communication with supporters and investment in Old Trafford, and holding out the possibility of the fans holding shares in the club. They were carefully written, nuanced and well-crafted, appearing to indicate a shift but rarely giving any quarter.

'We continue to believe that European football needs to become more sustainable,' Joel posted on the United website. 'However, we fully accept that the Super League was not the right way to go about it.'

The word 'sustainable' in this context is interesting. If he means keeping something running and not extracting cash, and making a return from it, that's one thing. If he means treating United as you would any other corporate investment so it produces a dividend, which you and your siblings take, regardless of the company's performance, and the asset's value increases, that's quite another.

'Over the past few days, we have all witnessed the great passion which football generates, and the deep loyalty our fans have for this great club.'

Had he not witnessed and indeed been on the receiving end of such 'great passion' during sixteen years of Glazer ownership, not just the last few days?

'You made very clear your opposition to the European Super League, and we have listened. We got it wrong, and we want to show that we can put things right.'

It was not a case of the Glazers 'listening'. They withdrew when the other teams withdrew, when there was no Super League left to speak of.

'Although the wounds are raw and I understand that it will take time for the scars to heal, I am personally committed to rebuilding trust with our fans and learning from the message you delivered with such conviction.'

The breakdown in trust between the Glazers and fans had nothing to do with the Super League, it had occurred sixteen years previously when the debt-free club was loaded with debt and when the people who loaded up the debt failed to attend matches or communicate with the paying supporters.

As for taking time to heal, Joel would have been well advised to read *The Daily Telegraph* and Henry Winter's column from 1 July 2005: 'A wound that will never heal'.

Joel went on. 'In seeking to create a more stable foundation for the game, we failed to show enough respect for its deep-rooted traditions – promotion, relegation, the pyramid – and for that we are sorry.'

It wasn't so much showing a lack of respect, it was attempting to demolish the pyramid completely, and failing to understand why that time-honoured structure was held so dear by so many.

'This is the world's greatest football club and we apologize unreservedly for the unrest caused during these past few days. It is important for us to put that right. Manchester United has a rich heritage and we recognize our responsibility to live up to its great traditions and values.'

So long as that means not attending the home of those traditions and values.

'We also realize that we need to better communicate with you, our fans, because you will always be at the heart of the club.

'In the background, you can be sure that we will be taking the necessary steps to rebuild relationships with other stakeholders across the game, with a view to working together on solutions to the long-term challenges facing the football pyramid.'

For which many read: we've not given up, we're going to try again with the Super League or something similar and this time we will make sure our lobbying effort is fully pumped, and we will get all the ducks in a row, and those we need to win over, first.

'In closing, I would like to recognize that it is your support which makes this club so great, and we thank you for that.'

Grand, offhand, dismissive.

He also responded to a letter to Woodward delivered during an emergency Fans' Forum with the United senior executive. In that, the supporters declared their 'disgust' at Joel's actions and said his apology was 'not accepted'. 'Joel's family have shown time and again that their sole motivation is personal profit at the expense of our football club,' said the letter.

Replied Glazer:

'I want to salute your service to the Fans' Forum, which I know is a vital channel for consultation between the club and our fans. As I recently stated publicly, I am personally committed to ensuring that we strengthen this relationship in future.'

It was so vital it did not exist until recently. As for the relationship with the fans, it's not a case of strengthening it: there wasn't one.

'Your heartfelt letter captured the unique spirit of Manchester United, forged through decades of triumph, adversity and tragedy, and still powerfully present in today's exciting team under Ole and the vibrant fan base which you represent.'

So exciting that Ole Gunnar Solskjaer was fired six months later.

'Our top priority is, and will always be, competing for the most important trophies, playing entertaining football with a team comprised of top-quality recruits and some of the world's best homegrown talent. Under Ole, we feel we are absolutely on the right track.'

Only competing in the finals of the Champions League and at the top of the Premiership will do. As for Solskjaer, they did not stay on the same track for long.

'Success on the field must be underpinned by solid foundations off it. We have supported sustained investment in the team over many years, and that will continue this summer. We recognize that we will need to significantly increase investment in Old Trafford and our training complex to ensure that the club's facilities remain among the best in Europe. As part of this, we will consult with fans on investments related to the stadium and the matchday experience.' Commercial first, playing second. Consulting with the fans about Old Trafford enables the Glazers to explain why they will not be spending hundreds of millions on the ground and how the supporters should lower their ambition.

'Indeed, one of the clearest lessons of the past few weeks is the need for us to become better listeners. To this end, I can commit the club will engage across all of the issues raised in your letter.' Another promise of a change in behaviour. Again, it's so radical as to be questionable.

'To highlight some specific points, as one of the few European football clubs listed on the public markets, we believe in the principle of fans owning shares in the club. We have previously engaged with you on fan share ownership and we want to continue and accelerate those discussions, together with provisions to enhance associated fan consultation.'

He continued. 'We recognize that the Government-initiated, fan-led review of football is a positive opportunity to explore new structures for fan engagement and influence. I can assure you that we will willingly and openly engage in the review, with the aim of putting fans at the heart of the game and ensuring their interests are advanced and protected.' Glazer had clearly been thrown by Boris Johnson's threat to drop a 'legislative bomb' on his Super League plans. He now wanted to work with the government, not against it.

'These commitments are a starting point for further dialogue, including all the specific points in your open letter, rather than final proposals. We want to work together to come up with an ambitious package of measures which will transform our relationship with fans and strengthen the club for the long term. In this spirit, we will reach out to you to discuss next steps.' It's taken an awfully long time, too long, to get to this.

'Thank you again for your work and your passion for the club.'

Woodward left United soon after the Super League shambles. He was one of those who had disagreed profoundly with the proposal; but then Joel went ahead anyway and signed the founders' agreement. He was going at the end of the year, now the announcement was brought forward.

'I am extremely proud to have served United and it has been an honour to work for the world's greatest football club for the past 16 years,' he said. 'The club is well positioned for the future and it will be difficult to walk away at the end of the year. I will treasure the memories from my time at Old Trafford, during a period when we won the Europa League, the FA Cup and the EFL Cup . . .

'I desperately wanted the club to win the Premier League during my tenure and I am certain that the foundations are in place for us to win it back for our passionate fans.'

Woodward had been there with the Glazers from the start. He was present when they got off on the wrong foot through appalling communication and remained throughout the years of fans' protest and anger. Better dialogue might have helped smooth relations, explaining that yes, while the club had debts and debt is bad, the commercial side of the club had roared ahead, so United was still able to invest in managers and players. That case was never made. If he had not been put in sole charge and given free rein over transfers, with only Joel to answer to, he would not have attracted such a degree of opprobrium. Woodward was a money man not a football man – players and their agents was not his natural domain. It didn't help either that on his watch, from 2016, the Glazers awarded themselves dividends, receiving more than £150 million in total, the only Premier League owners to do so, and this on top of other payments, consultancy and management fees and loans.

More illuminating than Joel's underwhelming missives or his now, similarly well-prepared occasional appearances on Zoom calls with select fans, was the impromptu, definitely unrehearsed session held by Richard Arnold, Woodward's successor, in the Boot Inn in Willington, Cheshire, on Saturday 18 June 2022.

He'd heard protestors were planning to march on his house. Twelve had assembled in his local pub, so Arnold went to meet them, buy them drinks, sit with them in the afternoon sunshine and attempt to head them off.

Channelling the spirit of David Brent he told them, 'I haven't promised anything I haven't done,' he said. 'I don't tell lies and I front the issues. I respect your passion and how you dealt with it. I need some help from you, because otherwise I can't do it.'

Time for some soul-searching. 'This sounds self-serving. We've not bottled you protesting. I love the passion of the fans. But it's been horrible, even though the performances are bad.'

In the beer garden, Arnold declared: 'I want to put us back together as a club and pulling to be successful. I'm going to do my bit and make sure the money is there – that's all I can do.'

He admitted that United had spent heavily, £1 billion, since Ferguson left, for no discernible benefit. 'We've fucking burned through cash. We spent a billion pounds on players, we spent more than anyone in Europe. I am not thrilled with where we are, it doesn't sit easy and we've got to get this sorted.'

He continued: 'We've blown through an enormous amount of money. Last year was a fucking nightmare. I was hating every minute of it.'

But in true Brent fashion, this was all about him. The fans sitting across the table from him in the pub garden were also hating it – which is why they were there – and, unlike him, they were paying hard-earned cash for the privilege.

He made it clear that unlike Woodward he would not be

conducting transfers. That would be the director of football, John Murtough. 'Do you want me buying the players? Doesn't that ring a bell?'

The dozen fans raised the condition of Old Trafford and Carrington. 'For the future, for investing in a new stadium and that sort of stuff, for a £250 million training ground, we've got to do something, we've got to get investors in.

'I need that to do what I want for the club – I've got to have more cash than I have now.'

They pointed out that he would have more cash if the Glazers did not take dividends and other payments. He batted criticism of the owners away. 'The money has got to come from somewhere. You may not like them but if you want someone else to come in, they have to love the club and the team.'

He stressed the Glazers were not going away. 'You know what it was like in 2005 and the pressure put on the owners not to buy the club, but they bought it anyway.

'If you think of them that way, they're rock hard. They're not frightened of people.'

A spokesperson for Manchester United summarized the pub encounter in that unmoved, detached, icy manner the Glazers had made their own. 'Richard heard that a group of fans had gathered in a pub near his house. He went to meet them, bought them all a drink, listened to their views, and explained what the club is doing to deliver success on the pitch, improve the stadium, and strengthen engagement with fans.'

How did Arnold describe the Glazers again? 'Rock hard.'

At Chelsea's Stamford Bridge, they've closed the gym. It was part of the stadium complex and was used by players, management and, for a membership fee, by outsiders.

Until he sold the club, Roman Abramovich liked to work out there. Its shutting was hardly a big deal, but its passing tells you something about the difference in approach between the Russian oligarch and Chelsea's new owners. Abramovich treated Chelsea as a trophy, a plaything, an indulgence, not as a money-making enterprise.

That's not how the new guard, led by US private equity tycoon, Todd Boehly, regard Chelsea. Each year, the biggest private equity get-together is the 'SuperReturn International' conference. Even the very name says everything about their approach.

The 2022 gathering was in Berlin's InterContinental Hotel. Among the speakers, behind closed doors, was Boehly. Billionaire Boehly partnered US private equity firm Clearlake Capital to buy Chelsea for a total of £4.25 billion in May 2022, after Abramovich was hit by sanctions following Russia's invasion of Ukraine.

Clearlake joined the likes of CVC, Oaktree Capital, RedBird Capital Partners and other private equity houses by moving into football. Lest there be any doubt, they are not doing so out of a sense of philanthropy – they are very much investors seeking a handsome – let's make that 'super' – return.

Former college wrestling star, Boehly, forty-nine, has amassed a $4.5 billion fortune via his Connecticut-based investment group, Eldridge Industries. His specialities are media, entertainment and sports. Chelsea, which finished third in the 2021–2 season, earning qualification for the lucrative European Champions League, now sits comfortably in his line-up.

This is how he calculates it. European football is watched by an audience of 4 billion, compared with the 170 million who follow the NFL in the US. But the NFL produces $15 billion in revenue from the networks, versus a 'fraction' of that generated by football. 'We think the Premier League itself is way undervalued. We think the approach with which those clubs go to market is years behind the US model,' said Boehly at SuperReturn.

Take baseball's LA Dodgers, which Boehly bought with a consortium a decade ago. He struck a deal with Time Warner to create a new regional network to broadcast all Dodgers games. 'Everyone said we were nuts [for buying the LA Dodgers]. We paid $2.15 billion, the largest price paid for a team, and the next year we sold the media rights for $9 billion.'

Using phraseology that is normal for private equity but alien to many football fans, Boehly described Chelsea as a 'portfolio' rather than a team, and said his analysts compile 'investment memos' on every player.

Those players now include England international Raheem Sterling for £56.2 million in the summer of 2022, Napoli centre back Kalidou Koulibaly for £33 million, Mykhailo Mudryk for £88.5 million, Enzo Fernandez for £106.8 million. In all, Boehly has spent more than £600 million in two transfer windows.

To circumvent the UEFA Financial Fair Play rules, designed to stop a club spending excessively to achieve success, they were signed on long contracts, with the cost spread over the contract.

They were bought not on an old-fashioned hunch, a feeling, but according to hard data. Analytics, Boehly told his private equity audience, were key to the LA Dodgers winning the 2020 World Series. 'When we bought [US baseball player] Freddie Freeman this year, we thought we'd moved our probability of winning the World Series from 17 per cent to 19 per cent. We are constantly looking at how to continue to modify and adjust our probabilities to win.'

As well as the US major leagues, Boehly cited Formula One as a model to follow. 'They've got the under-thirty-five-year-old demographic fully engaged, and they've got women fully engaged.'

One area ripe for the Boehly treatment, he said, is 'loyalty points', persuading supporters to spend more money in return for prizes and points, which provide them with access to tickets. 'We basically have 140,000 tickets a year we can sell to fans that aren't season-ticket holders. In order to get those seats, you become a member. If members engage in activities, that makes you more of a superfan, you get more points, and if you have more points, your odds of getting a ticket to Chelsea versus Liverpool go up. We're just scratching the surface on that.'

Gambling also features large in Boehly's thinking. Eldridge holds a stake in DraftKings, the sports betting platform. 'We are in the early days of sports betting,' he informed SuperReturn.

Clearly, there was no room for the small-scale gym in his grand plans. Other parts of the Chelsea firmament have undergone similar treatment.

Boehly's speech showed which ticket holders, which fans, matter to the money men more. While the likes of Chelsea and United can raise the price of season tickets, it's not by much, relative to what they can charge for the whole hospitality package, and each time they increase the price, they face a backlash (after one United rise, a car mistakenly thought to contain the Glazers was attacked by an angry mob outside the Lowry Hotel).

And such developments are not only taking place at the biggest clubs. At Fulham, they've just completed the new Riverside Stand. Alongside the bars and snack bars, including a sushi counter, there's a fine dining restaurant, hotel, swimming pool and spa, apartments and a private members' club. The most expensive seats are priced at £3,000, making them the costliest non-corporate seats in the world. At Fulham, at dear old Craven Cottage.

Fulham owner Shahid Khan is a US billionaire, one of the top 300 richest people in the world, says *Forbes*, who made his fortune from auto parts. He also owns an NFL franchise, the Jacksonville Jaguars.

'We're a small club and we need the fans, but we also need the money to invest in the squad and comply with [financial] fair play rules. This is striking a balance.'

Said Khan: 'I saw in the old Riverside Stand, where the Directors' Box used to be, they were supposed to be Fulham supporters but for some of those seats I never saw the same people twice. I found out it was people selling them or selling through ticket brokers and I was, "We need to have a formula where we harvest funds for the club, and they are not going to a third party."'

Continued Khan: 'So, it's about striking a balance in modern football where you get the revenue to invest in the squad and still have tickets for the hardcore fans that are more affordable. But there is a market for premium, we're calling it platinum, tickets.'

Which matters more, the affordable or the premium? One is a burden – ask any property developer charged with supplying a percentage of 'affordable' housing – the other is where the money is to be made. If only they could all be premium.

'It's sadly the case that "legacy fans" are increasingly irrelevant for the top clubs,' says Maguire. Legacy, that's what we've become. Same as the 'legacy' retailers on the High Street, the ones that have either disappeared or are hanging on, just.

Ideally, says Maguire, what they would like is lots of corporates paying large amounts for hospitality and 'football tourists', fans who buy tickets for individual matches and spend large amounts on the tickets (more than the price-per-game of a season ticket) and merchandise.

The mooted 'seat for a song' idea had no takers on high. Joel preferred to put the prices up, across all areas of the ground – in the by now not-so-cheap seats and hospitality. He introduced an Automatic Cup Scheme or ACS, which obliged all season-ticket holders to buy tickets for the early rounds of home cup games. This move sparked more anger among the fans.

A 'seat for a song' provides some clue as to where some wanted United to go, where the club and the game could go still. As well as issuing lanyards to ordinary fans so they can sing for their seats, there is the prospect of Augmented Reality or AR technology. The players, managers and referee will be given wearables made by the likes of Apple, so viewers can watch the match from their viewpoint, as if they are them, getting an 'as if you're this player or manager or the referee' experience of the action.

At United, AR would extend inside the dugout and in Old Trafford's Munich Tunnel, as the teams line up alongside each other. The thinking is that fans across the world, sitting in their homes or wherever they are with their mobiles, tablets or laptops and, in many cases, their online betting accounts, will be prepared to pay a premium fee for this service.

The economic landscape of top-class football could shift up several levels, prompting a vast amount of revenue pouring into the clubs – thanks to this disruptive technology – via micro-payments, avatars and wearables. They will narrow the gap between the fans and the club and the players – and in a way never thought possible before.

It won't just be the fans with the players standing in the tunnel, they will be able to pay to tune into the same music that United star Marcus Rashford is listening to on his Beats as he leaves the Lowry Hotel to board the team coach.

Maguire, for one, is in no doubt that the future will not stop there. The bosses of the big clubs, driven by money and constantly looking with fondness at the NFL, would like to truncate the ninety minutes into eighty minutes and four quarters, instead of two halves. That way they can sell more advertising. 'The action in an average NFL game lasts all of eleven and a half minutes but the whole game is on air for two and a half to three hours. The broadcast is crammed with advertising. Football, with its two halves of forty-five minutes, is a disaster by comparison.'

One factor they've convinced themselves about, he says, is newer fans. Younger people are not so hidebound, not so concerned with the traditions. 'They believe young fans don't have the same attention spans', and will readily accept US-style, shorter matches split into 'quarters'.

They believe they can buy success, although that is not borne out by the facts. In April 2023, after Chelsea were knocked out of the Champions League and after a string of defeats which meant they had no chance of qualifying for next season's Champions League, Boehly addressed another meeting, also in private. It came also after Boehly was verbally attacked by Chelsea fans when he attended the most recent game at Chelsea which saw his expensively assembled team taken apart by Brighton.

This meeting, in a function room at Stamford Bridge, was for his bankers and business associates. It was billed as an opportunity to hear him map out his vision for the 2023–4 season, but he began by admitting to having 'made mistakes' since buying Chelsea twelve months previously. He did not elaborate, but his mood was not as upbeat as it had been when he'd spoken at SuperReturn.

On Thursday 20 April 2023, Manchester United played Seville in the second leg of the Europa League quarter-final. In the first leg, at one point they had been 2–0 up and then conceded two late own goals, one from the world-record-breaking Harry Maguire. As it happened, United went on to finish third in the Premiership and claim a Champions League spot, but qualification cannot be left to chance, to human frailty such as Maguire exhibited. A re-run of the Super League or something like it, one that would have slicker PR this time, guaranteeing long-term Champions League football for both Chelsea and United, can only be a matter of time.

Buying Chelsea cost Boehly and his consortium £4.25 billion ($5.4 billion) after a bidding war. It was a princely sum, significantly in excess of what Chelsea were widely thought to be worth. Other owners did back-of-the-envelope calculations: if Chelsea have gone for that, what could I fetch for mine?

Among those doing the arithmetic were the Glazers and their advisors. If Chelsea went for $5 billion, then Manchester United, which is far bigger in terms of global reach, fan base and commercial power, could command a lot more. How much? Possibly twice the Chelsea price. Some said Manchester United could be worth $10 billion – they believed that with AR and the rapidly evolving environment it really had that much potential.

In November 2022, six months after Boehly paid all that money, the Glazers announced they were 'commencing a process to explore strategic alternatives' for United. The process would consider a number of options, 'including new investment into the club, a sale, or other transactions involving the company'.

Seventeen years after they took advantage of a row between billionaires and a football manager over a racehorse to buy the world's biggest football club, seventeen years of relentless personal abuse, seventeen years of barely watching their team play in person; finally, they had taken the decision to explore selling the club and collect their billions.

FOURTEEN

Billionaires all

Of the six Glazer siblings, only three – Joel, Avie and Bryan – ever displayed much enthusiasm for the football club. Joel and Avie were the most involved and were co-chairs, while the other four, Bryan, Kevin, Edward and Darcie, were directors. All of them enjoyed dividend and other payments.

Since they became owners in 2005, there were at least four attempts to gauge the Glazers' attachment to United, and whether they might consider selling. One was by the Red Knights – O'Neill and his fellow investors had raised substantial funds among themselves, and a wealthy Qatari with links to that country's ruling family was also thought to be willing to help them out. They could have afforded it if the Glazers were amenable.

Two approaches were made from Saudi Arabian businessmen. A fourth was from Sir Jim Ratcliffe, the British billionaire and owner of the chemicals group INEOS. He met them and described them as the 'nicest people', but got nowhere. 'We went to see them and they were charming,' said Ratcliffe. 'They [Avram, Joel, Kevin, Bryan, Darcie and Edward] are all very nice, despite the press they get. Josh was really hospitable. But the club is owned equally by siblings and you can't talk to that many siblings, really.'

Doubtless, there were other expressions of interest, which never developed into serious discussions; at every turn, the Glazers rejected the opportunity to explore further a possible sale even through intermediaries. No price was posited by the Glazers or their agents, no formal talks were ever held.

Throughout the Glazer years, there were fan protests, frequently of the most horrible, personal kind. Not once did the Glazers decide to walk away. 'The Glazers do what they want to do, they don't do what people tell them to do,' said someone who knows them well. He reiterated: 'Joel and Avie, they love it, absolutely love the sport. They're addicted to it, they watch every minute of every United game, just not at Old Trafford. They love the business side; they're very business focused. If they sold the club, they would no longer have a card which says, "owner of Manchester United".'

Joel had the largest individual stake and controlled 19 per cent of the voting rights. He was always more hands-on, involving himself in pretty much all aspects of the club. Avie was more the international ambassador.

At the most recent World Economic Forum at Davos, United set up a pavilion. It seemed incongruous: a lounge dedicated to a football club amid those from the multinational corporations, big tech, big pharma, banks and global institutions. In fact, United had partnered the forum since 2019 and attended in 2020.

Far from being out of place, Davos was somewhere the Glazers wanted the club to be, where they thought they belonged. Owning United entitled them to a place at the top table, at the annual gathering of the world's business elite. 'Manchester United is proud to be the first sports team to partner with the World Economic Forum,' said the club. 'Our global community of 1.1 billion fans and followers provide us with powerful opportunities to engage across cultural and geographical boundaries. We are in Davos to explore ways to maximize the impact of that extraordinary reach.'

Avie was there in person, rubbing shoulders with the titans of business and politics who had also flown in. He clearly loved being in such company. One delegate struck up a conversation with him, about football and United. A fan, he was chuffed when Avie gave him his card, thinking he'd got his personal contact details and he could follow up. He put it in his pocket. When he looked at it later, it said simply 'Avie Glazer, co-chairman Manchester United'. There was nothing else, no private email or phone number.

While avoiding Old Trafford, Avie did turn up at the 2023 Carabao Cup and the women's and men's FA Cup finals, all at Wembley. He also attended the 2022 World Cup in Qatar.

Avie was a guest, too, at the Bahrain Grand Prix in 2022, provoking speculation the Glazers were looking at diversifying into F1. They had already tried to buy an Indian Premier League cricket franchise in October 2021, but their bid at the auction, held at the Taj Hotel in Dubai, fell short.

Of the other siblings, Bryan had been closely involved in United affairs at first, but then backed away. Edward focused on a car sales business he set up in 2018, US Auto Trust, selling Jaguar Land Rover and Aston Martin in the US. Sister Darcie is more closely engaged with the Tampa Bay Bucs; Kevin looks after the family's property interests.

The family places great store by consensus – the obtaining of which can slow things. Wherever possible they must all agree. No one is to be seen or regarded as the leader, or as being above the rest. This explained their reluctance to do interviews. Nobody would ever do them for fear of enjoying a higher profile and appearing in charge.

They didn't want to provoke jealousy or discord among the other five. Always, they were together, as one.

The three less keen brothers, and sister Darcie, had always been happy to entertain thoughts of sale at the right price, but usually Joel and Avie would talk them down. United's value was only heading in one direction, Joel and Avie said, and that was upwards, so stick with it.

In late 2022 Chelsea was sold, and the price paid for the club by Todd Boehly and Clearlake Capital made even Joel and Avie sit up and take notice. For the first time, the Glazers decided to test the market. On 22 November 2022, the family announced it was 'commencing a process to explore strategic alternatives' for Manchester United. This will consider various options, 'including new investment into the club, a sale, or other transactions involving the company'. There was a catch, before their opponents rushed to celebrate: 'There can be no assurance that the review being undertaken will result in any transaction involving the company.'

When it came to choosing their financial advisor, they went for Raine, the small New York investment bank. Joe Ravitch, its co-founder and partner, had handled the Chelsea sale for Roman Abramovich, and liked to tell people how well he'd done, what a great price he'd secured. Impressed, the Glazers chose him and his operation over starrier, more celebrated City and Wall Street names.

From the off it was never clear what the Glazers desired. It was obvious, though, that the process was going to be slow. After seven months there was still no preferred bidder. The sale of Chelsea, by contrast, involved twelve serious bidders and took just three months from announcement to completion. To be fair, Chelsea had to rush – the government was forcing Abramovich's hand. But even so. The slowness at United was partly a result of the Glazers' determination to squeeze out the best possible price; it was also partly due to their natural caution, certainly on the part of Joel. It was that same hesitancy that had seen United squander transfer opportunities, delay the formation of a women's team when other clubs had one, and be slow to fund the youth development programme. Even some rudimentary improvements to Old Trafford seemed to take an age to be signed off.

As their initial statement said, this wasn't necessarily a sale – they were open to alternative ideas – and, in the end, they might not do anything at all. This lack of commitment to a firm conclusion provided a clue as to the machinations between the siblings – not all of them wanted to sell, especially if Raine could not achieve a knockout price reflecting what they thought the club was worth. Joel and Avie were also anxious to explore putting together the funding for a partial or staged payout to the family and a refurbished and expanded Old Trafford, to boost United's earnings power and value, while retaining some degree of ownership.

Either way, it highlighted how ineffectual the fans' protests had been in terms of influencing them. The Glazers were not being driven out, quite the contrary. They might yet remain, and nothing was guaranteed to rile the United supporters more than the prospect of the Glazers – Joel and Avie – staying in situ, but now in effective partnership (albeit as minorities) with someone else.

At the outset, the sale, or non-sale, or whatever it was, had been dealt a bad blow. On the very day the Glazers made their formal announcement regarding 'one of the most successful and historic sports clubs in the world', one of the most successful players of all time, a United player, was allowed to rip up the club's biggest playing contract.

Cristiano Ronaldo went on TalkTV and gave it to the Glazers straight. The frustrated Portuguese superstar compared the United he'd returned to with the one he'd left in 2009. 'They stopped on a clock, in my opinion. Since Sir Alex Ferguson left [in 2013] I saw no evolution, the progress was zero. You have some things inside the club which don't help United reach the top level [like] City, Liverpool, and even now, Arsenal. In my opinion, it will be hard for United to be in the top of the game in the next two, three years.'

The overall amount of money required to return United to that peak put off most suitors. Not only was there likely to be cash for the Glazers, but there were the club's debts to be settled (debts that were in the club's name, not the Glazers'), the cost of refurbishing Old Trafford, improving Carrington, and creating a playing squad capable of winning the Premier and Champions League. Around £10 billion might just cover it.

But then, there was the likelihood of spending such a sum but not achieving success. Winning is not a given, even after such sky-high spending. Then, too, there is the belief among some that football's bubble might already have burst. Some, though, beg to differ. They point to the tech add-ons and how they will take football to a whole new, bigger audience.

Others maintain that for a club like United, all sorts of other factors kick in that have little do with the state of the game and more to do with the global economy. This was a drawback to anyone wishing to buy United with borrowed money – Russia's invasion of Ukraine spelt the end for globally low interest rates. American investors who had been lining up to get into European football were suddenly not so positive.

After the Chelsea deal, Liverpool was also put up for sale by its Fenway Sports Group owners, then withdrawn. There were no takers, such that would detain FSG, and no one appeared interested even in spending less to take a significant holding.

The failure of Liverpool, United's great rival, to be sold or to seemingly attract serious attention, suggested football as an investment had indeed peaked. That is, football without the guarantee of riches provided by Project Big Picture or the European Super League. As the prices commanded by football clubs had risen exponentially, so too had the risk of financial ruin if a Premiership club does not qualify for Europe or, God forbid, is relegated.

Despite Ronaldo's condemnation, the Glazers received a boost when, in the US, the Washington Commanders NFL franchise secured its record asking price of $6 billion. It proved that people were still willing to invest heavily in sport.

There was also the trophy-asset factor. The argument could be made that United was not priced the same as other clubs, that – because of its prestige and history – it was a prized property, worth extra to the owner just to say it was theirs. That additional amount was incalculable, not based on sums or projections, but whatever someone would pay for a once-in-a-lifetime opportunity to own Manchester United.

So, what was the price the Glazers sought? According to the influential Lex column in the *Financial Times*, United was worth $1.6 billion; based on its stock-market capitalization, United was valued at just short of $3 billion; *Forbes* estimated it at $6 billion (they put Chelsea at $3.1 billion). Still others, meanwhile, believed that the application of new technology, of AR, avatars, micro-payments, wearables, together with the soaring popularity of betting on football, would soon put United at $10 billion.

Those in the UK around the club suggested £6 billion as the likely target – which neatly equated to roughly £1 billion for each sibling.

US firms that specialize in equity financing, in coming up with the sorts of packages that enabled the Glazers to buy United originally, circled. Elliott Management, The Carlyle Group, Oaktree Capital Management, MSD Partners and Ares Management were willing to discuss injecting cash into the club in return for equity. All were known for their low profiles, for remaining in the shadows. So, there was puzzlement in investment circles that they would make themselves a choice for fan hatred if they were to fund an arrangement that saw the Glazers remain.

All of them, though, had a record of funding European football: Elliott in AC Milan; Carlyle in Atalanta; Oaktree in Inter Milan; MSD in Southampton, Ares in Atletico Madrid.

Elliott manages £50 billion of assets and had put AC Milan on a better financial footing and won the Serie A title before selling out in 2022. Even so, United was a different proposition, especially if it meant keeping on the Glazers. 'They are very smart,' said one person who knows Elliott well. 'They're much cleverer than the Glazers. But they won't want the aggravation. I can't imagine them being willing to put up billions just so Malcolm Glazer's children can reduce their stakes, with all the attention that would bring. It's not what they're about.'

On a fact-finding visit to Old Trafford laid on by the Glazers for potential buyers and investors, however, Elliott's interest increased. They went from being open to the possibility of funding others who wanted to buy the club, to buying shares themselves. They toured Old Trafford and Carrington, and were then taken through the options for the development of the stadium prepared for the Glazers by firms of consultants. The visitors were given the breakdown of current ticket sales and hospitality revenues for Old Trafford, then they were shown the future possibilities.

There were two routes for expansion. One envisaged building an entirely new venue from scratch, on land adjacent to the present stadium. Including purchasing the land, this would cost more than £1 billion. The other entailed extending and modernizing the existing Old Trafford, expanding the Sir Bobby Charlton Stand, upgrading the hospitality areas and raising the capacity to 88,000. This could be done for £200 million. The extra income this cheaper option would generate was enticing, plus United and the fans would get to stay at Old Trafford, with its special atmosphere and famous past.

Finnish entrepreneur Thomas Zilliacus said he was serious about taking over and would share the club with the fans, only then to drop out and accuse the Glazers of wanting to prolong the sale process to secure a better price.

After months of canvassing, there were only two declared full takeover bidders left – Britain's richest man, Sir Jim Ratcliffe of INEOS, and Qatar's Sheikh Jassim bin Hamad Al Thani – although other finance houses still hovered. Neither was perfect, in the eyes of the fans, but then at that sort of price, who could be? There are very few individuals in the world who would splash many billions on a football club – without the certainty the ESL provided. It was a speculation, a gamble, and in the end hardly any were prepared to take it. No one seemed prepared to blow everybody else out of the water, to offer an eye-watering sum.

In some respects, Sir Jim Ratcliffe, aged seventy, ticks the boxes for an ideal Reds proprietor. Exceedingly wealthy, worth an estimated £29.7 billion, thanks to his vast INEOS petrochemicals group, he's a self-made Manc (he grew up in Failsworth outside Manchester and his family moved to Yorkshire when he was ten), and he's also a self-declared, lifelong United fan. His father went to the 1968 European Cup final at Wembley. A fifteen-year-old Jim was furious, as his dad explained he could only get one ticket. They went to United matches when the Reds played away, on their side, the Yorkshire side of the Pennines. Once at Leeds, they didn't have tickets, and Jim sought his father's permission to scale a wall. He did so and was almost crushed in the supporters on the other side. 'The crowd was solid, all standing, but I wriggled in. Within five minutes they were carrying out women, over our heads, because of the crush. I can remember helping to get these women out. I can't remember the score.'

His hero was Cantona. On his seventieth birthday in October 2022, Ratcliffe received a video of greetings from sports people. Three were United icons: David Beckham, Ferguson and Cantona.

'JR' as he is inevitably called, only became an entrepreneur aged forty, and quit the UK to become a tax exile living in Monaco in 2018.

When younger, Ratcliffe was a keen triathlete in his spare time. He decided he wanted to be more than just a participant in sports. He aspired to be an owner, using the lessons in management and motivation he'd gleaned from his business career.

His first foray into sports ownership was in November 2017, when he bought FC Lausanne-Sport, which played in the Swiss Super League. He described it later as 'dipping my feet in the water'. In that first season with Ratcliffe as owner, Lausanne were relegated. Since then, Lausanne have bounced up and down. Currently, they are in Swiss football's second tier.

David Walsh of *The Sunday Times* tells the story of how Sir Jim met Sir Ben Ainslie, four-time Olympic gold medal winner and Britain's greatest-ever sailor. They shared a drink in a London pub in March 2018. Ainslie was looking for funding to mount a British challenge for the America's Cup, which a British boat has never won. Ratcliffe was persuaded to invest. Great – except he also told Ainslie that he wanted to take over the whole campaign. Ainslie should get rid of all the existing backers and sponsors, and he, Ratcliffe, would take charge. Ainslie would only have to report directly to him, not to a group of investors.

Ainslie had secured funding from three of Britain's leading businessmen, all of them passionate and experienced ocean racing sailors: Sir Charles Dunstone, Sir Keith Mills and Chris Bake. He had to swallow hard and tell them one by one they were no longer needed.

'It's a poor show really when you think about it,' said Ratcliffe when announcing his partnership with Ainslie, reflecting on the lack of a British win since the cup's inaugural outing in 1851. 'One hundred and seventy years; it is an omission in our history.'

He went on. 'We are writing a cheque for £100 million and we're not casual with our money. We feel we have the Usain Bolt of sailing.'

Even with 'Usain Bolt' skippering and Ratcliffe commanding, they were pulverized. The INEOS team didn't get anywhere near landing the America's Cup. They were heavily beaten by the Italian boat *Luna Rossa Prada* in the final eliminator. The Italians were then crushed by

Emirates Team New Zealand in the America's Cup races. Britain's star yachtsman, Ainslie, it seems, had fallen foul of 'the curse of INEOS'.

In 2016–17, Nice was one of the very top clubs in France, challenging for the Ligue 1 title. Ratcliffe bought them in 2019 for €100 million (£88 million). 'The ambition is to reach Ligue 1's top four and regularly reach the [Champions League] within three to five years,' said Bob Ratcliffe, Jim's younger brother and chief executive of INEOS Football. Ratcliffe – Bob, that is – added: 'Without spending too much money on expensive transfers of players.'

Somewhat bizarrely, as well as appointing his brother, Ratcliffe put Sir Dave Brailsford, the former Team GB cycling coach and founder of Team Sky, in charge of Nice's finances and transfer policy. Ever since, there has been a regular revolving door at Nice – chaos is another way of describing it. The 2022–3 season was another disappointment and Nice finished mid-table.

In 2019, Ratcliffe bought Team Sky, the World Tour cycling team, winners of the Tour de France in six of the previous seven years. It was another considerable outlay (the team's annual budget is around £50 million) and, so far, another relative failure. Ratcliffe did enjoy some early success – three months after he took over, Team INEOS won the Tour de France with its twenty-two-year-old Colombian, Egan Bernal, but arguably that came so soon after Ratcliffe's purchase that it could not have made any difference. Certainly, that success was not repeated. Despite Brailsford's inclusion in the fold, INEOS Grenadiers cycling team dropped down the rankings and have not enjoyed anywhere near the success that Team Sky once did.

Sticking to his theme of targeting only the best, Ratcliffe sponsored the All Blacks, New Zealand's rugby union team, as well as the Mercedes team in F1. With the latter, he agreed a five-year £100 million sponsorship deal in February 2020. That coming season, Lewis Hamilton claimed the F1 drivers' championship. An enthused

Ratcliffe promptly bought a one-third share of the team for an estimated £350 million.

'This is a unique opportunity to make a financial investment in a team at the very top of its game, but which still has rich potential to grow in the future. We could not wish for better partners than Mercedes-Benz, and a team of proven winners led by Toto [Wolff],' Ratcliffe said.

When he came on the scene, Mercedes were the dominant F1 team, having won seven consecutive drivers' championships and constructors' championships, both of which they were about to win again. Ever since Ratcliffe became a co-owner, Mercedes has struggled behind Red Bull and Ferrari.

Invited to look at United's books and tour the facilities, Ratcliffe was accompanied by Brailsford. In cycling, Brailsford was known for his 'marginal gains' philosophy, the idea that if you broke down everything you could think of that goes into riding a bike, and then improved it by 1 per cent, you would get a significant increase when you put them all together. It extends into every aspect of the rider's life, not just training and how they perform in races. 'Do you really know how to clean your hands? Without leaving the bits between your fingers? If you do things like that properly, you will get ill a little bit less. They're tiny things but if you clump them together it makes a big difference.'

Will this doctrine extend to the managing of Manchester United? It would remain to be seen whether football, its players and fans, have the time and patience for such a holistic, micro-detailed strategy.

With Ratcliffe, too, there is the not inconsiderable concern as to where his heart genuinely lies. For years he was a Chelsea season-ticket holder when he could easily have afforded to fly to Manchester to see his professed 'first' team.

When Chelsea became available, he tried to buy them. Then, his statement said: 'We believe that a club is bigger than its owners who are temporary custodians of a great tradition. With responsibility to the fans and the community. We will invest in Stamford Bridge to make it a world-class stadium, befitting of Chelsea FC. We are making this investment as fans of the beautiful game – not as a means to turn a profit. We do that with our core businesses. The club is rooted in the community and its fans. And it is our intention to invest in Chelsea FC for that reason.'

When announcing his United bid he said: 'We would see our role as long-term custodians of Manchester United on behalf of the fans and the wider community. We are ambitious and highly competitive and would want to invest in Manchester United to make them the number one club in the world once again. We would want to help lead this next chapter, deepening the culture of English football by making the club a beacon for a modern, progressive, fan-centred approach to ownership. We want a Manchester United anchored in its proud history and roots in the North-West of England, putting the Manchester back into Manchester United and clearly focusing on winning the Champions League.'

To which you want to say: Jim, make your mind up. Is it Chelsea or United you love? Such is the tribal nature of football, you're not allowed both.

Chelsea, of course, was cheaper. He said that his Chelsea bid failed because by the time he made his move, the club was 'all wrapped up' for Boehly. 'An American mergers and acquisitions house was running the sale [for Roman Abramovich]. The only three parties they were talking to were private equity houses in America. They didn't want us involved at all. We did have a word with the government, and with the supporters' club, because football clubs are community assets, but Boris [Johnson] and company didn't want to know.'

A year previously, in 2021, Ratcliffe had tried to buy 50 per cent of Barcelona. Hearing that the club's newly elected president Joan Laporta planned to sell a proportion of the club's TV rights, Ratcliffe was horrified. 'We told them, "Don't do it, guys – we'll put in two or three billion, renovate the Nou Camp and have 50 per cent ownership – and sign a deed to say we'd never sell." Our interest was in football alone, not making money. I think it would have worked well. We talked about it but, in the end, they didn't think they could go to the fans with it.'

JR couldn't afford, or was not prepared to match, the whole United asking price. His offer was effectively less than what the Glazers thought it was worth, what they hoped Raine would raise, but with a clause keeping Joel and Avie on board for two to three years. He wanted only the Glazers' 69 per cent shareholding. Ratcliffe, advised by Goldman Sachs and J.P. Morgan, would take 49 per cent at first, leaving the Glazers with 20 per cent. Because the Glazers' shares were voting shares, 49 per cent would be enough to give him full control of the club. He would buy out their remaining 20 per cent in two or three years.

It was novel, but also hard to equate with the assertion that Ratcliffe was taking a 'fan-centred approach to ownership'. Many of the fans, as he surely must have known, could not abide the Glazers staying at Old Trafford in any shape or form, even on a promise to eventually go.

Ahead of United's game against Aston Villa on 30 April 2023, fans marched from central Manchester to the stadium behind a giant banner declaring 'Full $ale Only'. The Munich Tunnel for the players was closed for security reasons when the marchers arrived. Flares were let off. Throughout the game there was constant anti-Glazer chanting and more banners held aloft, 'Glazers Out', 'Full Sale Only' and 'Just Go'. The sinister-sounding group the 1958, 'an underground group of Reds intent on upholding the values of Manchester United, its culture and traditions', called for an eighteen-minute boycott of the match: 'one minute for each year the Glazers have driven our club into the ground.' The mood was also anti-Ratcliffe. One veteran United follower said he was shocked to hear fans in the toilets at half-time muttering, 'Die Ratcliffe, die.'

So, for United and their raging fans it was business as usual then, even when presented with the possibility of Ratcliffe, a Manc, buying the club, and with his pledges of involving the fans.

Qatar was hosting the World Cup when the Glazers made their announcement that they might be open to offers.

From the perspective of Qatar's rulers, the tournament had been a success. The tiny oil-rich nation were hospitable hosts, the finals passed without a significant hitch, the new stadia looked space-age, the crowds and atmosphere were good (even if some fans were paid to turn up and chant – an unintended precursor to the 'seat for a song' idea), and the matches were excellent. There was some negative coverage of Qatar's treatment of migrant workers, its attitude towards women and LGBT people, and its record on human rights. But once the football got under way, the criticism was relatively easy for them to ignore and – from the Qatari government standpoint – it was perhaps not as bad as it could have been.

Flush with that success, buoyed by the presence on the world stage that football had given them, Qatar's rulers wanted more. Since 2011, its sovereign wealth fund, Qatar Investment Authority or QIA, via a subsidiary, Qatar Sports Investments or QSI, has owned Paris Saint-Germain. But the Paris club, thanks to Qatar's cash, for all its glitz and the fielding of some of the greatest-ever players, including Neymar, Lionel Messi, Kylian Mbappé, is not United. Its Parc des Princes stadium holds 48,000, small compared to Old Trafford. And it has not got the history. PSG has won the French league eleven times, but a major European trophy, the Cup Winners' Cup, just once. PSG is among Europe's leading clubs, but despite QSI's investment, it has yet to land the top prize, the Champions League.

In theory, UEFA prohibits clubs owned by the same entity from competing against each other. So Qatari-state-funded PSG and United would not be able to take part in the Champions League (the same would also apply to Nice if it and a Ratcliffe-owned United qualified). But UEFA made an exception in the case of Leipzig and Salzburg, who both belonged to Red Bull. They were allowed to play each other in the Europa League tournament in 2018.

A bid backed by the QIA would also require UK government clearance, but it's hard to see how this could be withheld, given the number of businesses and properties already owned by the QIA in the UK. Besides, the government gave the nod to the Saudi Arabian Public Investment Fund buying Newcastle.

Sheikh Jassim chairs Qatar Islamic Bank. Born in 1982, he's the son of the former prime minister, Sheikh Hamad bin Jassim bin Jaber al-Thani, or 'HBJ' (famously, the giver of Fortnum & Mason bags stuffed with €3 million in cash to King Charles), and a member of the Qatari royal family.

Educated at boarding school in England and Sandhurst, Sheikh Jassim claims to be a United supporter. Only one picture appears to exist of him that bears this out. He's posing for the camera and wearing a 2022–3 United shirt. Doubts were immediately raised as to whether it was genuine. They were further raised when a spokesman for his bid said it was 'not an official picture' and he was 'not able to confirm its authenticity'.

Backed by Qatari state money, Sheikh Jassim would head up the bid, and, in a clever PR touch, the funding would come directly from his 'Nine Two Foundation', named, it was claimed, after the United 'Class of '92'.

Said his statement: 'The bid plans to return the Club to its former glories both on and off the pitch, and – above all – will seek to place the fans at the heart of Manchester United Football Club once more. The bid will be completely debt free via Sheikh Jassim's Nine Two Foundation, which will look to invest in the football teams, the training centre, the stadium and wider infrastructure, the fan experience and the communities the Club supports. The vision of the bid is for Manchester United Football Club to be renowned for footballing excellence and regarded as the greatest football club in the world.'

The Qatari sheikh, then, was going all out, for 100 per cent and no future involvement of the Glazers. Joel and Avie would head off, to enjoy their billions. There was nothing not to like about his intentions. In that sense, from the point of view of the supporters, the Qatari businessman was more appealing. He was, though, part of the political elite of a state with a reputation for oppression. Manchester is a city renowned for its outspokenness and independence of thought, to put it mildly, and it has a large LGBT community. The two would not be an easy match.

One supporter summed up the difference when he tweeted: 'A sovereign state-owned football club fundamentally changes what that club is and what you're supporting. It no longer stands as just a football club, it's de facto an extension of that state.' It would be the same as if the Norway Sovereign Wealth Fund or the Bank of England were buying the club. All the social and political baggage associated with that country comes with them.

To water down the criticism that the Qatari sheikh's ownership of United would be just the latest example of 'greenwashing' or 'sportswashing', arguments were made that the QIA owns Harrods, Canary Wharf, The Shard, Olympic Village, and much else besides in London and the UK. So why not United? As one fan tweeted in forthright fashion in response: 'I don't have a forty-eight-year emotional connection to the fucking Shard through birthplace and family, that's been collectively lived as community, culture, identity, experience, family, mates. To equate this shite with what supporting a football club means is weird as fuck.'

The supporters were stuck. Neither Ratcliffe nor Sheikh Jassim were ideal. Ratcliffe, because he would allow the Glazers to stay;

Jassim because of what he represented and his motive for buying the club. Nor were supporters keen on the US investment funds taking over. Gary Neville said he did not want the latter at any price. 'I don't see football as an ROI [return on investment] based, yield-based business. I see football as something far more emotive, that involves passion and community and people.' Said the former United star player, TV pundit and Manchester businessman: 'We've got Jim Ratcliffe, which is private money; Qatar, which is private money; and US equity. I'm against that. The club would just be run for a profit again . . . we would see dividends, we would see extraction, we would see cost-cutting, we would see commercial exploitation which may be unhealthy for the club.'

He preferred Ratcliffe or Sheikh Jassim, but without the Glazers. 'The Glazers just have to leave. So, if Jim Ratcliffe or Qatar came in without the Glazers, I'd be supportive of it on the condition of what they were pledging with respect to their manifesto to the club.'

The problem with the Neville argument is that the days of owners who grew up in the streets next to the ground buying a club out of love and putting something back and spending a large slice of their fortune on securing success, as Jack Walker, the steel magnate, did with Blackburn Rovers, rarely exist any more – not at the United, multibillion level. Walker's tearful TV interview when his beloved Blackburn won the Premiership is nerve-tingling. That was in 1995, the year before Sky dramatically raised the ante with live TV rights and changed the game for ever.

The pressure that Todd Boehly's purchase of Chelsea put on the process had meant that the Glazers were always going to struggle to find bidders at the £6 billion price they wanted. If they'd lowered their sights, they might have attracted more interest. As it was, they had to struggle to push Ratcliffe and Sheikh Jassim higher. They went through several rounds. Ratcliffe was prepared to pay £2.5 billion for part of the club now, based on a valuation for 100 per cent of £5.1 billion. But the Glazers would still remain until they were bought out completely in a few years. The feeling was that the Glazers were trying to draw out Sheikh Jassim, persuading him to go higher.

The process was torturous, going on and on. Both would-be purchasers vented their frustration, complaining at the lack of communication from the Glazer camp.

If the Glazers were split, so were the fans. On Twitter they overwhelmingly favoured Sheikh Jassim. In polls conducted behind paywalls for the readers of *The Athletic* and *United We Stand*, Ratcliffe emerged on top. The same was true of United's large Scandinavian supporters' club – they wanted Ratcliffe.

Whoever they chose, the Glazers would be making £5 billion on top of the millions they'd extracted from the club throughout their eighteen years of ownership. Theirs, by any standards, was a spectacularly successful return. They took a profitable, debt-free club and loaded it with £558 million of new debt (the equivalent to £918 million in 2022), which sucked out hundreds of millions in interest and fees. The debt had grown to £1 billion by 2023, with an additional £280 million of transfer debt. None of the £7 billion of revenue from the club, or the $830 million the Glazers raised from selling 52 million United shares, ever seems to have been used to pay down the debt.

United paid a total of £771 million in interest since the Glazers' leveraged buy-out in 2005. That's more than three-quarters of a billion pounds in interest payments since the Glazers landed. As the financial analyst and blogger Swiss Ramble posted: 'To place this into context, in the period since the Glazers' arrival up to 2022, Manchester United's £746 million interest payment was nearly three times as much as the next highest club, namely Arsenal with £255 million. Looked at another way, it was not far behind the rest of the Premier League combined, with the other nineteen clubs adding up to £862 million.'

Along the way, too, they withstood abuse that would have driven away less determined, less thick-skinned folk. Their perseverance had reaped a huge financial jackpot.

On 23 October 2022, in deepest, rural Ireland, a horse collapsed and died. Rock of Gibraltar had succumbed to a heart attack. Paddy Fleming, manager of the Castlehyde stud, where the horse was based, said: 'He was healthy and looking great right up to the end. He was a fantastic racehorse and a very good sire, who will be missed by all the staff here.'

On 31 July 2023, United secured a world-record kit deal: over ten years with Adidas, worth £900 million.

This, after a pre-season that saw Premier League players trial bodycams on tour in the United States. The camera was stitched to a thin vest under the shirt. A small hole was cut in the jersey so the lens could see the match. The camera was shatter-proof and was so small and light as to be invisible.

The players said they would be happy to wear one every week. For the owners, AR and a totally different way of viewing the game, as well as the prospect of the enormous riches this could bring, moved a significant step nearer.

With United back in the Champions League with the best manager in charge for some time, there was no sign of a complete sale, no puff of white smoke. Much to the annoyance of Ratcliffe and Sheikh Jassim – and the fury of the fans – the Glazers appeared to be in no hurry to cash in all their shares.

It's not known if the Glazers ever look heavenwards and give thanks to Rock of Gibraltar for their immense good fortune.

Acknowledgements

The idea for this book stemmed from the simple premise that here was a family, the Glazers, who seemingly sprang from nowhere to buy the world's biggest football club. For almost two decades they put up with relentless abuse, yet they carried on owning Manchester United. Rarely did they try and placate the protestors; if anything they made the situation worse by failing to engage or communicate with them – with anyone.

They bought the club using other people's money and at the end, they were sitting on an asset worth several billion pounds. Remarkable.

Along the way, they turned United into a commercial power-house, so much so that the 'beautiful game' appeared lost amid a welter of sponsorships, endorsements, tie-ins, partnerships and spin-offs. Incredibly, they chose to do this with the one club, above all others, that had the greatest, most famous history of all.

In telling this story, I spoke to numerous people in the UK and US, who could not, would not, be quoted. To them I am grateful.

Others felt able to be named. In no particular order I must thank: Andy Green, Jim O'Neill, John-Paul O'Neill, Tony O'Neill (all O'Neills but they are definitely not related), Andy Mitten, Mark Rawlinson, Roland Rudd, Paddy Harverson, Kieran Maguire, Paul Casson.

Those who provided valuable assistance: David Bick, Coolmore, Rory Godson, Simon Stewart, Duncan Drasdo, Chris Rumfitt, Sebastian McCarthy.

When I first mentioned what I'd like to do to my agent, Charlie Viney, he was immediately seized by it. He's been a source of encouragement and advice all along.

Mike Harpley, publishing director at Macmillan, was similarly enthused. He's been nursing the project along, choosing opportune moments to encourage and to dissuade.

Editor Mike Jones was a dream to work with. Someone who could see what I was trying to do without achieving it, then telling me what I had to do to achieve it. So too was copy-editor Penelope Isaac; her attention to detail and spotting of possible mistakes was extraordinary. Saying all that, Laura Carr at Macmillan also managed to find a few more when she read it through. Thanks to them all.

Special mention must go to the 'Fulham Massive' – family and friends who live the dream that – one day – Fulham will ascend to the very heights that others take for granted and believe are theirs and only theirs. Always, we go to matches with a spring in our step. Frequently, alas, that's not how we return. But there's always the next game, the next drink at the Winchester House Club in Putney, the next meal at Pappa Ciccia, the next discussion about the club we love but which frustrates in equal measure: Archie Blackhurst, Barney Blackhurst, Dominic Mills, Peter Welland, Gerard Lyons, Gerard

B. Lyons, Mark Lewis. Also, thanks to Michael McCarthy, another devoted Cottager, for listening and suggesting.

Simon Hayes supports Brentford but that does not mean he is barred. His thoughts on the game and his knowledge – as well of horse racing – were insightful and much appreciated.

As a member of the 1879 Club of Fulham supporters – the date of the club's foundation – I attend their social functions, where the guests are Fulham 'legends', past players, and others, including club executives. I don't take notes, it's not allowed, but much of the discussion, especially where it gets to the future of the game and the financial side, does go in. Thanks to the irrepressible David Roodyn for organizing.

At the other end of the football pyramid is my hometown club, Barrow. I love the Bluebirds dearly. They've had a tough time over the decades but, thanks to those who believe, they are still very much alive. Thanks to my brother-in-law David Houghton and Tom Houghton for getting me tickets and keeping me posted with analysis of a side that commands zero national attention but to the local community, especially to the likes of David and his fellow die-hards who think nothing of travelling hundreds of miles from Cumbria to an away match in the hope of witnessing a win – it is everything.

To Archie and Grace, thank you for putting up with a father who, for too long, was permanently upstairs in his office.

Finally, a special thank-you to my dear wife, Annabelle. How you stayed cheery and serene in the presence of someone who, for months on end, could only mutter 'book', 'deadline' and 'must go' is beyond me.

To all, my gratitude.

Source Notes

I have a loathing of footnotes in some books, believing that, in those that are telling a story, they can hold up the flow, that the reader's eye is drawn to a number at the end of a line and the pace is lost, so I've taken the liberty of not using them.

The material relied upon for this book came from a mixture of sources: interviews conducted by me, some on-the-record, many off-the-record, in the UK, US and elsewhere; newspaper and magazine articles; Manchester United fanzines, *Red News*, *United We Stand*, TV footage, websites, podcasts and blogs. And books. It should come as no surprise that more books have been written about Manchester United than any other football club. Some, the ones mentioned here, are outstanding.

Below are the sources used for each chapter.

1. RED DEVILS

The Liam Gallagher quote about the Pope is from the Oasis fan site *stopcrying-yourheartout.com*. The early history of Manchester United is from many published sources, from newspaper reports and feature articles, but Jim White's *Manchester United – The Biography* is enormously insightful on this period. Also particularly helpful was *Manchester United – The Betrayal of a Legend* by Michael Crick and David Smith. Patrick Barclay's *Sir Matt Busby – The Man Who Made a Football Club* contains everything you want to know and more about the great man. So much has been written about Munich and United's re-emergence, but again, White, Crick and Smith, and Barclay, all did the remarkable story proud.

2. ANYONE BUT MAXWELL

Again, too many United historians to choose from, but White and Barclay covered the European Cup win superbly. For Old Trafford regulars, 'Big Tony' O'Neill might need little introduction, but the former Red Army leader's accounts of 'away days' are colourful and, in their own way, gripping. O'Neill himself was delightful company, and especially helpful on this episode in the United story. I grew up on lurid tales from my late father about Louis Edwards – every time he appeared on the North-West TV news, I would be treated to another. Remarkably, it turns out, many of them were correct. Again, there was plenty of corroborative material to choose from, but White and Crick and Smith were authorities. The Michael Knighton story has been well aired, but not with the detail and colour contained in *Visionary – Manchester United, Michael Knighton and the Football Revolution 1989–2019* by Phillip Vine. It's written with Knighton's cooperation and it is fascinating. The Philip Green phone calls are from its pages. On the takeover history of United, Mihir Bose's *Manchester Disunited – Trouble and Takeover at the World's Richest Football Club* is a mine of authoritative information.

3. THE LEPRECHAUN

Even though he avoided the press, Malcolm Glazer did give interviews when he wanted something and he thought they might assist his cause. Two, in the *Baltimore Sun* and *Tampa Bay Times*, were especially illuminating. Fortunately, he was also serially litigious, and numerous US court reports contain many references to Glazer and the disputes he was involved in. Over the years, he was also the subject of repeated due diligence inquiries on Wall Street, and a former senior banker who led one of those provided valuable assistance in putting

Glazer into perspective and in describing the pattern of his business methods and tactics. The strange story of the Zapata Corporation and its links with George Bush and the CIA has been pored over by White House historians, and is the subject of many papers and books.

4. ENTER RUPERT MURDOCH

Interviews with the author and press reports from the time provided much of the detail in this chapter. Bose's *Manchester Disunited* was again an outstanding, minutely chronicled back-up. Sir Alex Ferguson has written not one but two autobiographies, as befitting someone with such a glorious, long career. They are both valuable sources on him and his time at the club, his dealings with the various boards and players and their agents. Tom Bower's *Broken Dreams – Vanity, Greed, and the Souring of British Football* is typically robust and uncompromising, and revelatory, containing tales that many other volumes choose to overlook or simply were not aware of.

5. 'IT ALL STARTED WITH THE HORSE'

The story of the Gimcrack dinner, Rock of Gibraltar and Sir Alex Ferguson was provided to me in interviews. Where there were gaps, Martin Hannan's remarkably detailed *Rock of Gibraltar – Ultimate Racehorse and Fabulous Prize in a Battle of Giants* would invariably come to my aid. For anyone who loves racing, Hannan's detailed, insider story of the remarkable horse and the twists and turns of its ownership cannot be bettered.

6. THE GLAZERS MAKE THEIR APPEARANCE

Interviews with the author provided much of the material for this chapter. The Glazers and Manchester United used advisors and those advisors felt free to talk. One of them, Tehsin Nayani, documented his work for the Glazers in a book, *The Glazer Gate Keeper – Six years' speaking for Manchester United's silent owners*. It captures delightfully the travails of the PR man, caught between a client who says nothing and a public always craving word from him. The row between Ferguson and J. P. McManus and John Magnier was described to me in interviews in the UK and Ireland with people I cannot name. To them I am grateful.

7. THE LEPRECHAUN RISES

The protests versus McManus and Magnier made headlines at the time and were covered in glorious detail. Again, I was able to conduct interviews with some of those close to the action. Bose's *Manchester Disunited* was also helpful on the machinations of the takeover.

8. 'A WOUND THAT WILL NEVER HEAL'

More interviews with the author, newspaper reports, *Manchester Disunited* assisted here. Some of those interviews focused on the formation of FC United. John-Paul O'Neill, one of the leaders of the breakaway, saw me and was helpful. He wrote his own account of the breakaway: *Red Rebels – The Glazers and the FC Revolution*, which was also useful. Andy Green is the investment genius who scrutinized the Glazers' shopping mall accounts. He was hugely patient with my questions and his explanations, and forthcoming with his original research.

9. THE BLACK BOX

Again, more interviews and press reports covered this period. Sources on the commercial side of Manchester United were especially helpful here. Much of the detail in this chapter derives from them. Nayani was also valuable. The Manchester United Supporters Trust was useful. On football's finances, Kieran Maguire cannot be bettered. He gave his time and appeared happy to answer my most inane questions.

10. CHARGE OF THE RED KNIGHTS

Interviews and cuttings supplied much of the material for this chapter. The first-hand accounts of Jim O'Neill and Mark Rawlinson on the Red Knights were hugely useful. Nayani's story, which ends with the retreat of the Red Knights, provided the other view. The Manchester United Supporters Trust were helpful. Maguire was again patient when explaining the money and business management side. His seminal book *The Price of Football* provides a masterclass in this aspect of the sport.

11. NEW YORK, NEW YORK

Interviews and press reports covered this period. United's filing with the Securities and Exchange Commission is a freely available, treasure trove of detail about the club under the Glazers. Ferguson's two autobiographies contain his retirement, non-retirement then retirement. Maguire was useful on succession planning, or rather, the lack of it.

12. NOT SO SUPER

The sources for this chapter were interviews and press reports. Maguire was essential reading on Project Big Picture. It was his analysis that showed up the project for what it was. Again, he was to the fore on the European Super League. Woodward was also useful. Andy Mitten of *United We Stand* was an especially valuable sounding-board on this period.

13. MEA CULPA, NOT

Joel Glazer's letters were analysed and scrutinized in the fanzines *United We Stand* and *Red News*. Barney Chilton of the latter went out of his way to provide assistance and, again, took the trouble to answer my most basic questions. Richard Arnold's impromptu session with the fans in the pub garden was the subject of numerous press reports. Todd Boehly's eye-opening address to SuperReturn International was made available to me by a private equity journalist Sebastian McCarthy, who was present. Again, Maguire is able to cut through brilliantly the sometimes deliberately opaque nature of football financing.

14. BILLIONAIRES ALL

Interviews with the author and press reports provided much of the material for this, the final chapter. *Grit, Rigour and Humour – The Ineos Story* was helpful on Sir Jim Ratcliffe and his support of Manchester United and his attempted investment in Barcelona. The financial analyst and blogger Swiss Ramble cuts through the United figures like no other. The ebb and flow of the sale process was covered on the business pages but, given the closely guarded talks and the fact they were subject to NDAs, discerning fact from speculation was sometimes difficult. Fortunately, there were those who were more informed, who could shine a light on what had been transpiring, but only anonymously.

Index

Picture Acknowledgements

1. Popperfoto / Contributor via Getty Images
2. Popperfoto / Contributor via Getty Images
3. Bentley Archive / Popperfoto / Contributor via Getty Images
4. Popperfoto / Contributor via Getty Images
5. Mirrorpix / Contributor via Getty Images
6. Paul Popper / Popperfoto / Contributor via Getty Images
7. Trevor Jones / Popperfoto / Contributor via Getty Images
8. PETER MUHLY / Stringer via Getty Images
9. Michael Steele / Staff via Getty Images
10. Julian Herbert / Staff via Getty Images
11. Matthew Peters / Contributor via Getty Images
12. ADRIAN DENNIS / Staff via Getty Images
13. Dario Cantatore via Getty Images and NYSE Euronext
14. Bryn Lennon via Getty Images
16. Robbie Jay Barratt – AMA / Contributor via Getty Images

Chris Blackhurst is an award-winning business writer and commentator. He is a former editor of the *Independent* and for ten years was City editor of the *Evening Standard*. Before that he was Westminster correspondent for the *Independent* and worked for *The Sunday Times* on its Insight investigative team and as a senior writer on its Business News. Throughout his career he has written widely on the business of sport, and his journalism has appeared in many of the world's major publications. He is the author of *Too Big to Jail* and *The World's Biggest Cash Machine*.